Media Scandals

Recent Titles in
Scandals in American History

Sports Scandals
Peter Finley, Laura Finley, and Jeffrey Fountain

MEDIA SCANDALS

Alan Bisbort

Scandals in American History

GREENWOOD PRESS
Westport, Connecticut • London

Library of Congress Cataloging-in-Publication Data

Bisbort, Alan, 1953–
    Media scandals / Alan Bisbort.
        p. cm. — (Scandals in American history, ISSN 1942–0102)
    Includes bibliographical references and index.
    ISBN 978–0–313–34765–8 (alk. paper)
    1. Scandals in mass media. I. Title.
P96.S29.B57   2008
302.23—dc22   2008022346

British Library Cataloguing in Publication Data is available.

Library of Congress Catalog Card Number: 2008022346
ISBN: 978–0–313–34765–8
ISSN: 1942–0102

First published in 2008

Greenwood Press, 88 Post Road West, Westport, CT 06881
An imprint of Greenwood Publishing Group, Inc.
www.greenwood.com

Printed in the United States of America

∞™

The paper used in this book complies with the
Permanent Paper Standard issued by the National
Information Standards Organization (Z39.48–1984).

10   9   8   7   6   5   4   3   2   1

CONTENTS

SERIES FOREWORD

Scandal is a part of daily life in America. The evidence is everywhere, from the business world, with its Enrons, Ponzi schemes, and insider trades, to the political arena, where scandals are so pervasive that, for shorthand purposes, we simply add "-gate" to each new one (Watergate, Travelgate, Spitzergate, and so on). Cultural phenomena that are designed to entertain, inform, and distract us—television, film, popular music, sports, media—have also been touched by the fickle finger of scandal. Even religion, the one area of life that is intended to uplift and guide Americans, has not been immune to the taint of scandal.

Scandal, which can be defined as something that offends propriety or established moral codes and brings disgrace on anyone or any organization associated with it, is not a modern invention. It has been with us since the days of the Salem witch trials and Boss Tweed, and it resurfaces in many of today's breaking news events. To bring this subject into the open and to offer a wider historical view of such a major and often overlooked aspect of U.S. history—one that is of abiding interest to students—Greenwood developed this series of reference works. These volumes examine the causes and impacts of scandal within key areas of American life—politics, sports, media, business, popular music, television, film, religion, and more. Prepared by field experts and professionals, the volumes are written to inform and educate high school and undergraduate college students as well as to engage and entertain students and general readers alike. As reference tools, they place scandals within a wider social and cultural context. But as general histories, they are fun to read from cover to cover.

The volumes have been carefully written and edited to ensure that a diversity of viewpoints surrounding each scandal is included. Because many of the issues that touched off scandals have never been resolved, the books in this series can be used to spark classroom debate as well as to examine the ethical issues that come into play. Each volume is enhanced with a timeline, illustrations, and a bibliography so that students can read further and in more detail about subjects that pique their interest, as well as to augment the reading and learning experience.

PREFACE

America's obsession with scandal—and the American media's boundless
capacity to report and sometimes even create it—did not start with
O. J. Simpson, Britney Spears, Michael Moore, or Rush Limbaugh. It
has been with us since before Paul Revere made his famous ride. Indeed, our
media's cherished right to free expression was hard-won and is now protected
by the First Amendment to the U.S. Constitution, but it comes with responsibilities and is fraught with peril. The tension between the two forces of free
expression and permissible subject matter has, throughout American history,
caused media scandals—public outcries, legal proceedings, denunciations, violence, and, in the case of Salman Rushdie's 1988 novel *The Satanic Verses*,
deaths. The early battles by the print media—newspapers, magazines, and
books—over censorship, book banning, book burning, obscenity, blasphemy,
and libel set the groundwork for the battles that would ensue as the media
expanded into radio, television, and the Internet. The latter has spawned its
own conduits of free expression, like YouTube, MySpace, blogs, and broadcast
streaming—and all of these are potentially scandal-making.

No matter how many media are eventually created, all will be fraught with
the same potential for scandal, and the same recurrent themes. This book,
therefore, is separated into two parts. The first part is broken down into three
chapters, each devoted to one of these recurrent themes (politics and the
media, race and religion, and sexuality and morality). These themes were there
at the start of the nation—built right into the foundation—and they, in all
likelihood, will be there as long as there is an American media. The second
part, broken down into four chapters, is devoted to the media itself as an
industry (books, newspapers/magazines, radio/television, and the Internet).
These are the "carriers," if you will, of potentially scandalous themes. By
themselves, they are neutral, merely conduits of information.

Within each chapter, the specific subjects are examined by theme, and in
chronological order within the theme. While historical precedents are covered—
to show how these themes established themselves in the American mind—the
emphasis of the book is on the twentieth and twenty-first centuries. Augmenting

the text is a detailed and unique timeline, which can help put these wide-ranging American media scandals into historical perspective. An exhaustive bibliography of books and materials on the American media is provided, to perhaps prod readers to learn more about the themes and events described herein. Wherever appropriate, cross references are included in the text to send the inveterately curious reader to another area that might help flesh out a subject. What emerges is a veritable tapestry of competing voices and distractions, opinions and break-throughs (or breakdowns). Students and general readers can use this book as a reference tool, as well as read it cover to cover in order to gain a better apprecia-tion for the complexity of the media and the power it wields in our daily lives.

ACKNOWLEDGMENTS

The author wishes to first thank his dear friends in Maryland, Mark Mattucci and Judy Furash, for introducing me to their neighbor, Wendi Schnaufer. Wendi, a senior acquisitions editor for Greenwood Press, displayed Job-like patience as she tried to find a project on which I might work. She ultimately put me in contact with Kristi Ward, Greenwood's popular culture acquisitions editor, who kept me busy for more than a year compiling this volume. Then, it was my turn to keep her busy trying to make sense of what I'd produced. I also want to thank Athena Angelos, picture researcher extraordinaire at the Library of Congress, for digging up some of the images for this book, as well as Tom Hearn, photographer extraordinaire, for lending me his talents.

This book is dedicated to my wife, Tracey Ann O'Shaughnessy, and our son, Paul James Bisbort, who is our shared hope for the future betterment of a scandal-filled world.

INTRODUCTION

I n this media-saturated age, scandal can be hard to define, or even notice. Public behavior that lands one celebrity or politician on the front pages of newspapers and Web sites (or in jail) barely registers when another celebrity or politician does the same thing. Likewise, a rash of plagiarism in newspapers and book publishing, or political corruption in Washington, D.C., will sometimes barely register on the scandal radar, perhaps because too many other scandalous things are occurring simultaneously or because these sorts of scandals have become too common to generate much outrage.

A guide for determining scandal was established by U.S. Supreme Court Justice Potter Stewart in the 1964 case *Jacobellis v. Ohio*, when he was asked to rule on whether a French film shown by an Ohio theater owner was obscene. In defining obscenity, Justice Potter famously said, "I know it when I see it, and the motion picture involved in this case is not that." The same may be said for scandal. You know it when you see it.[1]

Scandal is further defined by *Webster's Ninth New College Dictionary* as "A circumstance or action that offends propriety or established moral conceptions or disgraces those associated with it." Media is defined as any conduit of free expression, either in print form, broadcast through the public airwaves, or via the Internet. (Thus, motion pictures and music will not, for the most part, be considered in this volume.)

Media scandals have occurred when the "circumstance or action" of a media outlet has offended propriety, or the established moral conceptions, or disgraced those associated with it. That definition can be expanded to include any media circumstance or action that knowingly and willfully "offends" the truth by distortion, libel, outright lies, and manipulative propaganda. A celebrity scandal—like Britney Spears shaving her head or Paris Hilton being hauled off to jail—is not a media scandal, unless the media had a hand in the event. Just reporting the shaven head or the tearful trip to jail is the role of the media in a free society. Whatever scandal accrues to that individual is not the media's fault. Of course, some critics argue that, in our celebrity-obsessed society, the media shares blame for all scandal. Cases in point abound, including the deaths of

xiv   *Introduction*

O. J. Simpson's wife, Princess Diana, and JonBenet Ramsey. Though initially news events, these tragedies were transformed into media scandals by the collective excesses and insensitivity of the press coverage, as chronicled in Chapter 6.

Media is the plural form of *medium*. The widely-accepted use of *media*, to describe *mass media*, began with the advent of radio and television in the mid-twentieth century. Communications theorist Marshall McLuhan, in pioneering works like *The Gutenberg Galaxy* (1962) and *Understanding Media: The Extensions of Man* (1964), brought public awareness to the expanding power of these conduits of free expression. His theories were as timely as they were radical, and as disturbing as they were liberating. He theorized that each medium—print, radio, television, and film—had a different kind of impact on the user. Taken together, as media (plural), they surround humans on all sides, which he summed up in famous pronouncements like "The medium is the massage" and "The medium is the message."[2] McLuhan theorized that the days of print-dominated communication—the "Gutenberg Galaxy"—were numbered. He called print (books, newspapers, and magazines) a "cool" medium, because it chilled interaction with other humans, whereas electric media (television and radio) were "hot" because they created connections to what he called the "global village."[3] "Cool" media left users isolated. "Hot" media activated them. To ignore, resist, or fail to adapt to the new mass media, McLuhan said, would only bring anxiety, apathy, and alienation.

McLuhan's work in media was as revolutionary as Sigmund Freud's was in psychology. Though McLuhan died in 1980, before the advent of the Internet, Thomas Friedman, a *New York Times* columnist and author, used the metaphor "the world is flat" to update McLuhan's ideas for the Internet age. Friedman believed that free market capitalism and the Internet were transforming McLuhan's "global village" into a global shopping mall, which would spread prosperity and democracy. However, Friedman's ideas have also been critiqued and debunked by opponents of globalization, who decry the loss of regional identities and unique cultures as a result of this flattening. Regardless of how this ongoing debate plays out, it is clear that as the Internet stretches its tentacles into modern life, the definition of *media* will expand exponentially. The impacts of e-mail, blogs, the World Wide Web, downloading, file-sharing, YouTube, MySpace, Google, and others, have with unprecedented swiftness reshaped how we perceive the world.

Because of these more contemporary concerns, the vast majority of the material presented in this volume will pertain to media scandals that have occurred since the age of McLuhan and the advent of mass media—roughly, from the 1940s to the present day. Before fast-forwarding to post-World War II society, however, any study of American media scandals must flash back to the nation's origins. The underpinning of the mass media was made possible by the U.S. Constitution. The right to free expression is so sacrosanct to the American way of life that it is listed first among the Constitution's Bill of Rights.

The First Amendment reads, "Congress shall make no law respecting an estab-lishment of religion, or prohibiting the free exercise thereof; or abridging the freedom of speech, or of the press; or the right of the people peaceably to assem-ble, and to petition the government for a redress of grievances." This cherished right, while guaranteeing freedom of speech, also comes with responsibilities. The tension between these two pillars has, throughout American history, caused what can be called scandal—public outcries, legal proceedings, denunciations and even violence. (*See also* Chapter 2, "Race and Religion.") Media outlets can provoke such scandals by exposing criminal behavior, malfeasance, and lying by public figures and institutions, or by pushing the boundaries of what is deemed "fit to print" either through subject matter that some might find sacrilegious, deceitful, or obscene.

TIMELINE

1690

September 25   *Publick Occurrences Both Forreign and Domestick* was published in Boston; the four-page newspaper was summarily shut down by the colonial authorities for its controversial content.

1735

August   A jury acquitted newspaper publisher John Peter Zenger of seditious libel in New York City, setting a precedent for a free press that holds to this day.

1770

March   Boston engraver Paul Revere published a popular print that spread dissension throughout the colonies over "the bloody massacre perpetrated on King Street" (a.k.a. the Boston Massacre). Adding to the controversy, Revere had copied his print from an original work by another artist, Henry Pelham.

1776

January 10   Thomas Paine's history-changing pamphlet, *Common Sense*, was published, pushing the colonies toward a war for independence from Great Britain.

1806   Mason Locke "Parson" Weems published an expanded edition of his *A History of the Life and Death, Virtues and Exploits of General George Washington,* containing a fabricated anecdote about chopping down a cherry tree. Though this never happened in "real" life, it has been accepted as fact ever since.

1821   *Memoirs of a Woman of Pleasure* (illustrated!) was banned, arguably the first time a literary work in the United States was suppressed on grounds of obscenity.

1835

August 25   The *New York Sun* began a four-part series that claimed the moon was inhabited by all kinds of animals, including beavers and humans who could fly. The hoax made the *Sun* the widest-selling daily newspaper in the world.

1842
September 28   In New York, the first grand jury indictments in America against publishers of obscene books were issued against publishers Richard Hobbes and Henry R. Robinson, and the five book-stand proprietors who sold their books.

1852   John J. Jewett of Boston published *Uncle Tom's Cabin* by Harriett Beecher Stowe, the novel that, by exposing the institution of slavery to the average American, pushed the nation toward Civil War.

1873
March 3   Anthony Comstock successfully lobbied federal antiobscenity statutes through Congress, collectively known as the Comstock laws.

1873   The New York Society for the Suppression of Vice was founded by Anthony Comstock.

1906   In a speech, President Theodore Roosevelt coined the term *muckraker* to denote the new brand of investigative journalism embodied by the likes of Lincoln Steffens and the magazine he edited, *McClure's*.

1926
October 17   Father Charles E. Coughlin delivered his first radio sermon from the pulpit of his Michigan church, kicking off the career of one of America's most controversial media figures.

1928
March 19   The *Amos 'n' Andy* radio show, which would perpetuate negative racial stereotypes that took decades to defuse, debuted on WMAQ in Chicago.

1930
November 25   A member of Boston's Watch and Ward Society purchased a copy of D. H. Lawrence's *Lady Chatterley's Lover* at the Dunster House Book Shop in Cambridge. The manager of the shop and his clerk were both convicted of selling obscene literature and sent to jail.

1933
December 6   A federal judge ruled that James Joyce's *Ulysses* was "not written for the purpose of exploiting obscenity." It was one of the landmark rulings against censorship in U.S. history.

1937

July 27
Life magazine published Robert Capa's photograph captioned, "a Spanish soldier the instant he is dropped by a bullet through the head." The graphic image disturbed readers, and some critics insisted the photograph was a fake.

1938

October 30
Orson Welles's radio dramatization of H. G. Wells's classic *War of the Worlds* was mistakenly believed by listeners to be the report of a real Martian invasion. Panic ensued.

1943

September
With the War Department's sanction, *Life* began printing photographs of dead U.S. soldiers, to keep Americans on the home front from becoming complacent.

1948

August 4
Drew Pearson's "Washington Merry Go Round" column exposed the corruption of Rep. John Parnell Thomas, the powerful chairman of the House Un-American Activities Committee. Thomas resigned, was convicted of larceny, and was sent to prison.

1950

March 29
Herbert Block (a.k.a. "Herblock") published an editorial cartoon in the *Washington Post* in which he coined the term *McCarthyism*, after Sen. Joe McCarthy.

1954

March 9
On *See It Now*, TV journalist Edward R. Murrow warned viewers, "This is no time for men who oppose Senator McCarthy's methods to remain silent …"

September 16
A Comics Code Authority was adopted, covering 90 percent of all comic book titles in America. No torture, gore, or disrespect for authority was allowed. All comic books had to carry the code's seal on their cover or risk not being distributed.

1959

November 2
Charles Van Doren testified to Congress that he had cheated as a guest contestant on the television quiz show *Twenty-One*.

1960

February 10
Jack Paar, host of NBC's the *Tonight Show* (1957–62), stormed off the set on live television after having one of his planned jokes cut from his show-opening monologue. He said, "There must be a better way to make a living than this."

1963

November 24   Jack Ruby shot and killed Lee Harvey Oswald, the prime sus-
               pect in the assassination of President John F. Kennedy, in full
               view of live television coverage.

1964

March 13   In a landmark decision, a federal judge dismissed the copyright
               infringement suit brought by Irving Berlin against *MAD* maga-
               zine. The judge ruled, "We believe that parody and satire are
               deserving of substantial freedom—both as entertainment and as
               a form of social and literary criticism."

1968

February 1   Associated Press photographer Eddie Adams snapped a picture
               that would become the most famous, and upsetting, of the Viet-
               nam War. His image of a pointblank street-side execution in
               Saigon was deeply troubling to Americans who saw it in news-
               papers around the country.

February 27   CBS News correspondent Walter Cronkite hosted a special
               report on the Vietnam War, on which he said, "It seems now
               more certain than ever that the bloody experience of Vietnam is
               to end in a stalemate." President Lyndon Johnson remarked, "If
               I've lost Cronkite, I've lost middle America."

1969

November 12   The *New York Times* published Seymour Hersh's investigative
               article on the massacre of unarmed civilians at My Lai, in Viet-
               nam. The story won a Pulitzer Prize and changed the way many
               Americans viewed the unpopular war.

December 17   Tiny Tim married Victoria Mae Budinger ("Miss Vicki") on
               the *Tonight Show,* hosted by Johnny Carson. The outlandish
               spectacle, which critics called a shameless publicity stunt, was
               witnessed by 40 million viewers.

1972

June 13   The *New York Times* began printing a series of controversial
               articles on the history of America's involvement in Vietnam.

1973

May 17–   The "Watergate Hearings" were conducted by the Senate Select
August 7   Committee on Presidential Campaign Activities. The proceed-
               ings were carried live on television, and the broadcasts transfixed
               Americans that summer.

1974

August 12   Garry Trudeau, creator of the comic strip *Doonesbury*, published an installment depicting a stone wall being erected in front of the White House. The strip, which ran four days after President Richard Nixon resigned, was awarded a Pulitzer Prize.

1981

March 26   Five years after a libelous story about Carol Burnett appeared in the *National Enquirer*, a Los Angeles jury ordered the newspaper to pay the actress $1.6 million in damages and punitive recompense.

1984

June 18   Denver radio talk show host Allen Berg was gunned down in his driveway after several death threats had been made against him by members of a white supremacist group for his political commentary.

1985

September 26 Geraldo Rivera was scheduled to air an expose about Marilyn Monroe, the Mafia, and John and Robert Kennedy. But ABC President Roone Arledge—who was a friend of the Kennedy family—pulled the plug.

1986

January 28   The Space Shuttle Challenger exploded 73 seconds after liftoff, killing all seven crew members, including schoolteacher Sharon Christa McCauliffe, the first civilian to fly into space. Carried live on all three major networks, the tragedy was one of the darkest moments in U.S. broadcasting history.

1987

May 5–   The Iran-Contra hearings, which investigated the illegal activ-
August 3   ities within the Reagan White House, were broadcast live.

1988

June 7   A joint CNN/*Time* magazine broadcast accused the U.S. Army of using sarin nerve gas in a secret mission called "Tailwind," which targeted Americans who'd defected to Laos in 1970, as part of the Nixon war policy.

1990

July 25   At a baseball game between the Cincinnati Reds and San Diego Padres, Roseanne Barr sang the National Anthem. Her off-key rendition was followed by an off-color gesture. President George H. W. Bush called the TV broadcast "a disgrace."

1995

September 18   The *New York Times* and *Washington Post* both published the 35,000-word Unabomber manifesto.

1997

May 30   Comedian Ellen DeGeneres admitted that she was gay on an episode of her sitcom (*Ellen*), sparking celebration on the left and condemnation on the right.

1998

January 17   On his Internet gossip site *The Drudge Report*, Matt Drudge alleged that Bill Clinton had had an affair with White House intern Monica Lewinsky.

January 27   First Lady Hillary Clinton appeared on NBC's *Today* show to deny reports of her husband's affair with Lewinsky. She said, "The great story here for anybody willing to find it, write about it and explain it is this vast right-wing conspiracy that has been conspiring against my husband since the day he announced for president."

May 18   Stephen Glass's article "Hack Heaven" ran in the *New Republic*. None of it was true. Glass fooled his editors by creating a mock Web site and voice mail for the fake corporation.

2001

January 11   AOL purchased Time Warner for $164 billion, creating a giant media conglomerate that sparked fears of corporate news manipulation.

September 17   Bill Maher, host of ABC's *Politically Incorrect*, said, of the 9/11 terrorists, "We have been the cowards lobbing cruise missiles from 2,000 miles away. That's cowardly. Staying in the airplane when it hits the building, say what you want about it, it's not cowardly. Stupid maybe, but not cowardly." ABC fired him.

September 26   White House spokesman Ari Fleischer warned Americans, at a press conference, to "watch what they do and watch what they say." It was his answer to a reporter's question about Bill Maher's remarks on ABC's *Politically Incorrect*.

2002

October 13   Aaron McGruder's comic strip *The Boondocks* was dropped by several newspapers for unfavorably comparing George W. Bush to Adolf Hitler.

2003

July 14   Robert Novak revealed the identity of Valerie Plame, an under-cover CIA agent, in his syndicated newspaper column, a serious national security breach.

August 28	Pop singers Madonna, Britney Spears, and Christina Aguilera engaged in a sexually-suggestive "French kiss" during the MTV Video Music Awards ceremony.
October 2	Rush Limbaugh resigned as a commentator on ESPN's *Sunday NFL Countdown* after his racist remarks about Philadelphia Eagles quarterback Donovan McNabb created a furor against the network.

2004

February 1	At the 38th Super Bowl, Janet Jackson's breast was exposed during a halftime dance routine; though the mishap was blamed on a "wardrobe malfunction," it sparked an outcry against indecency on TV.

2005

August 4	Columnist Robert Novak stormed off the set of CNN's *Inside Politics*. At the time, Novak was under pressure for his role in exposing Valerie Plame's identity.
September 29	*New York Times* reporter Judith Miller was released from jail after spending 85 days incarcerated for refusing to reveal a White House source.

2006

January 26	On her TV talk show, host Oprah Winfrey confronted author James Frey about his fabricated "memoir," *A Thousand Little Pieces*. She had championed the book on her show, telling Frey, "I feel duped. But more importantly, I feel that you betrayed millions of readers."
April 29	Stephen Colbert gave a speech at the White House Correspondents' Association Dinner, mocking the assembled reporters and criticizing President George W. Bush, seated nearby. The speech angered Bush and the press corps, but made Colbert a media hero.
August 25	An agitated Christopher Hitchens made an obscene gesture at the studio audience during a broadcast of Bill Maher's cable television show.
September 10–11	ABC aired the two-part "docudrama" *Path to 9/11* that distorted the actual events so as to essentially blame the attacks on the Clinton administration. A former Clinton assistant said, "It is unconscionable to mislead the American public about one of the most horrendous tragedies our country has ever known."
October 23	Rush Limbaugh mimicked the Parkinson's disease of actor Michael J. Fox on his show, accusing Fox of "exaggerating the

effects of the disease" and, thus, being "really shameless," a criticism that would be leveled at Limbaugh afterwards.

2007

April 4   Don Imus made racist and sexist comments about the Rutgers University women's basketball team on his CBS Radio show *Imus in the Morning*, which was simulcast on MSNBC TV. He was fired from both venues over the comments.

2008

January   "Dr. Phil" McGraw tried to force his cameras into a hospital to film an intervention with the crisis-plagued Britney Spears.

Part I

RECURRENT THEMES

Chapter 1

POLITICS AND THE MEDIA

E
ven before the U.S. Constitution was ratified in 1788, precedents were set for the right to free expression by the American colonists. The seeds were planted for media scandals in America by the very first newspaper published in the colonies, *Publick Occurrences Both Forreign and Domestick*, printed by Richard Pierce and edited by Benjamin Harris. Harris vowed, as he wrote on the front page of his paper, to cure "that Spirit of Lying, which prevails amongst us."[1] The first issue reported a suicide by hanging, a smallpox epidemic, and scandalous rumors about the king of France. Though it began printing on September 25, 1690, the four-page newspaper was shut down by the Massachusetts Bay Colony authorities four days later for "printing without a license." The Colonial Governor and Council objected to the content, which they described as "Reflections of a high nature"—meaning highly inflammatory—and "sundry doubtful and uncertain Reports." That is to say, the "Reports" were seen as a threat to the Crown.[2]

While the scandal over its suppression was short-lived—*Publick Occurrences Both Forreign and Domestick* did not publish another issue—the push for press freedom was on. Indeed, as the colonies became more established and self-sufficient in the eighteenth century, Americans began to regularly make "reflections of a high nature" about their individual liberties. The liberty that proved most threatening to colonial rule was freedom of the press, which developed in the different colonies at varying speeds. Historian Clinton Rossiter wrote, "The establishment of a free press in eighteenth-century America was a fact of great moment for the future Republic. The struggle for a free and unlicensed press was long and frustrating, but by the time of the Stamp Act [passed by Parliament in March 1765] the victory had been sealed."[3] The Stamp Act—which required tax stamps for newspapers, among other public documents—was despised by the colonists, and it was ignored by most of them. Boycotts of British goods were organized, and threats were made against British stamp agents, most of whom resigned their posts in fear. Parliament repealed the Stamp Act in 1766, opening the way to free distribution of newspapers and, in effect, lighting the fuse for liberty.

Among the journalists whom Rossiter credits with expanding press freedoms were James Franklin of the *New-England Courant* (1721), the first paper in Boston to "be published without authority"; Andrew Bradford and nephew William Bradford, who both produced newspapers in Philadelphia; Benjamin Franklin, who published the iconoclastic weekly, the *Pennsylvania Gazette* (1729); William Parks, who published two important journals in two different colonies, *Maryland Gazette* (1727) and *Virginia Gazette* (1736); and Benjamin Edes and John Gill, who began publishing the *Boston Gazette* in 1755 and soon created enough in the way of scandal to be nicknamed "The Weekly Dung-Barge" by the Tories (colonists loyal to the British crown).

Rossiter saved his greatest praise for John Peter Zenger and the *New-York Weekly Journal*, which began printing on November 1, 1733, and soon developed a reputation for criticizing the excesses of British rule. William Cosby, the British governor of the Province of New York, was the embodiment of that excess. Known for his political corruption and kickback schemes, Cosby took the former British governor to court in April 1733 over a salary dispute. When the court ruled against him, Cosby suspended the chief justice of the provincial court (Lewis Morris). When Zenger's newspaper later criticized Cosby for this action—accusing him of violating both English and American laws—as well as for trying to rig the 1734 elections, the governor had the publisher arrested on a charge of seditious libel and ordered four editions of the paper burned. Zenger was held for ten months without being allowed to communicate with friends and family (his wife Anna continued to publish his newspaper). His resulting trial in August 1735 for "printing and publishing false, scandalous, malicious and seditious" statements was among the most important in American press history, establishing a precedent for freedom of the press eventually incorporated in the First Amendment of the U.S. Constitution. Zenger was represented in court by Andrew Hamilton, who argued that his client had not committed the crime because what he printed was true. The jury, ignoring the instructions of the pro-Cosby judge, returned a verdict of "not guilty" after only ten minutes of deliberation.

Rossiter wrote, "The Zenger trial is rightly celebrated as an epic of American liberty. Although the principles argued by Hamilton—the admissibility of evidence concerning the truth of an alleged libel and the right of the jury to decide whether a piece of writing is seditious or defamatory—were still many decades from final establishment in law, the release of Zenger was widely acclaimed and did much to put fiber in colonial editors and ginger in their political reporting."[4]

Reaction to Zenger's trial was dramatic. One *Connecticut Gazette* correspondent wrote, "The Liberty of the Press is the Foundation of all our other Liberties, whether Civil or Religious and whenever the Liberty of the Press is taken away, either by open Force, or any little, dirty infamous Arts, we shall immediately become as wretched, as ignorant, and as despicable Slaves, as any one Nation in all Europe."[5]

The most lasting impact the trial had was to set a precedent for—and a high value on—truthfulness in reporting. The Zenger decision maintained that the truth is never libelous, a "truth" that still holds today. Reporting the truth can be contested on grounds of national security—revealing classified material—or because it violates standards of decency, but it can never be libel.

BROADSIDED BY REVOLUTION

Though books were revered in colonial America, they were beyond the means of average citizens. Thus, pamphlets and broadsides (one-sheet documents distributed and displayed like posters) became the most popular—and opinion-shaping—medium of written expression before the Revolution. Pamphlets were booklets consisting of a few printers' sheets loosely folded and stitched. They were quicker to produce than books, spontaneous, timely, uncensored, and cheap.

One of the pamphlets most crucial to American history was Thomas Jefferson's *A Summary View of the Rights of British America* (1774), an early argument for the separation of the colonies from Great Britain. Anticipating a negative reaction from the king and his minions, Jefferson printed it in Williamsburg under the protective byline "a Native, and Member of the House of Burgesses." Another pamphlet crucial to American history was Thomas Paine's *Common Sense*. When published on January 10, 1776, it changed the course of world history. The forty-seven-page, two-shilling pamphlet was the first to raise the cry for America's full independence, without conditions or restrictions. Because of its incendiary nature, Paine did not put his name on the title page, referring to the author as "an American" (Paine was British). The pamphlet created a political scandal that has, in retrospect, been seen as the catalyst for the American Revolution. First printed in Philadelphia by "R. Bell, in Third-Street," *Common Sense* was reprinted in most major American cities and London. By June 1776, 120,000 copies had been sold; 500,000 copies would eventually be sold in Paine's lifetime. The author, who became an American citizen after Independence, refused royalties, saying it would demean his patriotic value to accept them. He continued his pamphleteering during the American Revolution with *The Crisis* series, one of which began with the famous line, "These are the times that try men's souls."

Once the new nation was established and its Constitution ratified, the new political establishment was not granted immunity from the same scrutiny that landed John Peter Zenger and Paul Revere in hot water.

UNDERGROUND PRESS

An underground press has existed on the edge of American society for most of its history. One could say that American journalism began as an underground press, with the first newspaper in the colonies, *Publick Occurrences*, which sparked a scandal with its first, and only, edition. Benjamin Franklin could be called an "underground" press figure, too, for his *Poor Richard's Almanack* (humor, advice, and sedition), John Peter Zenger's *New-York Weekly Journal* (suppressed by the Colonial government in 1735), *Freedom's Journal* (the first black-controlled newspaper, 1827, calling for abolition of slavery), *Cherokee Phoenix* (the first Indian newspaper, 1828, demanding more equitable treatment from the federal government), and the perennially controversial abolitionist papers of Frederick Douglass (*The North Star*) and William Lloyd Garrison (*The Liberator*). (*See also* Chapter 2, "Race and Religion.")

At the dawn of the twentieth century, a number of important papers began operating on the fringes of the political spectrum, not just to push ideological agendas, but to shed light on (or rake muck about) societal ills the mainstream press would otherwise ignore or dismiss, like poverty, hunger, illiteracy, lynching, alcoholism, and child labor. When these revelations reached a wide enough audience, they caused scandals that forced the authorities to address the problems. Among the best of the early underground publications were *McClure's* (1893–1911), *The Masses* (1911–17), *New Masses* (1926–48), *Liberator* (1918–23), *Workers' Monthly* (1924), the *Coming Nation* (1912), *Good Morning* (1919–21), *Big Stick* (Yiddish weekly, a.k.a. "Groyser Kundes," 1909–27), *Appeal to Reason* (1897–1922), *Daily Worker* (1924–58), *Mother Earth* (founded and edited by anarchist Emma Goldman, 1906–17), the *New Leader* (1924–present day), the *Catholic Worker* (founded by Dorothy Day, 1933–present day), the *Progressive* (founded by Senator Robert LaFollette as *LaFollette's Weekly*, 1909–present day), *Partisan Review* (1934–2003), and the *Guardian* (1948–92).

Some of the great names in advocacy journalism appeared in the pages of the above periodicals, including John Reed, Theodore Dreiser, Elizabeth Cochrane ("Nellie Bly"), Ida Tarbell, Lincoln Steffens, Upton Sinclair, Ida B. Wells, Dorothy Thompson (the first correspondent to be expelled from Nazi Germany by order of Hitler), Thomas Merton, and Philip and Donald Berrigan. Many of these publications were subject to harassment from the state and federal governments, for their alleged ties to Moscow, and for their unapologetically leftist and radical political advocacy, which by definition put them in opposition to the political and corporate status quo. Pressure was particularly intense during the years 1919–1921, in the wake of the Russian Revolution when anarchists and radicals had stepped up their activities. U.S. Attorney General Alexander Palmer ordered the Justice Department and Immigration Department to arrest suspected radicals in the United States. These so-called "Palmer Raids" briefly shut down some of these publications.

The Cartoonist Who Cleaned Up the City

Traditional media venues, like *Harper's Weekly*, *Puck*, and the *New York Herald Tribune*, also initiated their share of scandal. *Harper's Weekly* sparked

Cartoons like this one by Thomas Nast, in *Harper's Weekly*, created such outrage against William Marcy Tweed that he was hounded out of office in 1872 and into a jail cell. Tweed's corrupt regime was in power for two decades. Here, he leads a group of vultures. The caption reads, "Let Us Prey." Courtesy of Library of Congress, Prints and Photographs Division.

the biggest political scandal of the nineteenth century when its cartoonist, Thomas Nast, relentlessly exposed political corruption in New York City. Nast's main target was William Marcy Tweed (a.k.a. "Boss" Tweed), a politician who, as "Grand Sachem of Tammany Hall," was the most powerful man in New York. Because Tweed controlled city police, both political parties, and all poll workers, he was a virtual dictator for two decades before incurring Nast's wrath in 1869. Tweed's "Ring" plundered the city treasury, running up huge public debt while supporters lined their pockets. Nast's cartoons in *Harper's Weekly* fueled public outrage against the regime, even while Tweed "punished" Harper's (the magazine publisher) by stripping them of a city text-book contract. But that did not work because Nast's cartoons had tripled the circulation of *Harper's Weekly*. Responding to an attempt to bribe him into silence, Nast said, "I shall be busy here for some time getting a gang of thieves behind the bars!"[6] Nast created some of the most powerful editorial cartoons in U.S. history, including the often reprinted "Let Us Prey" and "The Tammany Tiger Loose, 'What Are you Going to Do About It?'" With unprecedented starkness and courage, Nast clearly depicted "good" v. "evil" without equivocation. His cartoons grew so ferocious by the election of 1872 that the Tweed Ring was soundly defeated at the polls, and many Tammany insiders went to prison, including Tweed. After Tweed escaped in 1875, he was caught in Spain by someone who recognized him from one of Nast's cartoons. Tweed was returned to prison, where he died in April 1878.

Raking the Muck

Muckraking was a term that came into popular use to designate writers, editors, and reporters who exposed corruption like Tweed's and advocated for reform. Lincoln Steffens, who became managing editor of *McClure's Magazine* in 1901, is generally regarded as America's first *muckraker*, though the term itself was not coined until 1906, in a speech by President Theodore Roosevelt. He compared the "fault finders" to a character in John Bunyan's 1678 fable *Pilgrim's Progress*: "the Man with the Muckrake who could look no way but downward." Though Roosevelt objected to the seemingly relentless negativity of the reportage, he also saluted the muckrakers thusly, "There should be relentless exposure of and attack upon every evil man whether politician or business man, every evil practice, whether in politics, in business, or in social life. I hail as a benefactor every writer or speaker, every man who, on the platform, or in book, magazine, or newspaper, with merciless severity makes such attack, provided always that he in his turn remembers that the attack is of use only if it is absolutely truthful."[7]

Steffens was committed to finding "the cause of political corruption and the cure."[8] With the support and encouragement of magazine publisher S. S. McClure, Steffens assembled a stable of fearless writers, to go along with staffers Ida M. Tarbell and Ray Stannard Baker. Wherever it occurred, Steffens rooted out big-city corruption, using the "shame of our cities" (the title of his 1904 book adapted from his *McClure's* work) to prod officials into implementing reforms. He made enemies—and inspired reform—in Minneapolis, St. Louis, Pittsburgh, Philadelphia, Chicago, Cleveland, Boston, Los Angeles, and New York. He also encouraged writers to investigate the monopolies that had risen, unchecked, since the Civil War. The attitudes of these monopolies were expressed by the head of one of them, thusly: "The public be damned!"

Tarbell was a century ahead of her time. After researching the oil industry, in particular, the Standard Oil Company ("Esso"), for five years, she wrote eighteen articles published in *McClure's* in the years 1902–1904. She exposed price-fixing, price-gouging, blackmail, and the extent of Esso's oil monopoly (they controlled 90 percent of the nation's oil). While regulation of monopolies had been addressed by the Sherman Antitrust Act of 1890, Tarbell's efforts prodded President Roosevelt—despite his denunciation of muckrakers—to create landmark "trust busting" legislation. Muckraking appeared in other magazines of the era, like *Collier's*, *Munsey's*, and *Everybody's*.

The other preeminent American magazine of its day, *Atlantic Monthly*, stirred up controversy too. The magazine, edited by William Dean Howells, revealed the dark underside of the Gilded Age long before such advocacy journalism was called muckraking. In 1881, Henry Demarest Lloyd offered the first inside look most Americans got of the nation's railroad and oil monopolies. Due to unprecedented demand for the story, it was reprinted separately from the magazine six times. In 1894, this pioneering work was fleshed out to book length in *Wealth against Commonwealth*.

Elizabeth Cochrane (a.k.a. Nellie Bly) was also fearless in pursuit of stories. In 1888, in order to secure a newspaper assignment for the *New York World*, she feigned madness so she would be admitted to the notorious insane asylum on Blackwell's Island. From that insider vantage point, she wrote arguably the first chronicle of what life was like in such institutions, "Ten Days in a Mad-House," in 1888. Her revelations of such scenes as starving inmates forced to eat garbage and doused by the staff with ice water unleashed a major public health scandal, leading to tightening of regulations in mental institutions. It also raised a scandal over whether it was "ethical" to go "under cover," a debate that's still going on. (*See also* Chapter 3, "Sexuality and Morality.") Bly also reported on prison life and gave firsthand accounts of executions.

Other important early muckraking works included:

By Bread Alone by Isaac Kahn Friedman (1901). The fictional but truthful insider story of an 1892 steelworkers' strike was printed by S. S. McClure; the American "radical novel" was said to begin with this book.

The Jungle by Upton Sinclair (1906). Arguably the most influential "radical novel," about working conditions in the meatpacking industry; the scandal unleashed by its publication led to changes in the nation's food laws. Another muckraking Sinclair novel, *Oil!* (1927), was the inspiration for the Oscar-winning film *There Will Be Blood* (2007).

Great American Fraud by Samuel Hopkins Adams (1906). An expose of the patent medicine scams that led to the passage of the Pure Food and Drug Act.

The Iron Heel by Jack London (1908). After his muckraking chronicle of English slum life, *People of the Abyss* (1903), London wrote this dystopian novel that, with eerie accuracy, prophesied the coming "Iron Age of Fascism."

When Things Were Doing by C. A. Steere (1907). A futurist fantasy in which five million socialists overthrow the U.S. government when the capitalists prevent change at the voting booth.

The Octopus: The Epic of the Wheat by Frank Norris (1901). Norris based
  this widely-read novel on the true story of the Mussel Slough Tragedy of
  1880, when railroad company mercenaries waged war with California
  wheat farmers who refused to pay the usurious price for land grabbed by
  the railroads.
The History of the Standard Oil Company by Ida Tarbell (1904). An
  expanded version of her study of the first giant oil company in America;
  the book influenced President Theodore Roosevelt in his efforts to bust
  up monopolies.
Out of Work by Frances Kellor (1904). A study of chronic unemployment.
Frenzied Finance by Thomas W. Lawson (1906). An early stock scandal
  involving Amalgamated Copper was dissected by this muckraking classic.
Bitter Cry of the Children by John Spargo (1906). Spargo proved that child
  labor wasn't just found in novels by Charles Dickens, or only in England.

Muckrakers Get Political

Largely because the previously-mentioned magazines were not overtly partisan or ideological, the scandals they sparked didn't cause a backlash against
them. The writers may have been denounced inside corporate boardrooms,
but no efforts were made to suppress or punish them. This was not true for
magazines like *The Masses* (1911–17), a radical monthly that focused on the
labor movement and social revolution, while it was also committed to high
artistic quality. Genevieve Taggard, a poet who contributed work to *The Masses*
and its offshoot, *The Liberator* (1918–24), said, "There was so much to be
said, done, thought, seen, tried out. The youth of the land was getting out of
doors and all winter taboos were being broken."

The spirit of Thomas Nast carried on in *The Masses*, particularly in the
political art by Art Young, Robert Minor, and John Sloan. Among the most
controversial was a June 1914 cover painting by John Sloan—an esteemed
member of the Ash Can School of painters—depicting a massacre of women
and children by strike breakers in the coal fields of Ludlow, Colorado. In
1913, *The Masses* set off a scandal within the ranks of journalism when the
editors accused the Associated Press (AP) of downplaying, even suppressing,
the facts of a coal miners' strike in West Virginia—at the behest of the mine
owners. The AP sued for libel but later dropped the suit.

The Masses pushed the reportorial boundaries to the breaking point, literally.
The magazine's most famous correspondent, John Reed, reported firsthand on
the Russian Revolution, unabashedly hailing the Bolshevik victory. His dispatches were later compiled for *Ten Days That Shook the World* (1919), for
which V. I. Lenin, the leader of the successful Russian Revolution, wrote the
foreword. The book, considered the definitive account of the Russian Revolution, is still in print today. Because Reed's dispatches were so pro-revolutionary,

the Post Office deemed *The Masses* "unmailable," using the Espionage Act as justification for putting it out of business by December 1917.[9] Reed returned from Russia to face the government's charge of sedition, along with Art Young, for "conspiracy to obstruct recruiting" for World War I. Before the case could be decided, Reed returned to Russia, where he died in 1920; he is the only American ever buried in the Kremlin.[10] In his honor, the American Communist Party named its arts organizations John Reed Clubs. Steffens also went to Russia and hailed the Revolution. He famously, and inaccurately, wrote in 1919, "I have seen the future, and it works."[11]

Photographing Scandal

Like Thomas Nast, Jacob Riis created scandal with pictures. Rather than editorial cartoons, he used photographs of the appalling conditions in New York's Lower East Side slums to fuel public outrage. Riis's crude photographs accompanied his written accounts (he started as a print reporter for New York's *Evening Sun*); he later compiled twelve years' worth of his tenement reportage and photographs in *How the Other Half Lives* (1890). The combination of impassioned

Photographs like this one of living conditions in New York City's tenements during the 1880s were scandalous enough to force the government to act. Courtesy of Library of Congress, Prints and Photographs Division.

words and damning pictures produced an indictment that could not be ignored. The ensuing scandals that he unleashed led to calls for "slum clearance" and a push for public housing.

Among the loneliest voice of the muckrakers was that of Helen Hunt Jackson. Inspired by her friend Harriett Beecher Stowe's *Uncle Tom's Cabin*, Jackson wrote the polemical *A Century of Dishonor* (1881), the first book to decry the government's policy toward Native Americans. She sent a copy of the book to every member of Congress, inscribing each cover in red-inked letters with the words, "Look upon your hands: they are stained with the blood of your relations." She also wrote *Ramona* (1884), an impassioned novel that raised awareness about Indian life. The book was an instant success and Jackson was named a special government commissioner in charge of examining living conditions for Indians in California. She died a year later, but the seed she planted bore fruit in the heightened awareness of Native American concerns.

Peerless Pearson

Drew Pearson was one of the first American journalists to straddle more than one medium, and the first bona fide muckraker to do so. From the early 1930s until his death in 1969, he hosted a radio show and wrote a syndicated column, both called "Washington Merry-Go-Round" (the title was taken from two books of political exposes he coauthored with Robert S. Allen in 1931 and 1932, respectively). The scandals unleashed by Pearson's pen and radio broadcasts led to, among other things, the imprisonment of four Congressmen, the resignation of President Dwight Eisenhower's chief of staff, Sherman Adams, and the downfall of Senator Thomas J. Dodd, who was censured in 1967 for corruption brought to light by Pearson's column.

From the outset, Pearson—raised a Quaker and hardened by foreign service among the world's destitute—was determined to be a government watchdog. On the strength of the "Merry-Go-Round" books, he and Allen were offered a syndicated column. Jack Anderson, later Pearson's partner, described the concept for his column: "It would appear not in several papers, but in several hundred. It would be read not only by intellectuals and liberals and political enthusiasts, but by great numbers of ordinary people running into the tens of millions who would be attracted by a formula that contained something for everyone. It would specialize in the butchery of sacred cows in papers which, elsewhere in their pages, held them sacrosanct: Presidents, charismatic generals, jingoes, supercops, noted divines, corporation heads.... It would be a voice that could not be silenced."[12]

Pearson was a veritable fountain of scandal, not to mention a powerful figure both feared and read religiously by Washington insiders. At his death, Pearson's (and Anderson's) column was carried in 650 newspapers, with a combined circulation of 60 million. Of the 275 lawsuits filed against Pearson by targets of his columns (including one by General Douglas MacArthur), he only lost one.

Among the most sensitive scandals Pearson sparked was over General George Patton. Because the nation was at war in 1943, Patton's harsh treatment of his soldiers was hushed up by the press corps in the interests of "national security." However, when Pearson learned from eyewitnesses that Patton had beaten two U.S. soldiers suffering from combat-related shell shock in Sicily on August 3, 1943, he could not hold his tongue. He was as angry at his fellow journalists for remaining silent as he was at Patton, whom he felt was "unstable."[13] On November 21, 1943, Pearson told a nationwide radio audience of Patton's "slapping incidents." The military command denied the report but relented when other military officials, emboldened by Pearson, confirmed it. Pearson reported on other incidents involving Patton that led some to question the general's sanity. Because of the scandal, Patton was reassigned to noncombat duty for the next year, and only reactivated after D-Day.

Similarly sensitive was the 1949 forced retirement of Defense Secretary James Forrestal, partly caused by Pearson and Anderson's relentless reportage. Forrestal, an ardent anti-Communist and the most powerful man in President Harry Truman's Cabinet, had exhibited signs of mental illness for some time. Pearson, fearing for the security of a nation led in part by a mentally unstable person with access to nuclear weapons, brought Forrestal's illness to light in his columns and on the radio, whereas the rest of the Washington press corps—knowing of Forrestal's illness—lapsed into gentlemanly silence. Forrestal was finally forced to leave office by President Truman, and was sent to Bethesda Naval Hospital suffering from "exhaustion." When Forrestal leaped to his death from the hospital's sixteenth floor six weeks later, Pearson and Anderson, as well as gossip columnist Walter Winchell, were blamed for the death. (*See also* "Winchelled, Parsoned, and Hoppered.")

At the beginning of the "Red Scare," when the Soviet Union became a world power and American politicians parlayed a fear of Communist infiltration into a tool of domestic control, Pearson was one of the few journalists not intimidated by the House Committee on Un-American Activities (HUAC). HUAC, formed in 1938, was mandated to investigate threats to national security posed by domestic extremist groups, but by the late 1940s, had become an intimidating political force aimed at all progressive and left-wing groups deemed "un-American." Chaired by the powerful John Parnell Thomas, HUAC had so cowed the film industry that it voluntarily created "blacklists" of suspected Communists and "fellow travelers"; once a name appeared on these lists, that person was not allowed to work in Hollywood. HUAC also prodded President Truman to implement a Loyalty Order that all government employees were required to sign; anyone suspected of "disloyalty," even if the source of an accusation was unverified, was subject to dismissal. After one of his friends, Laurence Duggan, was driven to suicide by HUAC harassment, Pearson doggedly pursued rumors of Representative Thomas's own corruption until he had documents to corroborate it. Pearson's "Washington Merry-Go-Round" column on August 4, 1948, citing Thomas's years of taking "kickbacks" from office staff, sparked a criminal investigation. Thomas resigned, was convicted of larceny, and sent to prison. More importantly, Pearson and his young "legman" Anderson had helped thwart America's move toward right-wing dictatorship.

Two years later, Pearson took on Thomas's political heir apparent, Senator Joseph McCarthy, who had earlier accused him—in collaboration with "international Communism"—of causing Forrestal's death. Pearson and McCarthy crossed paths at the Sulgrave Club, a Washington, D.C., women's organization. The gruff, hulking McCarthy cornered the smaller, pacifistic Pearson in the cloak room and kneed him twice in the groin.[14] McCarthy later bragged to the press about his physical confrontation with Pearson. In a speech, McCarthy called Pearson "the voice of international Communism" and "an unprincipled liar and a fake." McCarthy continued his Communist "witch hunt" until he crashed and burned on television in 1954.[15] (*See also* "The End of McCarthyism.")

Pearson's fearlessness rubbed off on his young collaborator, Jack Anderson. When Anderson took over the "Merry-Go-Round" column in 1969, the political scene had changed dramatically. The Vietnam War had escalated and a former associate of Senator McCarthy, Richard M. Nixon, was in the White House. For the next six years, Anderson doggedly pursued Nixon in his column. Though Bob Woodward and Carl Bernstein of the *Washington Post* have been credited with breaking the Watergate story, Anderson was the first to report on the break-in and cover-up—Anderson actually reported on *two* break-ins at the Watergate offices of the Democratic National Committee; only on the second break-in were the perpetrators caught. His use of secret documents to embarrass the White House earned him the 1972 Pulitzer Prize. His refusal to back down from the Watergate affair kept the story alive until the young *Post* reporters began devoting daily coverage, leading to the televised hearings on the Watergate scandal by the U.S. Senate. (*See also* "Watergate Hearings.") Anderson's scoops hit so painfully close to the truth that Nixon associates E. Howard Hunt and G. Gordon Liddy "discussed in oblique terms a project to assassinate Jack Anderson one day over lunch ... They concluded that the best tradecraft to use would be to make it look as if Anderson had been a victim of street crime."[16] In honor of his long career and defense of the First Amendment, an annual Jack Anderson Award is now given to investigative journalists (or, muckrakers).

The Censored Centenarian

The career of one of America's great champions of press freedom, George Seldes, paralleled both Pearson's and Anderson's (he died in 1995, at age 104). An acolyte of Steffens, regarded as the father of American muckraking, Seldes was a link between the early age of muckraking and modern investigative journalism. As a foreign correspondent for the *Chicago Tribune* in the 1920s, he filed dispatches from every "hot zone" in the decade. For his efforts to push press freedom to its limits, Seldes was court-martialed by the U.S. Army for interviewing the supreme commander of the German Army, Paul von Hindenburg, at the end of World War I. Hindenburg, the man who would later appoint Adolf Hitler German chancellor, admitted to Seldes that Germany was defeated when the United States entered the war in 1917. This revelation, had it been widely shared, would have deflated the myth of national betrayal that Hitler later used to secure and expand power in Germany. That is, Hitler rose to prominence by proclaiming that Germany had been "stabbed in the back" by Jews, Socialists, and Communists, which weakened them sufficiently to lose the war and accept the severe restrictions of the final Treaty of Versailles. This explanation appealed to the German masses. Struggling as they were under postwar conditions, Germans wanted to believe that there was some other explanation for their plight than defeat on the battlefield. Seldes provided what would have been the counterargument straight from von Hindenburg himself.[17] Seldes was also expelled from the Soviet Union for a confrontational interview with Lenin in 1921, and he was expelled from Italy for linking Benito Mussolini to the death of Giacomo Matteotti in 1924, head of an opposition party. After leaving the *Tribune* in 1928, Seldes published two books, *You Can't Print That!* (1929) and *Can These Things Be!* (1931), containing material censored by the government. He published the first expose of the global arms trade, *Iron, Blood and Profits* (1934), followed by an account of Benito Mussolini, *Sawdust Caesar* (1935), and two books on the newspaper business, *Freedom of the Press* (1935) and *Lords of the Press* (1938). He was one of the first American journalists to confront the right wing, in his prescient book, *Witch Hunt* (1940), for which Senator McCarthy later accused him of being a Communist.

From 1940 to 1950, Seldes published a political newsletter, *In fact*, with a circulation of 176,000. In this newsletter, he broke some major stories, including revealing the link between cigarette smoking and cancer in 1941. Seldes argued that story was suppressed by every major newspaper in the country for fear of losing advertising money from the tobacco companies—a campaign of silence that cost the lives of millions of Americans. Seldes, because of his outspokenness, was blacklisted by a number of newspapers during the McCarthy era, but he continued to write books. His last one contained the fitting title *Witness to a Century* (1987).

At War with the Warren Commission

When President John F. Kennedy was assassinated in Dallas on November 22, 1963, Americans turned to the media for solace and answers. A week later, President Lyndon Johnson appointed a commission to investigate the assassination, led by the chief justice of the U.S. Supreme Court, Earl Warren. After nearly a year of research, interviews, and discussions, the commission issued an 888-page, 296,000-word report on September 27, 1964; the "Warren Report" concluded that the killer was the lone gunman Lee Harvey Oswald and that he was not part of a wider conspiracy. While this "official" story placated some people, the report unleashed a torrent of criticism that it was a "whitewash," or worse, a "cover up." Many books disputing key points in the report were published in its wake; they have continued to be published as more material related to the crime is declassified and made available to researchers. Among the most controversial of the books were *Rush to Judgment* by Mark Lane (1966), *They've Killed the President!* by Robert Sam Anson (1975), *Appointment in Dallas* by Hugh C. McDonald (1975), *The Assassination Tapes* by George O'Toole (1975), *Conspiracy* by Anthony Summers (1980), *Deadly Secrets* by William Turner and Warren Hinckle (1992), and *Deep Politics and the Death of JFK* by Peter Dale Scott (1993). New Orleans District Attorney James Garrison spawned his own mini witch hunt with his book, *On the Trail of the Assassins*, and Garrison's attempt to pin the assassination on Clay Shaw was covered in a controversial book by James Kirkwood, *American Grotesque*.

As a result of the contrarian views expressed in most of these books, suspicions about a conspiracy to kill the president became widespread. "Conspiracy theory" became a buzz phrase that launched a separate publishing genre in the 1960s, stretching its tentacles into all the corridors of power in Washington, D.C. These publications, and their huge and enduring sales, are often cited as proof that millions of Americans no longer trust their government. As Seymour Hersh learned on the Pentagon beat, the abyss between the government's "official" story and reality as perceived by most Americans came to be known as the "credibility gap." That gap has continued to grow with the string of dubious explanations—now largely dismissed as "spin control"—for subsequent events like the Vietnam War, Watergate, Iran-Contra, the Savings and Loan crisis, and the Iraq war.

Hersh Goes First

Originally assigned by the Associated Press to cover the Pentagon beat in 1965, Seymour Hersh was convinced that official press briefings were unreliable. By ferreting out more trustworthy "off the record" sources within the Pentagon, Hersh was able to extricate the truth from the "official" story. His first big scoop for AP was about how universities and corporations, on contract to the Pentagon, were making chemical and biological weapons in 1966, later substantiated in his detailed first book, *Chemical and Biological Warfare* (1970). After leaving the AP in 1968 to pursue a freelance career, Hersh heard about a U.S. Army criminal investigation of Lieutenant William Calley at Fort Benning, Georgia. Calley was accused of murder for leading his platoon in a massacre of

Vietnamese civilians at the village of My Lai in March 1968. The Army wanted to complete its probe in secret and, if necessary, conduct a quiet court-martial proceeding. Hersh tracked down other eyewitnesses to the massacre, and learned that Army officials—including Major Colin Powell, future Secretary of State Colin Powell—ignored revelations about the massacre.[18] Hersh reconstructed the events from eyewitness accounts, and on November 12, 1969, the *New York Times* published his investigative article on My Lai. The story not only won a Pulitzer Prize, but it also unleashed a scandal that changed the course of history. The article reported how on March 16, 1968, U.S. soldiers gunned down 347 unarmed Vietnamese civilians—children and babies included. This prompted widespread condemnation around the world and reduced public support for the war. It also led to a lengthy court-martial of the commanding officer, Lieutenant Calley, from November 1970 to March 1971. Calley was convicted of premeditated murder of 22 civilians and sentenced to life imprisonment, but only served three years of house arrest. His sentence was commuted in 1974 by President Nixon. The antiwar movement was further radicalized by the My Lai revelations and stepped up their demonstrations.

After winning the Pulitzer Prize, Hersh worked for the *New York Times* from 1972 to 1979. Hersh uncovered, among other things, the CIA's violation of its charter—which bans the agency from any intelligence gathering within the United States—by conducting domestic spying on antiwar groups for President Nixon, as well as the CIA's aiding the military junta that murdered the democratically elected president of Chile, Salvador Allende. Hersh also wrote a series of books that countermanded the government's "official" stories. In 1986, his book *The Target Is Destroyed* revealed that the accidental shoot-down of a Korean commercial air flight by Soviet jets was the result of a U.S. intelligence operation designed to confuse Russian surveillance efforts. At the time of the tragedy, President Ronald Reagan blamed the Soviet Union for the "act of barbarism, born of a society which wantonly disregards individual rights and the value of human life and seeks constantly to expand and dominate other nations."[19] CIA documents later corroborated Hersh's story.

In recent years, Hersh has written for *The New Yorker*, most notably about the political deceptions that preceded the U.S. invasion of Iraq in March 2003, the Bush administration's push for war with Iran, and the possibility of nuclear weapons being used on a preemptive basis. Hersh so angered one of the architects of the Iraq war, Richard Perle, a member of the powerful Defense Advisory Board, that he told CNN, "Sy Hersh is the closest thing American journalism has to a terrorist."[20]

The Pentagon Papers

One of the media figures embodying this new skepticism toward the federal government was Daniel Ellsberg, whose name was synonymous with "The

Pentagon Papers." On June 13, 1972, the *New York Times* began printing a series of controversial articles on the history of America's involvement in Vietnam. Though the two lead articles carried the bylines of Neil Sheehan and Hedrick Smith, respectively, the stories were actually based on a classified (read: top secret) 47-volume study commissioned by former Secretary of Defense Robert S. McNamara. That study, called "History of U.S. Decision-Making Process on Vietnam Policy, 1945–1967"—mandated by McNamara to be "encyclopedic and objective"—came to be known as "The Pentagon Papers." The text of these 47 volumes was prepared by a Pentagon-based staff of 36 military officers, civilian policy experts, and historians under the leadership of Leslie Gelb. The Papers included 4,000 pages of actual documents from the 1945–1967 period, and 3,000 pages of analysis.

While the scandal resulting from the publication focused largely on the alleged breach of national security by Daniel Ellsberg—the Rand Corporation consultant and ex-U.S. marine who worked on the papers and whose own intense misgivings about the Vietnam War led him to secretly release the papers to the *Times*—no one disputed or debunked the papers' startling conclusions. Among these were that U.S. presidents from Harry Truman to Lyndon Johnson had covertly been "directly involved" or played a "direct role" in the events that took place in Vietnam, dating back to when it was a French colony. Further, U.S. presidents authorized sabotage, harassment, and provocation of established governments. Perhaps the most disturbing revelation was Sheehan's description of what Sanford J. Ungar called "the build-up of a secret 'provocation strategy' and the drafting of a congressional resolution as a blank check for escalation to be held in reserve."

In other words, U.S. policy had been to provoke an incident, and then use that provocation as a pretext to start open warfare. That incident, in the Gulf of Tonkin, did occur and led to the escalation of American troops and years of combat. The American people, it appeared from the Pentagon Papers, had been led into war by their presidents or, as Ungar put it, "systematically misled by their elected and appointed leaders."

The initial *New York Times* articles were, noted Ungar, "the opening round in what would become one of the most dramatic conflicts between press and government in American history." To produce this series, the *Times* devoted four reporters, plus editors and staffers, and stationed them under tight security on the eleventh floor of the New York Hilton Hotel. Here, the 7,000 pages of the "papers" were sifted through over a period of three months, and the results were finally ready to be printed beginning on June 13.

Once the stories ran exclusively in the *Times*, the reporters (and Ellsberg) thought that other prominent newspapers and radio and television news outlets would begin running rewritten and abbreviated versions of the same material. However, as Ungar noted, "the *Times*'s great journalistic coup was met with dead silence from the outside world."[21] The government's cat was out of the bag, largely due to McNamara's sincere effort to come to grips with a devastating war for which he was largely the architect. (McNamara goes into some detail about this in the Errol Morris documentary film, *The Fog of War* [2003].) What Ungar found "was enlightening about the collected Papers was the total picture they presented of the United States planning and waging an arguably illegal and undeniably immoral war, all in the name of 'peace.'"[22]

Later, Senator Mike Gravel would write, in an introduction to one abridged edition of *The Pentagon Papers*, "The papers show that we have created, in the last quarter-century, a new culture, a national security culture, protected from the influences of American life by the shield of secrecy." They were a damning indictment of U.S. policy gone amok.

The Nixon administration—whose policies were not under scrutiny in the papers—nonetheless sought an injunction against the *New York Times* to cease publication of the series in the name of "national security." A federal judge, Murray I. Gurfein, granted a temporary restraining order on the *Times* on June 16. Ellsberg, frustrated that the series was losing momentum, offered copies of the papers to NBC and CBS news departments; both refused. Ungar noted, "The networks' reluctance to touch the Papers was perhaps the clearest evidence of the extent to which they felt intimidated by the Nixon administration's attitude toward the press."

Then, Ellsberg tried the *Washington Post*, to which no injunction had been leveled, funneling 4,400 pages of the papers to them. The *Washington Post* began their own series of articles based on the papers, on June 18, with the byline of Chalmers Roberts. The *Washington Post* was warned by Assistant Attorney General William Rehnquist (later chief justice of the Supreme Court) that publication of the material violated the Espionage Law. The *Washington Post* refused to stop publishing. A federal lawsuit was filed. The issue was whether a newspaper (or any media outlet) could be permitted to publish classified material, at risk of national security. *Washington Post* lawyers argued, "The case represents a critically important principle involving the relationship between the press and the government. For two hundred years we have operated under a system of free press. We have two choices now: Either we go on with it or we inject the courts into the relationship."[23]

On June 26, the U.S. Supreme Court merged both cases under one heading, *New York Times Co. v. U.S.* On June 30, the court ruled, in a 6-to-3 vote, the injunctions against the two newspapers amounted to "prior restraint" that the government was required to prove rather than to simply state. Each of the nine justices wrote a separate opinion in this landmark case, now seen as a rejection of censorship and a strengthening of First Amendment protections. Nonetheless, the sense of victory was tempered by the sobering reminders of the limits of press freedom, when "national security" is invoked, in the nation's newsrooms. Columnist Jack Anderson referred to this as, "Those fifteen fateful days in June when the freedom of the press was suspended."[24]

The version of the *Pentagon Papers* that was published had the 4,100 pages that Senator Gravel placed in the public record on June 29, 1971, through his subcommittee on buildings and grounds. The full 7,000 pages of the papers, now kept under lock and key at the Lyndon Baines Johnson Presidential Library, have yet to be published.[25]

Ellsberg turned himself in to the U.S. Attorney's Office on June 28, 1971, charged with theft, conspiracy, and espionage. While Ellsberg was in custody, members of Nixon's "Plumbers" (officially, the White House Special Investigation Unit) broke into his psychiatrist's office, looking for Ellsberg's files. Because of this illegal activity and harassment, all charges against Ellsberg were dropped, and he was released.

Saving Nature and Protecting Consumers

When authors tackle controversial subjects, a good indication of their truthfulness is the reaction from the powerful political interests targeted in their books. Two of the most important books in modern American history—one credited with inspiring modern environmentalism and the other with inventing the concept of consumer activism—sparked scandals simply because their authors told the truth.

The first of these, *Silent Spring* by Rachel Carson, was published in 1962. In it, Carson, a respected field biologist, asked readers to "imagine a world without birds." In no uncertain terms and with the backing of rigorous scientific data, Carson called out the chemical industry, which was, in its effort to "control nature" with indiscriminant spraying of DDT and other deadly synthetic insecticides, destroying the fabric of life on earth. She warned that first the birds would go—silencing the spring—and then other species would follow, eventually *Homo sapiens*. *Silent Spring* unleashed a tsunami in its wake. Indeed, few books of investigative reportage can equal the changes it wrought. The book stayed on the *New York Times* bestseller list for thirty-one weeks and led to the world's first environmental regulations. By throwing the gauntlet at the feet of the government—turning it into a public health issue— Carson's book transcended the genre of nature writing that preceded hers and reached a general audience receptive to her warnings. Though aimed at the misuse of chemical pesticides, in particular the spraying of DDT, the book was the first to address the entire issue of pollution and the damage mankind had done to what she called "the balance of nature" (Aldo Leopold's 1949 *A Sand County Almanac* first spoke of the "interconnectedness" of life and need for a "land ethic"). The effort to "control nature" was, she said, "conceived in arrogance" and "born of the Neanderthal age of biology and philosophy, when it was supposed that nature exists for the convenience of man." It was, she further said, "death by indirection." While we were trying to kill mosquitoes, we were ultimately killing ourselves.

Though Carson won a legion of fans, including President Kennedy, the chemical companies and their powerful Congressional allies were not so enamored. Rather than address the substance of her work, they unleashed a toxic spray of "spin," mocking her work, stirring up fears of a malaria plague that never materialized, and portraying Carson—a National Book Award winner (for *The Sea Around Us*; 1951)—as a "Communist" and an "embittered spinster." On the fortieth anniversary of *Silent Spring*'s publication, radio host Rush Limbaugh (*See also* "Broadcast Journalism") posed a quiz to his audience: "Who caused more deaths—Adolf Hitler, Josef Stalin or Rachel Carson?" His answer was Carson, for her efforts to stop spraying for mosquitoes, which he said led to deadly malaria outbreaks that never actually occurred. As *New York Times* reporter Philip Shabecoff noted, Carson was proven right. DDT is gone, PCBs are gone, and no plague of locusts or malaria epidemic materialized; eagles and ospreys (birds nearly rendered extinct by DDT) have made comebacks. Carson "lit the fuse for environmentalism in the United States."[26]

The other book, *Unsafe at Any Speed* (1965), was compiled by a young Harvard-trained lawyer named Ralph Nader, who stood up against the most powerful corporation in America at the time: General Motors (GM). A self-styled "public crusader," Nader documented the systemic disregard for public safety at the company; in particular, the Corvair had serious defects that caused it to crash at high speeds. He showed how GM had spent only $1 million of its $1.7 billion profits on safety research, with tragic results like the needless fatalities linked to the Corvair.[27] Rather than address the points Nader raised, GM hired private investigators to dig up dirt on him and prostitutes to proposition him. The ascetic Nader would not be cowed or tempted. GM was forced to apologize and implement safety procedures. This victory was the first of many for Nader, whose crusading inspired an entire generation to become involved with grassroots political issues like environmentalism, tax reform, and energy policy.

Essential Reading by Modern Muckrakers

The Hidden Persuaders by Vance Packard (1957).
American Power and the New Mandarins by Noam Chomsky (1969).
The Fate of the Earth by Jonathan Schell (1982).
The Monkey Wrench Gang by Edward Abbey (1985).
The End of Nature by Bill McKibben (1989, 1999).
Backlash by Susan Faludi (1991).
The Geography of Nowhere: The Rise and Decline of America's Man-Made Landscape by James Howard Kunstler (1993).
Makes Me Wanna Holler: A Young Black Man in America by Nathan McCall (1995).
No Logo: Taking Aim at the Brand Bullies by Naomi Klein (1999).

How to Overthrow the Government by Arianna Huffington (2000).
Nickel and Dimed: On (Not) Getting By in America by Barbara Ehrenreich (2001).
When Corporations Ruled the World by David Korten (2001).
Fast Food Nation: The Dark Side of the All-American Meal by Eric Schlosser (2001).
The Best Democracy Money Can Buy by Greg Palast (2002).
The Death of the West by Patrick Buchanan (2002).
Bias: A CBS Insider Exposes How the Media Distorts the News by Bernard Goldberg (2003).
The Republican Noise Machine by David Brock (2004).
An Ordinary Person's Guide to Empire by Arundhati Roy (2004).
American Theocracy: The Peril and Politics of Radical Religion, Oil, and Borrowed Money in the 21st Century by Kevin Phillips (2006).
An Inconvenient Truth by Al Gore (2006).
The Shock Doctrine by Naomi Klein (2008).

POLITICS IN PRIME TIME

At various times in the past half century, Americans have come together around their television sets to watch an unfolding political scandal. One question is raised by the following examples: Without television's unforgiving eye, would the scandals that these events/hearings spawned have been as big?

The Mob Speaks: The Kefauver Hearings

Until the U.S. Senate went on a fact-finding mission in the early 1950s known as "The Kefauver Hearings," the American people were in the dark about organized crime, in particular about the so-called "Mafia." Senator Carey Estes Kefauver, chairman of the Special Committee on Organized Crime in Interstate Commerce, convened hearings in May 1950 to investigate the growing threat of organized crime. The hearings lasted fifteen months and were held in fourteen cities, with 800 witnesses called to testify. Though not all of the hearings were televised—and only CBS and NBC carried any at all—those that were broadcast attracted a sizeable audience. Although few homes owned TVs in 1950, many people watched in bars, restaurants, and workplaces. This was the first time Americans had heard members of the Mob—until then, an "enemy within" that seemed more mystery than real—speak in public. The highlight was the week of hearings held in New York on March 12–20, 1951, when fifty witnesses described the nation's most powerful crime "family," led by Frank Costello (who had taken over leadership from Charles "Lucky" Luciano). According to *Life* magazine, "the week of March 12, 1951, will occupy a special place in history … people had suddenly gone indoors into living rooms, taverns, and clubrooms, auditoriums and back-offices. There, in eerie half-light, looking at millions of small frosty screens, people sat as if charmed. Never before had the attention of the nation been riveted so completely on a single matter."[28] Despite ample evidence to the contrary, these hearings created the public perception of a "Mafia" that came from Sicily and had run organized crime in the U.S. since the 1920s when they started as bootleg liquor distributors during Prohibition. As a result of the Kefauver Hearings, the Senate set up a Permanent Subcommittee on Investigations (a.k.a. "Rackets Committee"). This committee later riveted TV viewers when special counsel Robert F. Kennedy grilled Teamsters Union boss Jimmy Hoffa in 1957.

The End of McCarthyism

From April to June 1954, an unprecedented television event took place when the "Army-McCarthy Hearings" were broadcast live from the U.S.

Daniel Fitzpatrick of the *St. Louis Dispatch* captured the flavor of Sen. Joe McCarthy's witch-hunting. McCarthy paralyzed the press with his threats and innuendos against editors, writers, and cartoonists. That began to fade by May 13, 1953, when this cartoon appeared in newspapers around the country. Courtesy of Library of Congress, Prints and Photographs Division.

Senate by the American Broadcasting Company, a fledgling rival to NBC and CBS. These were among the first large-scale governmental proceedings televised live into American homes; they were, in fact, an excuse for many Americans to purchase their first television sets. For the fledgling TV industry, the hearings were a phenomenon. As many as 20 million Americans watched at a time during the 35 days and 187 hours of live coverage, and most Americans watched at least some of the proceedings.[29]

Senator Joseph McCarthy was chairman of the Senate Committee on Government Operations and its Subcommittee on Investigations. A powerful anti-Communist crusader, McCarthy had used this platform for the previous two years to wage a campaign against alleged Communists or their "fellow travelers" within the ranks of the federal government. The "Army McCarthy Hearings" grew out of what seemed an inconsequential matter—the drafting by the U.S. Army of David Schine, an associate of Roy Cohn, McCarthy's investigative assistant. Private Schine was alleged to have received preferential treatment through the intercession of McCarthy and Cohn, and the Pentagon was investigating the matter. During basic training, for example, Schine went AWOL. He was also allowed to skip rifle range practice during rainstorms and was released from drills to make or accept 250 long-distance telephone calls.

McCarthy accused the Pentagon of trying to force him to call off his probe of the Army's security practices and of holding Schine "hostage" in order to curtail his anti-Communism investigations. In retaliation, McCarthy convened these hearings. That McCarthy would accuse others of intimidation struck many as hypocrisy, given that for the previous ten years he and his Republican colleagues in Congress had waged a relentless campaign against political opponents under the guise of Communist "witch-hunting." TV journalist Sidney Kline wrote, "McCarthy was riding high on ruthless demagoguery. The Cold War, the Korean War, the Alger Hiss case, the Russian acquisition of the atom bomb—all contributed to an atmosphere of fear in America. McCarthy capitalized on this fear as he attempted to smear those whom he considered to be America's internal enemies, but his accusations were rarely founded on fact."[30]

The Army-McCarthy Hearings came in the wake of similar hearings in the House of Representatives, starting with the Dies Committee (1938–44), which morphed into the House Un-American Activities Committee, or HUAC (1946–75). These committees fanned out beyond their original mission, pushing into the private lives and careers of thousands of loyal Americans. HUAC published lists of names of hundreds of people purported to be associated with the Communist Party or "fellow travelers." Self-appointed private citizens distributed damning material, like Elizabeth Dilling's *The Red Network: A Who's Who and Handbook of Radicalism Patriots* (1935). Business groups distributed publications like *Red Channels: The Report of Communist Infiltration in Radio and Television* (1950). The vast majority of those whose names appeared on these "blacklists" were innocent of nefarious activity, yet it was enough to destroy their livelihoods.

Simultaneously, Senator McCarthy had, since 1950, conducted his own unofficial campaign against the State Department, which he accused of being infested with Communists. For many Americans, inside and outside the government, the "Army-McCarthy Hearings" were the last straws, the ones that broke the back of "McCarthyism"—a term coined in 1950 by political cartoonist Herbert Block to mean fear-mongering, career-ruining accusations against political opponents based on little or no evidence. Because the hearings were televised live, the public got to see McCarthy in person; they did not like what they saw. Though he'd swiftly ridden his crusade to national prominence, his fall was just as quick. The biggest blow occurred on June 9, 1954, the thirtieth day of the hearings, when the Army's special counsel Joseph Welch (working *pro bono*) confronted the senator. McCarthy had accused an attorney who worked for Welch of having been a member of a Communist front organization while in college, a diversionary tactic the Senator had used to silence opponents in the past. Welch cut him off. "Until this moment, Senator, I think I never really gauged your cruelty or recklessness," he said. When McCarthy tried to shout him down, Welch asked, "Have you no sense of decency, sir? At long last, have you left no sense of decency?" Welch's outburst inspired sustained applause from visitors in the gallery and provided one of the highlights of television broadcasting history. Though the hearings ended inconclusively, they led to a resolution to censure McCarthy for contempt of the Senate and "habitual contempt for people." McCarthy was censured by the Senate on December 2, 1954, by a 67–22 vote, the symbolic end of his career.[31]

"I've Lost Cronkite"

The Vietnam War divided the country and put American media to the test. CBS News was at the heart of two of the biggest scandals during this time. First, CBS News (and later *60 Minutes*) correspondent Morley Safer was among a handful of courageous network TV reporters to send filmed dispatches from the front lines. In one segment, aired in 1965, Safer showed U.S. Marines setting fire to the thatched huts of Vietnamese villagers (which he said the troops called "Zippo jobs"). This tactic fit in with the famous pronouncement, attributed to an Army major at Ben Tre in 1968, "It became necessary to destroy the village in order to save it." Correspondent David Halberstam noted of the Safer report, "[It] was like watching a live grenade going off in millions of people's homes. Watching American boys, young and clean, our boys, carrying on like the other side's soldiers always did, and doing it so casually. It was the end of the myth that we were different, that we were better."[32] It was also the end of the myth about Walter Cronkite, the venerable anchor of *CBS Nightly News*, who had long evoked an air of a well-meaning father, presenting the news dispassionately and without taking sides. After visiting Vietnam in the wake of Safer's broadcast, and then again in 1968 in the wake of the bloody Tet Offensive, Cronkite returned to New York and presented a special report that when aired on February 27, 1968, altered national history. On it, the avuncular newsman advocated a U.S. withdrawal from Vietnam ("It seems now more certain than ever that the bloody experience of Vietnam is to end in a stalemate"). A forlorn President Lyndon Johnson noted at the time that "If I've lost Cronkite, I've lost middle America." A week later, Johnson announced that he would not seek reelection to the presidency, opening the doors of the White House to Richard Nixon.

Watergate Hearings

From May 17 to August 7, 1973, the nation was transfixed by another political scandal unfolding on their television screens. The "Watergate Hearings" were conducted by the Senate Select Committee on Presidential Campaign Activities into the matter of the break-in at the Democratic National Committee headquarters on June 17, 1972, by operatives for the Richard Nixon reelection committee. The committee of U.S. senators (Howard Baker Jr., Edward Gurney, Lowell Weicker Jr., Daniel Inouye, Herman Talmadge, and Joseph Montoya) and counselors was chaired by Senator Sam Ervin Jr., the "country lawyer" whose homespun manner and impassioned defense of the Constitution captured the fancy of viewers and made him a modern folk hero. Adding to the drama, the hearings were held in the same caucus room as the Army-McCarthy Hearings.

Each of the three major networks alternated coverage of the hearings, while public television carried the hearings in full, rebroadcasting them in the evening. Over the course of all this programming, 85 percent of American TV owners watched at least some of the broadcasts. The cast of characters and the unfolding plot captivated people who normally avoided politics. The tone was set by White House Counsel John Dean's day-long "opening statement," a 245-page, 55,000-word confession of criminal wrongdoing by the Nixon White House, from which all the subsequent witnesses were forced to distance themselves, defend, or deny. Dean told the panel that the president was involved in the cover-up soon after the break-in and that the White House had conducted political espionage and "dirty tricks" for years. Despite the evasive, sometimes surly and defiant testimony of Nixon's closest advisors (Attorney General John Mitchell, National Security Advisor John Ehrlichman, and Chief of Staff H. R. Haldeman), the entire Watergate scandal unraveled on July 13, when a relatively minor witness, Deputy Assistant to the President Alexander Butterfield, admitted to a relatively minor interrogator, Assistant Minority Counsel Donald Sanders, that a taping system had been set up in the White House to record all calls to and from the Oval Office. With the

tapes of these calls, the committee could definitively verify or disprove assertions by the White House. The tapes were soon subpoenaed by special prosecutor Archibald Cox and the Senate. Nixon refused to hand over the tapes,
citing the principle of "executive privilege," a ploy that backfired, giving the
impression that he was covering up a crime. Many, in hindsight, have insisted
that the cover-up was more serious than the crime. Either way, it led to Nixon's resignation on August 8, 1974.

Besides the "smoking gun" of Butterfield's admission, several other exchanges
entered the political lexicon, due entirely to their exposure on live television.
Among these were Senator Howard Baker's question, "What did the President
know, and when did he know it?", John Dean's warning to Nixon about "a cancer on the presidency," Senator Ervin's response to Ehrlichman, "Because I can
understand the English language. It's my mother's tongue," and Senator Weicker's accusation that John Mitchell was "stone-walling."

The Watergate scandal spawned another theatrical TV moment, when President Nixon held an hour-long press conference on November 17, 1973. During the course of this televised event, Nixon famously said, "People have got
to know whether or not their President is a crook. Well, I'm not a crook. I've
earned everything I've got."

Iran-Contra Hearings

Another televised political scandal unfolded during the summer of 1987
when the U.S. Senate opened hearings into the so-called "Iran-Contra affairs."
Though the issues involved confused many viewers, the hearings made compelling television, especially when National Security Advisors John Poindexter and
Robert McFarlane, and Lieutenant Colonel Oliver North—McFarlane's top
"action officer"—took the stand. Americans sat glued to the tube as this scandal
unfolded. From May 5 to August 3, 1987, President Reagan's inner circle was
exposed to bright TV lights and tough questioners like Senator George Mitchell,
Senator Daniel Inouye, and Chief Senate Counsel Arthur Liman.

In a nutshell, the Iran-Contra accusations were that, at Reagan's orders—
and with the tacit approval of Vice President George Bush and Secretary of
Defense Caspar Weinberger—Oliver North undertook covert operations to sell
arms to an alleged enemy (Iran) in order to raise funds for right-wing Contra
insurgents against another alleged enemy (the democratically elected government of Nicaragua). Both the sale of arms to Iran and the funding of the
Contras were illegal; the Arms Export Control Act forbade the former, and
the Boland Amendment forbade the latter. At the center of the scheme was
North, whose gap-toothed smile and patriotic posturing scored well in the
court of public opinion (even though North was later found guilty in a court
of law). It also featured some entertaining bit players like Fawn Hall, who illegally shredded documents under orders from North, and Saudi arms dealer

Adnan Khashoggi. Though the scandal's players received little, if any, punishment, and the Reagan White House weathered the storm, the televised hearings added to a growing cynicism about politics in America. Many of the participants in Iran-Contra—including Poindexter, Elliott Abrams, John Negroponte, Otto Reich, and Robert Gates—were later given high-ranking posts in the administration of George W. Bush.

PARTISANSHIP: MEDIA TURNS HOSTILE

Clarence Thomas Confirmation Hearings

The Senate confirmation hearings for Supreme Court justice nominee Clarence Thomas, televised from September 10 to October 15, 1991, gripped the nation. When the Senate Judiciary Committee, chaired by Senator Joseph Biden, deadlocked on a 7–7 vote on Thomas's fitness for the highest court in the country, the nomination was sent to the full Senate in the U.S. Capitol Building. Here, the high drama ensued, and was broadcast live on television to a huge national audience.

Thomas, many argued, was an inexperienced, unqualified right-wing ideologue.

Adding to the politically partisan nature of the appointment by President George H. W. Bush were the scandal-ridden issues of race and sex. To wit, Thomas was nominated to replace the retiring Thurgood Marshall, one of the most revered African American leaders in the nation's history. Thomas's supporters were not above implying that those who opposed him were racists, even though two leading civil rights groups, the NAACP and Urban League, opposed the nomination because Thomas had been harshly critical of affirmative action in the past. In addition, the most compelling witness against Judge Thomas's unfitness to serve was University of Oklahoma law professor Anita F. Hill, a former associate of Thomas, who described the nominee's chronic sexually inappropriate behavior and unwanted advances toward women in his office. The latter accusation reached a pinnacle when Hill described one of Thomas's "practical jokes"—placing his pubic hair on the top of a canned soda that he offered to women in his office.

Rather than address the evidence that Ms. Hill brought forward, Thomas called her testimony "a high-tech lynching for uppity blacks who in any way deign to think for themselves, do for themselves, to have different ideas, or to refuse to kowtow to an old order, this is what will happen to you. You will be lynched, destroyed, caricatured by a committee of the U.S. Senate rather than hung from a tree."[33] Thomas further fanned the flames of racism and sexism by accusing the Senate of "ruining the country" and charged that "our institutions are being controlled by people who will stop at nothing." Republican senators followed by attacking Hill personally, despite the fact that four other credible associates of Thomas corroborated her testimony. On October 15, 1991, the full Senate confirmed the lifetime appointment of the forty-three-year-old Clarence Thomas to the U.S. Supreme Court, by a vote of 52–48.

Given what critics of Hill had said—that she was lying under oath—she would have faced legal consequences for perjury. But no charges were ever brought against Hill, buttressing the substance of her claims about Thomas. David Brock wrote a bestselling book, *The Real Anita Hill*, that undermined Hill's credibility, a book he later disavowed as having been filled with half-truths and unsubstantiated material that he had been paid to write. Partly in penance, Brock devoted his energies to running a Web site called Media Matters for America, whose mission was "comprehensively monitoring, analyzing, and correcting conservative misinformation in the U.S. media."

Partisanship Pumps up the Volume

Historian Daniel J. Boorstin has noted that a celebrity was a "human pseudo-event ... a person who is known for his well-knownness."[34] In more recent times, even political activists or partisan commentators have achieved this status. That is, they are famous for being well-known, and often their political views are secondary to their ability to provoke outrage. On the left, these activists/celebrities have included Michael Moore, Janeane Garofalo, and Al Franken. On the right, these have included Bill O'Reilly, Sean Hannity, Mike Savage, and Ann Coulter. They have commanded large audiences and accrued large fortunes because they were able to present their views in many media simultaneously, including print, radio, television, film, and the Internet.

The beginning of this trend toward openly partisan punditry began during the 1992 presidential election, when the media began scrutinizing Bill and Hillary Clinton's past—his alleged infidelities and her investments. The couple, hoping to fend off the spate of tabloid stories about his alleged long-term affair with Gennifer Flowers and investigative "attack" articles by Jeff Gerth in the *New York Times* and Jeffrey Birnbaum in the *Wall Street Journal*, agreed to appear on *60 Minutes* before the first presidential primary in New Hampshire. In the television interview, they affirmed their strong marital bond and tried to allay doubts about their honesty and integrity. Bill Clinton reportedly told his campaign staff afterwards, "Nobody's ever had this kind of personal investigation done on them, running for president, by the legitimate media ... I think that it is almost blood lust ... an insatiable desire on the part of the press to build up and tear down. And they think that is their job, and not only that, their divine right."[35]

"A Vast Right-Wing Conspiracy"

The "blood lust" continued during Clinton's eight years in the White House. A seemingly nonstop spate of books, articles, and tabloid TV segments

A selection of New York City's newspapers show headlines on President Clinton's testimony on the Monica Lewinsky affair in 1998. The nation weighed his suspenseful testimony in the Monica Lewinsky case and his prime-time declaration that he had "misled people, including even my wife." AP Photo/Marty Lederhandler.

appeared that claimed incontrovertible proof of the Clintons' involvement with everything from White House counsel Vince Foster's death to a secret plot to turn America into a Communist state (due, mainly, to Hillary Clinton's attempt to revamp the nation's healthcare system). Richard Mellon Scaife, a right-wing billionaire and owner of the _Pittsburgh Tribune-Review_ newspaper, spent almost two million dollars underwriting foundations that attacked the Clintons. The Scaife-funded Arkansas Project was responsible for underwriting _American Spectator_'s probe of the Clintons' alleged role in Foster's death. In January 1994, the _Spectator_ also published a story by David Brock that detailed an affair between Paula Jones and Bill Clinton, when he was Arkansas governor. The story was wrong (its author, David Brock, later admitted so), but Jones still demanded apologies from both Clinton and the magazine. Jones persisted, making appearances on media outlets owned by Republican-friendly fundamentalists Jerry Falwell and Pat Robertson, keeping the stories alive.

Also fueling the media frenzy were bestselling books like *Unlimited Access: An FBI Agent inside the Clinton White House* by Gary Aldrich and *Slick Willie: Why America Cannot Trust Bill Clinton* by Floyd Brown, who also published a monthly newsletter called *ClintonWatch: Proving Character Does Count in a President* and hosted a nationally syndicated radio show called *Talk Back to Washington*. The *New York Post*, owned by the conservative Rupert Murdoch, resurrected the Vince Foster story in January 1994, claiming the death was not a suicide and suggesting Foster was killed because he "knew too much." Though the *Post* article was also proven wrong, its reappearance coincided with the emergence of the Internet. Sherman Skolnick, the first of the Internet's now-ubiquitous conspiracy theorists, featured the Foster story on his Web site *Conspiracy Nation*, while G. Gordon Liddy, who had his own radio show, *Radio Free DC*, gave extensive airtime to the alleged conspiracy. (*See also* Chapter 6, "Broadcast Journalism.")

Bill Clinton's so-called "bimbo eruptions" reached a crescendo on January 17, 1998, when Matt Drudge included an item on his Internet site *The Drudge Report* about allegations that Bill Clinton had an affair with an intern named Monica Lewinsky, during the time she worked at the White House, from November 15, 1995, to April 7, 1996. (*See also* Chapter 7, "Internet Scandals.") The belated revelation of the affair was the result of the continued probe of Paula Jones's allegations of Clinton's sexual improprieties as Arkansas governor. Lewinsky was asked to testify by Jones's lawyers, who wanted evidence to substantiate their client's allegations. This affair came to the attention of investigators through Lewinsky's coworker, Linda Tripp, who secretly taped their phone calls during which Lewinsky detailed her affair with Clinton.

The media scandals that erupted from the Lewinsky affair were the biggest of the Clinton presidency. On NBC's *Today Show* on January 27, 1998, Hillary Clinton said of this nonstop media blitz, "The great story here for anybody willing to find it, write about it and explain it is this vast right-wing conspiracy that has been conspiring against my husband since the day he announced for president." Scaife's Arkansas Project had one main priority: to create a political atmosphere conducive to initiating impeachment proceedings against President Bill Clinton. To some extent, it succeeded.

Post-9/11 Media Commentary

After the terrorist attacks of September 11, 2001, the two political wings hardened into polar opposites and the volume and hostility of the rhetoric increased dramatically in the media. The rhetoric of Ann Coulter and Bill O'Reilly, in particular, went beyond partisanship into attacks on entire ethnic or interest groups. O'Reilly, in the wake of the terror attacks, suggested on his television show, *The O'Reilly Factor*, that Bill Clinton bore some responsibility for not eliminating Osama bin Laden; in 2005, O'Reilly said that illegal immigration was the cause, blaming the attacks on "Muslims who overstayed their visas."[36] Coulter, however, in syndicated columns and bestselling books, exhibited far more intolerance toward homosexuals, "the godless," Arabs, Muslims, and, especially, "liberals." Her publications include: *Treason: Liberal Treachery from the Cold War to the War on Terrorism*, *How to Talk to a Liberal If You Must*, and *Slander: Liberal Lies about the American Right*. Her books, however, have also been shown to be filled with factual errors, misquotes, exaggerations, and dubious statistics.

On the left, Michael Moore accrued his share of detractors for his one-sided takes on the issues. Several Web sites were established to do nothing but document Moore's various alleged hypocrisies and inaccuracies. On TV shows, like his *TV Nation* (1994) and *The Awful Truth* (1999), and in his documentary films, Moore was criticized for "gotcha" journalism. He was known for setting up his subjects in a way to produce the most unflattering responses and, thus, buttress his own viewpoint. As a wealthy man with a populist agenda, he opened himself up to charges of being a "pseudo-muckraker" and "limousine liberal" who sent his child to private schools while championing the common man. An anti-Moore book, *Michael Moore Is a Big Fat Stupid White Man* (2004) by David T. Hardy and Jason Clarke, even made the bestseller list.

Michael Moore's biggest scandals involved his documentary films *Bowling for Columbine* (2002) and *Fahrenheit 9/11* (2004). He won an Academy Award for the former, and at the Oscars ceremony in March 2003, gave a controversial acceptance speech on television broadcast live worldwide. The speech came only days after George W. Bush had authorized the invasion of Iraq. Moore said, "We live in a time where we have a man sending us to war for fictitious reasons … Shame on you, Mr. Bush, shame on you."[37] For that television appearance, Moore was targeted by the right wing as a "traitor," and worse.

Moore's published work also produced controversy. The biggest scandal occurred after the 9/11 attacks, when the publisher of *Stupid White Men*, Rupert Murdoch-owned HarperCollins, refused to release Moore's book, 50,000 copies of which had already been printed. Because the book criticized Bush harshly, Murdoch was wary about the reaction in the wake of the terror attacks, when the nation was united. Murdoch considered destroying all existing copies and killing the project, though Moore was given a chance to change the title, delete inflammatory material (including the chapter, "Kill Whitey!"), and pay for the changes out of his pocket. He refused. His cause was taken up by a group of librarians who began a nationwide protest via e-mail to protect Moore's First Amendment rights. Not publishing Moore's book, they argued, was the same as censoring him, regardless of whether one agreed or disagreed with what he wrote. HarperCollins published the book under pressure, but made no effort to promote it or connect their name to it. Nonetheless, the publisher did not refuse to accept the profits when *Stupid White Men* became the biggest-selling nonfiction book of 2002.

Franken versus Fox News: "Wholly without Merit"

A similar scenario unfolded when satirist Al Franken published *Lies and the Lying Liars Who Tell Them: A Fair and Balanced Look at the Right* (2003), a follow-up to his surprising bestseller *Rush Limbaugh Is a Big Fat Idiot and Other Observations* (1996). Because the book attacked Fox Channel's credibility, featured Fox's Bill O'Reilly on the cover, and used Fox News' "Fair and Balanced" slogan in its title, the network sued Franken and his publisher (E. P. Dutton/Penguin) for trademark infringement, saying his use of "fair and balanced" would "blur and tarnish" the slogan. Fox's lawsuit backfired. Their legal complaint created a miniscandal of its own, by provocatively calling Franken "neither a journalist nor a television news personality.... He is not a well-respected voice in American politics; rather, he appears to be shrill and unstable. His views lack any serious depth or insight." Fox lawyers also called Franken a "parasite." The publisher responded, "In trying to suppress Al Franken's book, News Corp. is undermining First Amendment principles that protect all media by guaranteeing a free, open and vigorous debate of public issues. The attempt to keep the public from reading Franken's message is un-American." U.S. district judge Denny Chin agreed, ruling that Fox's lawsuit was "wholly without merit, both factually and legally." Franken's book became a bestseller in hardcover, paperback, and audio-book formats.

Caught in a Webb

Gary Webb won a Pulitzer Prize for a three-part investigative series for the *San Jose Mercury News* on the connection between the CIA-supported Contra insurgency in Nicaragua in the 1980s and the sale of cocaine in the nation's inner cities. He expanded the articles into the book *Dark Alliance* (1996), in which he alleged that American officials, including Oliver North, facilitated the influx of the Nicaraguan cocaine, using the profits to fund the Contras' efforts, and that these drugs led to a crack cocaine epidemic around the nation that resulted in thousands of deaths and destruction of families. The *Mercury News'* stories were, in the assessment of the *Columbia Journalism Review*, "the most talked-about piece of journalism in 1996 and arguably the most famous—some would say infamous—set of articles of the decade."[38] However, the White House and the CIA denied any connection between the drugs and the Contras. The *Mercury News's* editors aired much of the criticism over the next year before reassigning Webb to another bureau at the paper to avoid any further controversy. Despite his many awards, Webb was unable to find another investigative job with a large newspaper and, according to his family, had grown despondent over this. On December 11, 2004, he was found dead, from two gunshot wounds to the head. Though the coroner ruled the death a suicide, it is difficult for some to understand how Webb could have shot himself in the head a second time. The fate of Webb had a chilling effect on investigative reporters with plans to take on the CIA or White House on this issue.

Unfortunate Son

One of the strangest scandals in modern publishing involved a former convict named J. H. Hatfield, who published *Fortunate Son: George W. Bush and the Making of an American President* in 1999, a full year before Bush became president in 2000. Among the book's scandalous claims was the bombshell that Bush was arrested in 1972 for cocaine possession and the crime was expunged from police records through his father's intercession. The scandal rose not just for the book's subject—though Bush had not yet become president—but for its author too. Soon after *Fortunate Son* was published, reports surfaced tying Hatfield to a 1987 attempted pipe-bombing of his boss, a crime for which he served five years of a fifteen-year prison sentence before being paroled. Because of the controversy about Hatfield's past and the fact that many of his choicest revelations came from "unnamed sources," his publisher (St. Martin's) recalled all copies of *Fortunate Son*. The book was later reprinted by Soft Skull Press, which took the position that Hatfield's past had no bearing on the veracity of what he wrote. Indeed, some of his revelations about Bush proved true, though some were impossible to confirm (including the cocaine bust). The scandal came to an abrupt end on July 20, 2001, when Hatfield was found dead in an Arkansas hotel room. His death, due to a drug overdose, was ruled a suicide, though rumors persisted that foul play was involved.

Partisan Publishing Bulks Up

Publishing houses of both left- and right-wing persuasions have long competed for the hearts, minds, and eyes of American readers. Among left-wing publishers have been stalwarts like Beacon Press, Nation Books, Common Courage, and Verso. Among the right-wing publishers have been Regnery, World Ahead, Cato Institute, and Noontide. (*See also* "Holocaust Deniers.") And then there are mainstream presses that publish books from both sides of the political divide, like St. Martin's, which in 2007 published Patrick J. Buchanan's *Day of Reckoning* and Thomas Oliphant's *Utter Incompetents: Ego and Ideology in the Age of Bush*; HarperCollins (owned by professed conservative Rupert Murdoch), which in 2007 published Neil Boortz's *Somebody's Gotta Say It* and Barbara Estrich's *Soulless: Ann Coulter and the Right-Wing Church of Hate*; and Simon and Schuster, which has two separate imprints devoted to conservative subjects—Threshold Editions and The Free Press—but no liberal or progressive equivalents.

Partisan political groups have engaged in the controversial practice of buying bulk shipments of books that reflect their political view, thereby propelling the book onto the prestigious *New York Times* bestseller lists. Once the book has reached the *Times* list—so the thinking goes—others will be compelled to purchase it. When this practice began to get out of hand in the 1990s, the *Times* implemented a "dagger" icon to denote titles on the bestseller list that benefited from bulk purchases. Richard Mellon Scaife has been known for bulk buying, but the practice is not just a right-wing phenomenon. Both Ann Coulter and Michael Moore have had dagger icons next to their books' listings. Nor is bulk buying limited to political groups. Individual authors have done the same thing. In 2002, David Vise, author of *The Bureau and the Mole*, purchased 20,000 copies of his own book to spike it onto the bestseller list. After it had made the list, Vise then tried to return 17,500 copies of his book to Barnes and Noble for a refund.

In 2007, the conservative publisher Regnery was sued over its bulk-sales policies. Five of Regnery's authors—Jerome R. Corsi, who wrote *Unfit for Command*, the controversial book that "Swift-Boated" John Kerry during the 2004 presidential campaign; Bill Gertz; Robert "Buzz" Patterson; Joel Mowbray; and Richard Miniter—filed a suit against the publisher for fraudulent accounting practices related to royalties. The publisher sold their books at a bulk-order discount to the Conservative Book Club, which in turn, discounted them to its members. As a result, Regnery authors were denied royalties due them if the book had sold at a retail venue. Miniter claimed that a sale to the book club earned the authors 10 cents, but a sale at a retail outlet would have earned them $4.25. He told the *New York Times*, "They've structured their business essentially as a scam and are defrauding their writers."[39]

PUBLIC RELATIONS

Wartime Censorship

Periodically, in the name of national security, the U.S. government has monitored content on the media; it has also used the media as a conduit for propaganda. In World War I, for example, President Woodrow Wilson unleashed a propaganda campaign he dubbed "Making the world safe for democracy," to prod an isolationist nation into the conflict. When the war in Europe began in 1914, George Creel, director of the Committee on Public Information (CPI)—Wilson's propaganda chief—was in charge of creating public support for overseas intervention. To do this, Creel's committee created propaganda—films, cartoons, posters—that played on crude anti-German stereotypes like the "bloodthirsty Hun." (The term *Hun* derived from tribes of Asian nomads who swept through Europe in the fourth century under Attila; their name has since been used as a pejorative for any marauders in Europe.) They also planted stories in the press comprised of fantasized scenes of "Hun" brutality that all but demanded retaliation. Though these stories were reported in the media with little attempt to verify their accuracy, they were not effective enough to prod the United States into the war until April 1917, two years after it began. After World War I—and in response to Creel's excesses—the Institute of Propaganda Analysis was formed in New York with a grant from Edward Filene, the Boston merchant and philanthropist. The Institute determined that there were three ways to deal with propaganda: suppress it; meet it with counter propaganda; or, analyze it rationally.

Because of these groundbreaking efforts, during World War II the government used the media to gain support for the campaign against Germany and Japan. New Deal liberals like Archibald MacLeish—then Librarian of Congress and director of the Office of Facts and Figures—insisted that the Nazi propaganda flooding American shores be fought with counter propaganda that relied on "aggressive truth." Theirs was a moral crusade of good versus evil. MacLeish saw the war as "a revolution aimed at the destruction of the whole system of ideas, whole respect for the truth, the whole authority of excellence" for which he felt America stood, at least in the eyes of those under Nazi or Japanese occupation.[40] However, the government did tightly restrict the media during the war. On December 19, 1941, two weeks after Pearl Harbor, President Roosevelt signed Executive Order 8985, which established the Office of Censorship, with Byron Price as director. He gave Price the power to censor international communications in "his absolute discretion."

Despite the tight lid on reporting, one scandal threatened to change the course of the war—for the worse. Stanley Johnston, who covered the Pacific theater for the *Chicago Tribune*, wrote an article on June 7, 1942, headlined, "Navy Had Word of Jap Plan to Strike at Sea." Johnston had learned that U.S. cryptologists had cracked the Japanese Navy's radio code, which had helped reverse Allied fortunes in the Pacific. Indeed, the intelligence had been decisive at the Battle of Midway, one of the turning points of World War II and just after which Johnston's article appeared. U.S. military officials were outraged by this breach of national security, fearing that the Japanese would see the article and, in response, alter their radio communication codes, thus ending the Allies' advantage and potentially costing thousands of American lives. The Justice Department prepared a case against Johnston and the *Tribune*, charging them with violations of the Espionage Act. Immediately after the article appeared, the Japanese did not change their codes, suggesting that their intelligence agents had not seen the *Tribune*. However, when Johnston was brought before a grand jury two months later, the publicity of the case alerted them to the fact that the U.S. had cracked their codes. The Japanese then changed their codes, wiping out an Allied advantage.

The Father of Spin

Before the modern science of public relations, "spin" was crude, comprising anything from penny press ads for snake oil and curative medicines to sensational notices about traveling circuses with their freaks and sideshows that always promised more than they delivered and "dime novels" that purported to offer the "true adventures" of mostly fictitious pioneers. Inheriting this mantle for hyperbole, "yellow journalism." (*See also* Chapter 5, "Newspapers and Magazines.") engaged in sensationalism and outright propaganda to sell newspapers and nudge the nation toward the publishers' political views. Simultaneously, press agents for Hollywood stars used gossip columnists like Walter Winchell, Hedda Hopper, and Louella Parsons to spread rumors or break "news" that would keep a client's name in the newspapers. However, the person responsible for turning these clumsy early efforts into the efficient science of public relations was Edward Bernays. Bernays, a nephew of Sigmund Freud, called his work "crystallizing public opinion," which was also the title of a book he published in 1923 detailing his theories. One recommendation was to hire "experts" to say what you want them to say, even if it's not true.

Bernays's biggest coup with this technique was to normalize cigarette smoking, to not only increase the number of men who smoked, but also to ply what he saw as an untapped "gold mine" of women smokers. For eight years (1928–36) while working for the American Tobacco Company, Bernays waged a relentless campaign to make cigarettes attractive to women. Prior to this, "proper" women did not smoke. Bernays inundated newspapers and radio broadcasts with ads and even got restaurants to offer cigarettes ("instead of a sweet") on dessert menus to take advantage of American women's new weight consciousness ("Thin is in"). His techniques were attacked from all corners, and Senator Reed Smoot called it "fraud." The scandal worked to Bernays's advantage, by keeping the issue of female cigarette smoking in the news. His biggest coup was to enlist A. A. Brill, a noted psychoanalyst and translator of Freud's work, to offer an "expert opinion" on why women should smoke. Brill's opinion that cigarettes were "torches of freedom" was cited in a flood of advertisements, and Bernays organized a successful "Torches of Freedom" parade down Fifth Avenue on Easter Sunday 1929, with hundreds of women proudly strutting while puffing on cigarettes. The result was that cigarette smoking in women increased dramatically, as did tobacco company profits (by $32 million alone in the first year). Some have argued that Bernays signed the death warrants for thousands of American women with this campaign. Biographer Larry Tye said Bernays was familiar with medical reports about the dangers of smoking even while he conducted his propaganda campaign. Nonetheless, he was willing, wrote Tye, "to employ whatever antics or deceptions it took to do that crystallizing, including trying to discredit new research linking smoking to deadly disease."[41] Bernays had misgivings when the Surgeon General's 1964 report revealed a clear link between cigarette smoking and cancer. To expiate his guilt, Bernays led the effort to ban cigarette advertising from radio and television (The Public Health Cigarette Smoking Act, passed by Congress in 1970, did just that). The most telling irony of all is that neither Bernays nor Brill ever smoked.

In his book *Crystallizing Public Opinion* (1923), Bernays also showed how to use these same advertising techniques to sell political candidates. He demonstrated their effectiveness by working to "sell" the dour Calvin Coolidge to the American people as president in 1924. Political consultants have since utilized the same techniques to sell their candidates to the American people, and then to sell those elected officials' policies. Bernays may have had more influence on American media than any single figure other than Marshall McLuhan. Public relations, which Bernays created, is now the fastest-growing segment of the American media, with more publicists than journalists graduating each year from U.S. universities.

Our Hidden Persuaders

By 1957, Bernays's propagandistic techniques had made their way to the most powerful medium in America—television. A muckraking journalist named Vance Packard became alarmed at the ability of television advertising to psychologically manipulate consumers into buying specific brands or impulsively buying products for which they had no real need (that is, advertising artificially created that need). Packard's book *The Hidden Persuaders* (1957) was a shock to Americans who liked to think of themselves as individuals with free will. Instead, Packard revealed the use of "motivational research" by ad agencies to play on consumers' weaknesses and fears. He was the first journalist to document how advertising techniques were used in politics to "sell" candidates. The 1956 presidential election was the first to use professional advertising consultants to reshape the "brand" of the candidates to get undecided voters to choose their leaders the way they would a laundry detergent. Packard's observations about the 1956 campaign in *The Hidden Persuaders* mirror present-day political reality. Candidates, Packard noted, were made to exude "personality" and to stay "on message," that is, the message that has been decided ahead of time by focus groups. Packard quoted one ad executive who cynically dismissed "independent" voters as nothing more than "switch voters" who "switch for some snotty little reason such as not liking the candidate's wife." A fiftieth-anniversary edition of Packard's book was published in 2007 and found a new generation of readers, caught up in the 2008 election process.

Richard Nixon and John F. Kennedy Debates

A good example of how television can alter political reality occurred in 1960, when two presidential candidates, Richard M. Nixon and John F. Kennedy, took part in four televised debates between September 26 and October 21, 1960. Both men were gifted speakers, but the first of the debates proved Nixon's Achilles' heel—and not for anything he said. The image he projected, historians have argued, led to his defeat. Gaunt from a recent hospital stay, Nixon wore a shirt that was too large; he also refused cosmetic attempts to lighten his 5 o'clock shadow. Under the studio lights, he seemed to be pale, sweating, and angry, which contrasted starkly with Kennedy, who appeared tanned, fit, and rested, and exuded cheery confidence. While radio listeners judged Nixon to have won the debate, the considerably larger TV audience (70 million viewers) found Kennedy to be the clear winner. The power of those initial images helped to boost the lesser-known Kennedy to national prominence. Nixon, after all, had been the vice president of the United States for the previous eight years and was favored to win in November. After his loss, Nixon refused to participate in televised debates in the presidential campaigns of 1968 and 1972—both of which he won.

Political Propaganda

During campaign seasons, the American media has, in the past, been flooded with advertisements touting the virtues of candidates. In recent years, however, rather than tout a candidate's virtues, the ads have more often sought to demonize the opponent and suggest that the opponent's policies will put Americans in harm's way, destroy the economy and environment, or even empty the prisons and mental hospitals. This media blitz, dubbed "going negative," has been employed by all political parties. Though critics have decried the practice and candidates have threatened legal action against opponents, the political demonizing continues apace. The Federal Communications Commission has stipulated that political ads on America's airwaves must contain a disclaimer that clearly indicates the source of the funding for the ad (e.g., "The sponsor shall be identified with letters equal to or greater than four percent of the vertical picture height that air for not less than four seconds.").

The first shot in this modern media war was fired in 1964, when the committee to reelect Lyndon Johnson aired an ad against Republican opponent Senator Barry Goldwater. The ad, broadcast once on September 7, 1964, exploited the fear generated by the conservative Goldwater's suggestions that he favored the use of nuclear weapons against Communist forces in Vietnam. Few television ads have equaled the scandal created by this one Johnson ad. It opened with a shot of a young girl in a meadow, plucking petals from a daisy and counting them as they fell. When she reached "nine," a man's voice took over, counting down from "nine" for the launch of a missile armed with a nuclear warhead. The little girl stared in horror at the sky, as the screen faded to black when the countdown reached zero. After a pause, a mushroom cloud appeared on the screen and a voice intoned, "These are the stakes. To make a world in which all of God's children can live, or to go into the dark. We must either love each other, or die ... Vote for President Johnson on November 3. The stakes are too high for you to stay home." This jarring ad only appeared once, as a paid political spot, but it was rebroadcast several times on news programs, due to the scandal it unleashed. Johnson won the election by a landslide, much of the credit for which was given to this fear-mongering ad.

Selling Dick Nixon

Similar demonizing ads were aired by Richard Nixon against Hubert Humphrey and George McGovern in the 1968 and 1972 campaigns, respectively, but none approached the level of enmity of Johnson's "daisy" ad. Nixon had long been a canny politician, but he suffered from a poor public persona. For the campaign of 1968, he hired "media consultants" who helped him project the "New Nixon" image. Using time-honored techniques developed by Bernays and the advertising industry, Nixon was able to "sell" that image through television advertising and carefully staged television appearances. His reliance on television was likened by Joe McGinnis, author of *The Selling of the President 1968*, to "the way a polio victim relied on an iron lung." The consultants wanted to humanize the often stiff and standoffish Nixon, and show flashes of his sense of humor. Even Nixon was wary about the reliance on image makers; he was quoted by McGinnis saying, "It's a shame a man has to use gimmicks like this to get elected."[42] McGinnis's book—which raised the same warning cry Packard had raised about the 1956 presidential election—resonated with an increasingly skeptical American audience distressed over Vietnam, the assassinations of Martin Luther King Jr. and Robert F. Kennedy, and racial unrest. *The Selling of the President 1968* was on the *New York Times* bestseller list for seven months, and was number one for four months.

Enter Lee Atwater

The media game changed with the arrival of Lee Atwater, a political consultant and campaign advisor to Ronald Reagan and George H. W. Bush. Atwater was renowned for such tactics as using third parties to spread half-true or fraudulent rumors about an opponent, and employing "push polls"—citing phony pollsters or using rigged questions—to produce "findings" that made the opponent appear to hold dangerous views. These tactics forced the Democratic candidates to play defense throughout the campaigns he managed, taking the heat off his candidates. After helping to get Reagan elected, and then reelected, Atwater developed a series of television ads for George H. W. Bush in 1988 about a black convicted murderer named Willie Horton who had, while on furlough in Massachusetts, raped a woman. The ad campaign Atwater devised—suggesting that dangerous black men would soon be lurking in America's backyards if Massachusetts Governor Michael Dukakis were elected president—was enough to nudge reluctant voters into the Bush column. Prior to the ads' appearance, the Democratic challenger held a seventeen-point lead in the polls.

Atwater later expressed regret over his tactics. In 1991, while in the last throes of a fatal brain disease, he wrote in *Life*, "My illness helped me to see that what was missing in society is what was missing in me: a little heart, a lot of brotherhood ... It took a deadly illness to put me eye to eye with that truth, but it is a truth that the country, caught up in its ruthless ambitions and moral decay, can learn on my dime."

Row, Row, Rove the Boat

After Atwater died, the media tactics he developed, and then repudiated, were adopted and expanded by Karl Rove, a former Atwater assistant. After working on a few campaigns for Republican candidates, successful and unsuccessful, Rove became George W. Bush's campaign manager, for both Texas gubernatorial races (1994, 1998) and both presidential races (2000, 2004). Because of his alleged political acumen and uncanny sense of how far he could push the media envelope on behalf of his boss, Rove earned the nickname "Bush's Brain." Once Bush was vaulted into the White House in January 2001, Rove was named deputy chief of staff. As head of the Office of Political Affairs, the Office of Public Liaison, and the White House Office of Strategic Initiatives, Rove was the architect of White House political operations, which included manipulation of the mainstream media (network news and daily newspapers). For a hired consultant, Rove had unprecedented power, and his unapologetic, ruthless wielding of that power created some major scandals for the Bush White House.

Foremost among the scandals was what became known as the "Plame Affair," a scandal that put the media on trial along with the White House. It involved Valerie Plame Wilson, an undercover CIA agent, whose husband Joseph Wilson had previously been ambassador to Iraq under President George H. W. Bush. In looking for a pretext to initiate an invasion of Iraq, the Bush White House claimed that Iraqi leader Saddam Hussein was creating weapons of mass destruction (WMDs). To determine if reports of Saddam's acquisition of enriched uranium were true, Joseph Wilson traveled to Africa, the alleged source of Saddam's uranium. After determining the reports to be false, Wilson relayed the information to the White House. Yet the president continued to assert that Saddam was making WMDs. In his 2003 State of the Union address, Bush said, "The British government has learned that Saddam Hussein recently sought significant quantities of uranium from Africa." Wilson was so dismayed by the deception that he wrote a *New York Times* op-ed denouncing reports of Saddam's WMD capabilities.

Though it was not known at the time—and would not be until *Newsweek* reported it in July 2005—Rove revealed the identity of Wilson's wife to Matthew Cooper at *Time* and to syndicated columnist Robert Novak. Since Plame was an undercover CIA agent whose expertise was terrorism, this act constituted a national security breach, a serious federal crime. Rove sanctioned the leak to retaliate against Wilson for his *Times* editorial. When Novak "outed" Plame in his July 14, 2003, column (Cooper chose not to reveal the classified information), he was working as a political operative for the White House, not as a journalist. Though Novak faced no legal consequences, Cooper and *New York Times* reporter Judith Miller were threatened with prison sentences if they did not reveal their sources. Cooper named Rove as his source and Miller was jailed for contempt of court for eighty-five days when she would not reveal her source (it was Lewis Libby, Vice President Dick Cheney's Chief of Staff, who would be convicted and sentenced to prison). After the scandal broke, sixteen former CIA and military intelligence officials asked Bush to revoke Rove's security clearance, and Plame filed a lawsuit against Cheney, Rove, and Libby for conspiring to destroy her career. In April 2007, Rove was investigated by the Office of Special Counsel for his role in several other scandals, including having "improper influence over government decision-making." The cumulative weight of the scandals forced Rove's resignation on August 31, 2007.

Scandal Fatigue

During the years in which Rove held sway in the White House (2001–7), the presidency and the Republican Party were visited by a wave of scandals, some of which were sparked by media scrutiny. The 9/11 attacks and the war in Iraq briefly healed a rift between the press and the White House, as journalists put aside their skepticism in the interest of national unity. However, as the war dragged on into its fourth year, and then surpassed the length of the U.S. military involvement in World War II, that gap reopened. Among the books published during these years, some were particularly damaging to the reputation of the Bush White House and the Republican Party. These included:

Big Lies: The Right-Wing Propaganda Machine and How It Distorts the Truth by Joe Conason (2003).
The Lies of George W. Bush by David Corn (2003).
Bushwhacked: Life in George W. Bush's America by Molly Ivins and Lou DuBose (2003).
The Great Unraveling: Losing Our Way in the New Century by Paul Krugman (2003).
The Book on Bush: How George W. (Mis)leads America by Eric Alterman (2004).
Against All Enemies: Inside America's War on Terror by Richard A. Clarke (2004).
The Politics of Truth: Inside the Lies that Led to War and Betrayed My Wife's CIA Identity by Joseph Wilson (2004).
The One Percent Doctrine: Deep Inside America's Pursuit of Its Enemies Since 9/11 by Ron Suskind (2006).
Bush on the Couch: Inside the Mind of the President by Justin A. Frank (2007).

Chapter 2

RACE AND RELIGION

RACE AND MEDIA SCANDALS

It could be argued that scandals generated by the American print media brought slavery to an end. Before the Civil War, editors, writers, and novelists who tackled this thorny issue faced harassment, libel suits, jail, violence, even death for daring to speak the name of what pro-slavery Senator John C. Calhoun, in an 1837 speech, dubbed "our peculiar institution." Among the first to risk life and limb to address this issue was William Lloyd Garrison. In 1829, as editor of *Genius of Universal Emancipation*, a Baltimore abolitionist weekly, he proposed the immediate emancipation of slaves with no compensation to slave owners. He wrote, "We are resolved to agitate the subject to the utmost; nothing but death shall prevent us from denouncing a crime which has no parallel in human depravity." Garrison was jailed for two months for "criminal libel." When, after resuming publication of his Baltimore weekly, he was threatened with another libel suit, Garrison relocated to Boston and started *The Liberator*, a weekly that would kindle the abolitionist movement and inspire the establishment of 1,350 separate local branches of the American Anti-Slavery Society throughout the United States. In the South, laws were passed that prohibited African Americans (free or enslaved) from receiving *The Liberator*. The state of Georgia offered a $5,000 reward for Garrison's capture, and even in "free" Boston, Garrison faced regular threats of tarring and feathering. On October 21, 1835, in fact, an angry mob tied a rope around Garrison and pulled him through the streets of Boston. The city mayor ordered Garrison jailed, for his own protection. After the Thirteenth Amendment banned slavery, Garrison shut down his paper.

Other editors followed Garrison's example, raising public awareness about slavery (the vast majority of Southerners did not own slaves). In Cincinnati, James G. Birney, editor of antislavery papers, had his printing press destroyed by a mob in 1835. In Louisville, Cassius Clay, editor of the *True American*, had to shut down operations when a mob stole his printing equipment and hid it in Cincinnati in 1845. In St. Louis, Elijah Lovejoy, who published the abolitionist paper the *Observer*, had his press equipment destroyed on three

THE LIBERATOR.

VOL. I.]   WILLIAM LLOYD GARRISON AND ISAAC KNAPP, PUBLISHERS.   [NO. 33.

BOSTON, MASSACHUSETTS.]   OUR COUNTRY IS THE WORLD—OUR COUNTRYMEN ARE MANKIND.   [SATURDAY, AUGUST 13, 1831.

THE LIBERATOR

IS PUBLISHED WEEKLY

AT NO. 10, MERCHANTS' HALL.

WM. LLOYD GARRISON, EDITOR.

TERMS.

Two Dollars per annum, payable in advance.
No subscription will be received for a shorter period than six months.
Agents allowed every sixth copy.
All letters and communications must be POST PAID.

AGENTS.

JOSEPH C. LOVEJOY, Bangor, Me.
DANIEL C. COLESWORTHY, Portland.
EDWARD J. POMPEY, Nantucket, Mass.
HARVEY KIMBALL, Amesbury.
BENJAMIN COLMAN, Salem.
WILLIAM VINCENT, New-Bedford.
HENRY E. BENSON, Providence, R. I.
ALFRED NIGER, "
J. L. CROSS, New-Haven, Ct.
JOHN WM. CREED, "
WILLIAM SAUNDERS, Hartford.
Rev. JEHIEL C. BEMAN, Middletown.
PHILIP A. BELL, New-York City.
GEORGE HOGARTH, Brooklyn, N. Y.
NATHAN BLOUNT, Poughkeepsie, N. Y.
EDWIN SCRANTOM, Rochester, N. Y.
JOSEPH CASSEY, Philadelphia, Pa.
JOSEPH SHARPLESS, "
THOMAS HAMBLETON, Jennerville, Pa.
WILLIAM WATKINS, Baltimore, Md.
BENJAMIN LUNDY, Washington City, D. C.
WILLIAM WORMLEY, "
GEORGE CARY, Cincinnati, Ohio.

THE LIBERATOR.

Robbers invade the property, and murderers the life of human beings; but he that holds another man in bondage subjects the whole sum of his existence to oppression, bereaves him of every hope, and is, therefore, more detestable than robber and assassin combined.—THOMAS DAY.

CHRISTIAN SECRETARY.

A NOBLE COMMENTARY.

NOVEL INCIDENT.

William Lloyd Garrison's abolitionist weekly, *The Liberator*, was started in Boston in 1831 and kept the scandal of slavery alive, despite threats against his life. Courtesy of Library of Congress, Prints and Photographs Division.

different occasions. After relocating across the river in Illinois, Lovejoy was killed while trying to protect his fourth press from an angry mob. In St. Cloud, Minnesota, Jane Grey Swisshelm—credited with opening the U.S. Capitol press gallery to women journalists in 1850—saw the press equipment for her abolitionist paper, the *Visiter* [*sic*], destroyed by an angry mob, and was then harassed into bankruptcy by a libel suit.

Among the most famous of those who claimed Garrison as an inspiration was Frederick Douglass, a former slave who in 1838 fled from Maryland to Massachusetts. Douglass not only gained national fame with his *Narrative of the Life of Frederick Douglass, an American Slave* (1845), but also became the face of abolition, the living proof of slavery's evil. In 1847, he started his own abolitionist weekly, *The North Star*, in Rochester, N.Y. Loren Ghiglione wrote that despite threats to "dump Douglass's press into Lake Ontario and banish him to Canada," his publication tackled previously "taboo" issues like slavery, women's rights, public education, and labor policy.[1]

After the Civil War, another ex-slave named Ida B. Wells began her writing career. As a reporter for and part owner of the Memphis-based *Free Speech*, Wells focused on the grim topic of lynching. After investigating the circumstances of a number of lynchings in the South, she decried the barbaric practice in *Free Speech*, even provoking Southern white men by saying they "will overreach themselves and a conclusion will be reached which will be very damaging to the moral reputation of their women." In response, the Memphis *Commercial Appeal*—still the daily newspaper in Memphis today—editorialized, "The black wretch [Wells] who had written that foul lie should be burned at the stake." Soon thereafter, an agitated mob destroyed the *Free Press* equipment and Wells, threatened with lynching, moved to New York. She continued to document the atrocities of lynching in booklets like *Southern Horrors* and *A Red Record: Tabulated Statistics and Alleged Causes of Lynchings in the United States, 1892–1894*, vowing to show "that a large portion of the American people avow anarchy, condone murder and defy the contempt of civilization."[2]

Harriett Beecher Stowe's *Uncle Tom's Cabin, or Life Among the Lowly* (1852) was one of the most influential novels in U.S. history, due to the scandal it created by exposing the institution of slavery. Prior to the novel's appearance, white Americans in the North and South assumed that slaves were, as Mel Watkins writes, "a fortunate lot, who basked in the comfort of plantation hospitality and sought nothing more than a continuation of their merry lives as servile chattel, free from the practical responsibilities that burdened whites."[3] The publication of Stowe's novel ended this delusion, and the ensuing scandal is credited with hastening the arrival of the Civil War. When it was published, public opinion on slavery was divided, but *Uncle Tom's Cabin* turned the tide against the "peculiar institution." Coming in the wake of the Fugitive Slave Law of 1850, which allowed Southern slave owners to enter the North to retrieve human property, the novel revealed the human impacts of slavery, and, for this, the sale of Stowe's novel was banned in the South. Stowe, daughter and wife of ministers, saw the slave system firsthand on a visit to Kentucky in 1833. She was also influenced by the book *The Life of Josiah Henson, Formerly a Slave, Now an Inhabitant of Canada* (1849). When she finished, she declared, "I wrote what I did because as a woman, as a mother I was oppressed and broken-hearted, with the sorrows and injustices I saw, because as a Christian I felt the dishonor to Christianity—because as a lover of my country I trembled at the coming day of wrath."

Uncle Tom's Cabin was first serialized in the *National Era*, an abolitionist weekly, in 1851–1852. It was published by John J. Jewett of Boston in 1852, with the subtitle changed from "The Man That Was a Thing" to "Life Among the Lowly." The first printing of 5,000 sold in two days; 300,000 sold by year's end. Eight presses worked day and night to meet the demand. When President Lincoln met Stowe, he reportedly said, "So you're the little woman who wrote the book that made this great war."[4]

Broadcasting Stereotypes

Though *Uncle Tom's Cabin* was, as James Baldwin put it, "the ultimate protest novel" and led to the war that ended slavery, the depiction of "Uncle Tom," the long suffering but uncomplaining old "Negro," leaped far beyond the printed page. The Uncle Tom character became a staple of the minstrel show, a popular nineteenth-century stage entertainment in which black performers—or, more often, whites in black face—portrayed stereotypes like "Tom" and "Sambo," who had affinities for indolence and watermelon. As Mel Watkins noted, "[The white performers] were unaware that they had stumbled upon a notion that would transform American entertainment and firmly establish the image of blacks as happy-go-lucky plantation darkies and outrageously dressed, ignorant dandies."[5] The minstrel troupes were most popular in the North; the first, the Virginia Minstrels, was formed in New York City and debuted on February 6, 1843, at the Bowery Amphitheatre. Despite the tragedy of the Civil War and savagery of Reconstruction, the minstrel show stereotypes lingered, partly because they were also popular with black audiences. Among the most popular of the earliest recordings, on Edison's wax cylinders, were minstrel songs with titles like "Little Pickaninnies" (1899) and "Coonville Cullid Band" (1904) by Arthur Collins. Collins was white. The race stereotypes filtered into other media, including magazines, where black people were regularly referred to—even in the respectable *Munsey's*—as "kind, slavish and picturesque" and "darky." Visual depictions on the newspaper funny pages, too, were relentlessly insulting. Popular strips like *Mutt and Jeff* and *Gasoline Alley* depicted the black characters (always maids or servants) with tar-black faces and giant lips ringing O-shaped mouths, shuffling around docilely and mangling the English language. Such demeaning ethnic images, found in two of the most popular comic strips in the country, reinforced the worst sort of stereotypes about black people to millions of young and impressionable Americans.

Race Flames Fanned by Media

One of the worst race riots in American history took place in Tulsa, Oklahoma on Memorial Day, 1921. The racial hostility that drove the riot was largely fanned by the *Tulsa Tribune*, the city's dominant daily paper. The white-owned-and-operated *Tribune* regularly referred to the city's black residential area as "Little Africa" or "Niggertown," when its official name was Greenwood. Greenwood, which Booker T. Washington once called "the black Wall Street," rivaled Harlem as a national center of urban black culture. After the riot of 1921, Greenwood was obliterated. The precipitating event that touched off the riot was an alleged assault of a white woman by a black man. The event, at least as depicted in the pages of the *Tribune*, never took place. But the unsubstantiated story was enough to inflame an angry white populace. Goaded by the Ku Klux Klan, which had a large presence in Tulsa, a white mob gathered at the courthouse. Now 10,000 strong, the mob marched on Greenwood. In the ensuing mayhem, 36 city blocks were razed, 3,000 homes burned, 1,000 people injured, and as many as 300 killed—some bodies were dumped in the Arkansas River and never recovered. It was as total a destruction of an intact community as has ever been perpetrated in U.S. history. A correspondent for *The Nation* called it "the worst instance of racial violence in America since slavery." The commander of the National Guard, which was summoned the morning after the riot, said, "I have never witnessed such scenes ... Twenty-five thousand whites, armed to the teeth, were ranging the city in utter and ruthless defiance of every concept of law and righteousness. Motor cars, bristling with guns, swept through the city, their occupants firing at will." The *Tribune* showed no remorse after the riot. Indeed, the paper continued to fan the flames of race hatred, blaming the riot on "black agitators" and running headlines like "PROPAGANDA OF NEGROES IS BLAMED" and "BLOOD SHED IN RACE WAR WILL CLEANSE TULSA."[6] Most black residents moved away from the city, never to return.

Uncle Remus versus Aunt Jemima

The publishing equivalent of Stepin Fetchit, the stereotypically servile and shiftless black man portrayed in popular early Hollywood films by Lincoln Perry, was Uncle Remus, the fictional ex-slave created by white Atlanta journalist Joel Chandler Harris. Harris published the first of seven *Uncle Remus* books in 1881. Though the stories about Br'er Rabbit and Br'er Fox were based on authentic folktales, Harris had a regressive attitude toward slavery. In his introduction to the first of his books, he called his series a "sympathetic supplement to Mrs. Stowe's wonderful defense of slavery as it existed in the South. Mrs. Stowe, let me hasten to say, attacked the possibilities of slavery with all the eloquence of genius; but the same genius painted the portrait of the Southern slave owner, and defended him." Today, Uncle Remus—like Stepin Fetchit—is seen as an embarrassing relic of American racism.

At the same time Harris was presenting this benign image of life in the South for black people, other white authors were creating their own false realities. Among these was Thomas Dixon Jr., a North Carolina minister and nephew of the Grand Titan of the Ku Klux Klan. In his novel *The Leopard's Spots* (1902), Dixon decried the treatment accorded white men in the South during Reconstruction, but he created a much bigger scandal with his 1905 novel, *The Clansman*, which revealed the "leopard's spots" of the author to be one of a race-baiting bigot. *The Clansman* was adapted by director D. W. Griffith for his controversial, and influential, 1915 film *The Birth of a Nation*.

Minstrel Stereotypes Meet the Radio

The minstrel show stereotypes did not create a scandal until two forces collided—the black middle class and the radio. Though some regional radio shows traded on the "darkie" stereotype, the most popular show was *Amos 'n' Andy*, which debuted on March 19, 1928, on WMAQ in Chicago. The show chronicled the misadventures of Amos Jones, Andrew H. Brown, Lightnin', Kingfish, and Sapphire, and the ongoing business woes of the Fresh Air Taxi Company. Airing nightly from 7 to 7:15 P.M., *Amos 'n' Andy* was an immediate hit, and soon moved to NBC, where it was broadcast nationwide from 1930 to 1943. With 40 million nightly listeners, *Amos 'n' Andy* was one of the most popular shows in any medium in U.S. history. Families arranged evenings around it, and newspapers ran summaries of the previous night's episode for those who missed it. *Amos 'n' Andy* was created by Freeman Gosden and Charles Correll, two white men who also performed the voices. At first, only scattered protests of the show were heard from black leaders. Bishop W. J. Walls of the AME Zion Church and the *Pittsburgh Courier*, a black newspaper, mounted petition drives to get the show canceled. These protests failed to register with a national audience, perhaps because the show was one of the few in any medium that featured the lives of black Americans, regardless of how they were depicted or by whom. *Amos 'n' Andy* was also seen as an improvement over "Stepin Fetchit," a popular movie character created by Lincoln Perry around the same time. Touted as "the Laziest Man in the World," Fetchit was the star of popular movies in the 1930s. He was, to blacks, the equivalent of the drunken, bloodthirsty savage that Hollywood had created to represent Native American cultures. Both were false, demeaning, and damaging stereotypes.

The real scandal began when CBS adapted *Amos 'n' Andy* for television. Using an all-black cast—Gosden and Correll fooled radio listeners into thinking they were black, an impossible feat on TV—*Amos 'n' Andy* ran on CBS from 1951 to 1953. Despite strong performances by Tim Moore (as Kingfish) and Ernestine Wade (as his shrewish wife Sapphire) and its popularity with black viewers unaccustomed to seeing black faces on TV, the show irked upwardly mobile African Americans. The NAACP campaigned to get it canceled on TV and radio, saying it depicted "Negroes as inferior, lazy, dumb and dishonest ... every Negro is a clown or a crook ... Negro doctors are quacks ... Negro lawyers are without ethics ... All Negroes dodge work."[7] Eventually bowing to pressure from the NAACP and the civil rights movement, CBS canceled the show.

A similar trajectory was charted by Eddie Anderson, another black radio and TV personality popular with a multiracial audience. Anderson portrayed Rochester, comedian Jack Benny's valet and sidekick. The scandal Rochester created was twofold. Because he was that rarest of characters—a black man who regularly challenged white authority figures—Rochester was deemed too "uppity" for Southern white listeners, even though he was also criticized by the NAACP for being a demeaning stereotype. Soon enough, the civil rights movement consigned all these characters to the archives. In the ensuing years, *Amos 'n' Andy*, Rochester, Stepin Fetchit, and the like came to be seen by many African Americans as shameful artifacts from an unhappy era. Watkins noted, "Except for bootleg films and later video tapes, the original *Amos 'n' Andy* characters, clearly embarrassing for most middle class blacks, had been banished from earshot and public view."[8] The irony of this banishment was that, until the mid 1960s, black Americans were effectively absent altogether from television programming. That is a media scandal in and of itself—one of omission rather than commission.

Anticipating Adolf: Eugenics Rears Its Head

Reinforcing the fears of a rising black race in America were "scientific" tracts like *The Rising Tide of Color Against White World Supremacy* (1920) and *The Revolt Against Civilization: The Menace of the Under Man* (1922) by Lothrop Stoddard. Bestselling works like these popularized the now roundly decried eugenics movement, the goal of which was to discourage breeding by "unfit" people and encourage the "fit" to procreate in larger numbers. Though the movement had been widely discredited by the 1930s, Hitler used its theories to underpin the racialist theories he put into practice with tragic results. Stoddard also railed against the dangers of immigration, the explosion of population among nonwhite populations. He went so far as to divide the white race into three types: Nordic, Alpine, and Mediterranean. Nordic was, by general consensus among the eugenicists, to be the superior type. Though his books and theories generated heated debate in academia, Stoddard proved to be correct about some things. He anticipated the rise of Japan as a world power, the Second World War, the end of colonial rule in Asia and Africa, and, with remarkable prescience, the rise of Islam as a world power.

Race Radio/Race Records

Prior to the payola scandal (*see also* Chapter 6, "Broadcast Journalism"), radio's biggest scandal involved race. That is, the radio industry was segregated and discrimination was rampant, with the larger white-owned stations seldom hiring black employees, or playing music by black musicians. Thus, two entirely different radio universes existed, side by side, on the radio dial, like the "white" and "colored" water fountains outside the radio station doors. Nowhere was this more evident than in the schism at the heart of rock 'n' roll. By the late 1940s, if a white station played hit songs by white artists, the music was known as "pop" and, in the 1950s, "rock 'n' roll." If the identical music was performed by black artists—and most of the white pop stars simply borrowed songs by black performers—it was called "rhythm and blues." Robert Palmer noted that "Rhythm and blues was a catchall rubric, coined by future Atlantic Records producer Jerry Wexler when he was writing for *Billboard* [the music industry magazine whose charts determined a record's success] ... to refer to any sort of music that was made by and for black Americans ... Compared to Perry Como and Patti Page, even the most formulaic rhythm and blues seemed to sizzle."[9] Rhythm and blues records were generally referred to as "race records," and only independent black-owned radio stations, whose low-power signals reached a comparatively small audience, would play them.

Until deejay Allen Freed began playing the original records by black artists, rather than the white cover versions, white radio audiences were as unaware of their existence as black audiences were unaware of Pat Boone and Elvis Presley. Radio's segregation extended to the station employees. Most high-power stations (50,000 watts and above) had all-white staffs. However, some stations hired black "coaches" to teach white deejays how to talk in hep-cat slang, which appealed to young white audiences. Among the first stations to hire black deejays was WDIA in Memphis, followed by Nashville's WLAX. This created crossover demand for black music by white listeners.

Strange Fruit

One of the songs that received airplay on race radio stations was Billie Holliday's version of "Strange Fruit." The song derived from a 1937 poem by Abel Meeropol (written under the name Lewis Allan), inspired by the lynching of two black men. After Meeropol set the poem to music and performed it at Madison Square Garden in New York City, it came to the attention of Billie Holliday. Her version of the song was a staple of her live repertoire and a popular recording that was used as the title of a novel about interracial love by Georgia writer Lillian Smith. *Strange Fruit* (1944) was a dissection of forbidden love damned and destroyed by racism. As the *Georgia Encyclopedia* noted, "This novel of interracial love was denounced in many places for its 'obscenity,' although sex is barely mentioned. Massachusetts banned it for a short time; so did the U.S. Post Office." In spite of—or perhaps because of—these efforts to suppress it, *Strange Fruit* was the biggest selling novel in America that year, selling as many as 30,000 copies a week, proving once again that nothing sells like scandal.

Invisible Men and Coming Fires

His "invisibility" was a theme explored earlier by Ralph Ellison in his novel, *Invisible Man* (1952), which created a scandal for its graphic depiction of the blood-lust that underscored racial hostility in America. Ellison's "Battle Royal" chapter described a party held by the leading citizens of a Southern town in which a white woman disrobes for a group of young black men who are then blindfolded and tossed into a boxing ring. The winner of the free-for-all "battle royal" must then give the high school valedictorian address, during which he is jeered and shouted down. At the end he is given a scholarship to a black college. This, metaphorically, is what Ellison said the gifted black male faced in the United States during the 1950s. Though *Invisible Man* was praised by critics and earned the 1953 National Book Award, it was derided by black critics for its harsh depiction of black people.

Ellison's warnings echoed earlier warnings by novelist Richard Wright in his controversial *Native Son* (1940), which one critic called, "the most important novel of the Black American tradition ... the vanguard of a new rawness and frankness."[10] In the novel, the main character, Bigger Thomas, murders and mutilates the daughter of the white man for whom he works, and burns her remains in the family mansion's furnace. He then murders his black girlfriend to keep her from going to the police. After he is arrested and put on trial, Thomas can't articulate his rage, a paralyzing racial vision that would later inspire James Baldwin's and Eldridge Cleaver's controversial writings. Wright was attacked by critics for implying that the murders were the system's fault, and not the fault of the individual who committed them.

Ellison's warning also anticipated the work of James Baldwin. In May 1963, on the centennial of the signing of the Emancipation Proclamation, Baldwin published a piece in *The New Yorker*, "Letter from a Region in My Mind," that would later make up the bulk of his book, *The Fire Next Time* (1963). Ostensibly about the black Muslims, the piece and the book that followed captured the rising sense of frustration and hostility in racial attitudes in the United States. Baldwin's face was featured on the cover of *Time* (May 17, 1963), next to his warning from *The Fire Next Time*: "What I am asking is impossible. But in our time, as in every time, the impossible is the least that one can demand."

Because of Baldwin's sudden notoriety, Attorney General Robert Kennedy met with him and other black leaders to address the rising racial tension in the South—in the wake of James Meredith's enrollment at the University of Mississippi, the firebombing of a church in Birmingham, Alabama, that killed four black girls, and the March on Washington, where Martin Luther King Jr. gave his "I Have a Dream" speech. However, Baldwin's blunt remarks to Kennedy only frustrated the attorney general. Ultimately, the writer was investigated by the FBI after he was quoted in response to President Kennedy's assassination,

"For many generations black men's heads have been blown off and nobody cared. Because it wasn't happening to a person, it was happening to a 'nigger.'" Baldwin had also expressed interest in writing a book about "the FBI in the South," which alarmed J. Edgar Hoover. Baldwin's name was added to the FBI's Reserve Index of people who, in times of national emergency, "will receive priority consideration with respect to investigation and/or other action following apprehension of Security Index subjects." In his FBI file, which runs to 1,302 pages, Baldwin was described by the agent tailing him as "a dangerous individual who could be expected to commit acts inimical to the national defense and public safety of the United States in a time of an emergency."[11]

Black Like Me

The preface to John Howard Griffin's book *Black Like Me* (1961) opened with "For years the idea had haunted me." The "idea" was to find out, as a white man, how it felt to be a black man in America. To conduct his undercover mission, Griffin needed someone to underwrite the cost of travel and medical consultations required to "pass" for being black. *Sepia* magazine, an internationally distributed magazine for and about black readers that was modeled on *Look*, agreed to these terms if Griffin wrote about his experiences for the magazine. Griffin lived in Texas; to assure his anonymity, he traveled to New Orleans to undergo an accelerated process of skin pigmentation change. He took medication normally given to skin disease victims and augmented the drugs with sunlamp sessions. He shaved his head and added a final coat of a dark staining cream. After a week, Griffin had been transformed, as far as the world knew, into a black man. He spent the next four weeks traveling the Deep South at a time (1960) when lynching was common and hostility on the rise due to the beginnings of the civil rights movement.

Griffin found himself routinely refused service in restaurants and in entry to restrooms. "Though I was the same person with the same appetite, the same appreciation and even the same wallet," he wrote, "no power on earth could get me inside this place for a meal." Water fountains, public beaches, and jobs were also denied him. Griffin tirelessly looked for work, touting his writing skills, but all he could find was a job shining shoes. He ate catfish head stew with the other street vendors and winos and lived at the YMCA or in flophouses. On a bus trip from New Orleans to Hattiesburg, he and other black passengers were not allowed to get off the bus at the trip's midpoint, when white passengers were given a restroom break. Thus, some black passengers were forced to urinate on the floor of the bus.

In *Black Like Me*, the book that grew out of the experience, Griffin described how things were so bad for black citizens that they were driven to despair. He cited a government report that detailed "the rise in suicide tendency among Southern Negroes. This did not mean that they killed themselves, but rather that they had reached a stage where they simply no longer cared whether they lived or died."[12] *Black Like Me* sold 12 million copies and was translated into fifteen languages. The book sparked a scandal not just for what it revealed about racism in the South at the time—far worse than white Americans were led to believe—but also for Griffin's methods of impersonation. This wasn't his first venture in undercover reportage; he'd lived as a "blind" man in New Orleans on another writing assignment. However, his posing in *Black Like Me* as someone he was not was, to some critics, tantamount to entrapment. Rather than taking money or valuables from a person, he "entrapped" their racism. This issue has resonated among journalists ever since Jack London posed as a tramp, Nellie Bly feigned mental illness to get inside Blackwell's Island Insane Asylum, Gloria Steinem posed as a Playboy Bunny, and Barbara Ehrenreich worked menial jobs as a "single mother" while writing *Nickel and Dimed: On (Not) Getting By in America* (2001).

From Nat Turner to H. Rap Brown

Though it seems a huge leap from *Amos 'n' Andy* to Black Power, chronologically it was only one decade. Indeed, by 1968, when William Styron published his controversial novel *The Confessions of Nat Turner*, the stakes had been raised. Black leaders like Medgar Evers, Malcolm X, and Martin Luther King Jr. had been gunned down, and the nation's cities were torn by riots and shootouts between police and "militants." Styron's novel was a fictionalized account of a bloody 1831 slave uprising in Virginia, which became a bestseller and won a Pulitzer Prize, perhaps because it tapped into the turbulent tenor of its times. Despite its prescient theme, Styron's novel unleashed a torrent of resentment in the black community. It was an unusual standoff—a Southern white man taking up the case for a black revolutionary and coming under attack by black intellectuals. It was also indicative of the trigger-finger racial tension in the country during a year in which the nonviolent Dr. King was murdered and the gun-toting Black Panther Party rose to prominence. At its most basic, Styron's book raised the question, how can a white man presume to speak for the black people?

Yet, there was more to it, as became clear in a book published in the wake of Styron's novel, *William Styron's Nat Turner: Ten Black Writers Respond*. The most scandalous of the criticisms leveled at Styron was that he distorted history by claiming, among other things, that Turner's rebellion was "the only effective sustained revolt in the annals of American Negro slavery." They also took issue with his depiction of "loyal" slaves as "complaisant plantation Sambos" who willingly helped put down the rebellion, and Turner as a celibate man beset with wild sexual fantasies (Turner was married in 1831).[13] Styron's detractors included fellow novelists John A. Williams and John O. Killens. Styron and his defenders claimed that, in a historical novel, an author was given creative license, and what coursed through the minds of the "characters" was, ultimately, a product of the author's "creative unconscious." Questions of historical accuracy aside—after all, Styron could reasonably claim his was a novel and, therefore, fiction—the language put into the mouth and mind of Styron's Nat Turner was that of a classically educated white intellectual.

Fiction based on historical events has long been a staple of the U.S. publishing industry. In recent years, such bestselling novels as *Cold Mountain* by Charles Frazier and *A Widow of the South* by Robert Hicks both took real events from the Civil War and built narratives around them (as did the book that created the whole genre, Margaret Mitchell's 1936 novel *Gone with the Wind*). Thus, many of the charges leveled against Styron could be leveled against any of these other authors.

The Original Rappers

While there were many militant or revolutionary books that created flurries of scandal during the racially tense 1960s, few rivaled the reaction generated by Eldridge Cleaver's *Soul on Ice* (1968). Cleaver wrote his bestselling book of essays while in California's San Quentin Prison. Though the book was one of the first to argue for black "self-defense," the most scandalous passages were about sex—in particular, the rape of white women. Cleaver admitted to having raped white women and of "practicing on black girls in the ghetto." He wrote, "I had stepped outside of the white man's law, which I repudiated with scorn and self-satisfaction. I became a law unto myself ... rape was an insurrectionary act."[14] These words created a furor that drowned out his political polemic. Many have argued that had *Soul on Ice* been published while he was in prison (he got out in 1966), Cleaver would not have been paroled.

Asked to clarify his comments in 1969, Cleaver told *Playboy*, "It was my delight in violating what I conceived of as white men's laws, and my delight in defiling white women in revenge over the way white men have used black women ... rape was simply one of the weird forms my rebellion took ... it was a combination of business and pleasure." In *Soul on Ice*, he concluded that "I could not approve the act of rape" and told *Playboy*, "I felt I had become less than human." But, by then, the damage was done.[15]

Other Incendiary Books on Race in America

Wretched of the Earth by Franz Fanon (1963).
Nigger by Dick Gregory (1964).
The Autobiography of Malcolm X (1965).
Black Power: The Politics of Liberation in America by Stokely Carmichael and Charles V. Hamilton (1966).
Custer Died for Your Sins: An Indian Manifesto by Vine Deloria Jr. (1969).
Die Nigger Die by H. Rap Brown (1969).
Seize the Time by Bobby Seale (1970).

Soledad Brother by George Jackson (1970).

If They Come in the Morning: Voices of Resistance by Angela Davis (1971).

Ain't I a Woman: Black Women and Feminism by Bell Hooks (1981).

Hunger of Memory by Richard Rodriguez (1982).

Faces at the Bottom of the Well by Derrick Bell (1992).

Race Matters by Cornel West (1992).

Two Nations: Black and White, Separate, Hostile, Unequal by Andrew Hacker (1992).

Volunteer Slavery: My Authentic Negro Experience by Jill Nelson (1993).

The All American Skin Game by Stanley Crouch (1998).

The Bell Curveball

The reaction to the 1994 publication of *The Bell Curve: Intelligence and Class Structure in American Life* by Richard J. Hernstein and Charles Murray was unprecedented for a scholarly work. Though the word *race* is not mentioned in the title, and is seldom mentioned in the text, *The Bell Curve's* message was clear and unequivocal: black people were inferior to white people. To Hernstein and Murray, the deciding factor was IQ (intelligence quotient), which they saw as hereditary, not—as was accepted since the 1920s—environmental. In other words, the authors argued that you were born inferior if you were black, and no public policy or accelerated attempts to redress the inequality would change that. In a book that was published in response the following year, *The Bell Curve Wars*, editor Steven Fraser called *The Bell Curve* "the most incendiary piece of social science to appear in the last decade or more ... [It] is an explosive device. Its premises, its purported findings, its prescriptive advice for what ails American society are shocking." While the authors insisted their book was not driven by ideology, the reaction to the book was split between conservatives who hailed it and liberals who said it harkened back to Hitler's theories of racial superiority. *Harper's* magazine editor Michael Lind called *The Bell Curve* "a body of racialist pseudoscience."[16]

Native Americans Get Their Manifesto

Native American scholar Vine Deloria Jr. had a long career, but his most notable accomplishment may have been the first of his more than twenty books, *Custer Died for Your Sins: An Indian Manifesto* (1969). This bestselling polemic hit like a bombshell at a time when the nation was focused on the racism encountered by African Americans. Deloria's book reminded Americans that another large group demanded their say. *Custer Died for Your Sins* was part history lesson, part political tract, and it shocked Americans to read Deloria's characterization of Colonel Custer as "the Adolf Eichmann of the Plains" who was "not defending civilization; they were crushing another society." Thus, the massacre of Custer and his soldiers at Little Big Horn was an event to be praised and reexamined by contemporary Americans. Deloria paved the way for the militant American Indian Movement, which drew national headlines with their November 1969 "occupation" of Alcatraz Island, and he continued to write correctives about American history, such as *We Talk, You Listen: New Tribes, New Turf* (1970) and *Behind the Trail of Broken Treaties: An Indian Declaration of Independence* (1974).

Churchill and State

One of the scholars who followed in Deloria's wake was Ward Churchill, an activist and author of books on Native American genocide and the FBI's COINTELPRO program, which infiltrated and sabotaged militant groups during the 1960s and 1970s. Churchill, whose claims of Native American ancestry have been disputed, was known for his incendiary writings, but provoked real outrage in the months after the terrorist attacks on September 11, 2001. Churchill, then a University of Colorado professor, was invited to speak at Hamilton College in New York in February 2005. In anticipation of his appearance, the campus paper ran a story that quoted from an essay Churchill wrote just after the attacks, "Some People Push Back; On the Justice of Roosting Chickens." In the essay, Churchill called those who worked in the World Trade Center and the Pentagon the "technocratic corps at the very heart of America's global financial empire." Echoing Deloria, he called them "little Eichmanns."[17] The campus article came to the attention of the Fox Channel's Bill O'Reilly, who called on the university to fire Churchill, a motion seconded by Colorado Governor Bill Owens, who said Churchill should be "terminated." The University of Colorado Board of Regents voted to review and monitor all of Churchill's speeches and writings. Hamilton College rescinded Churchill's invitation, and he resigned as chairman of the Ethnic Studies Department; he was fired by the University of Colorado in July 2007.

The Poem That Blew Up

In 2002, two months after being named New Jersey's poet laureate, Amiri Baraka, wrote a poem, "Somebody Blew Up America," which he then read at an arts festival. In the poem's most controversial lines, Baraka suggested that Israel may have had a "heads up" about the terror attacks of 9/11. Baraka wrote, "Who knew the World Trade Center was gonna get bombed/Who told 4,000 Israeli workers at the Twin Towers/To stay home that day." Because then-Governor James McGreevey could not fire Baraka, he asked for his resignation, which Baraka refused to give. Months later, with McGreevey's push, the state legislature eliminated the poet laureate position. Baraka sued the state, but the U.S. Supreme Court refused to hear the case in November 2007. After the ruling, Baraka called the decision "a confirmation of the ignorance, corruption, racism, and criminal disregard for the U.S. Constitution."

RELIGION AND MEDIA SCANDALS

The freedom to practice one's chosen religion without fear or repression is among America's most treasured rights, guaranteed, along with freedom of speech, in the First Amendment to the U.S. Constitution. Also implied in that guarantee is the need to maintain a clear separation between church and state. The precedent for this was the Statute of Virginia for Religious Freedom, which Thomas Jefferson authored as a member of the House of Burgesses in colonial America. Jefferson felt so strongly about this sacrosanct—and uniquely American—separation of church and state that he left instructions for his tombstone to contain, for his accomplishments, "author of the Declaration of Independence and the Statute of Virginia for Religious Freedom, and the father of the University of Virginia." Throughout the nation's history, scandals have occurred when the boundaries between church and state are blurred, or when religious leaders push the boundaries on what is accepted to say, do, write, or preach in America, or impinge on the rights of other to worship as they choose.

One of the most controversial religious books in U.S. history was the *Book of Mormon*, published in March 1830. Subtitled *An account written by the hand of Mormon, upon plates taken from the Plates of Nephi*, the book resulted from a series of religious visions experienced by Joseph Smith Jr., in which an angel named Moroni led him to a hill in upstate New York. Here, gold plates engraved with a narration were allegedly buried. In 1827, Smith began to translate this narration and dictate what he saw to scribes. The result was the *Book of Mormon*. The sect, now officially the Church of Jesus Christ of Latter-day Saints, moved west to Ohio and Missouri, trying to escape the hostility that greeted them at each stop. They settled in Illinois, establishing a city at Nauvoo, but their religious rites, secrecy, prosperity, and political clout created suspicion among non-Mormons. Among the many controversial tenets contained in the writings of these "Mormons" was the divinely blessed practice of polygamy. Mutual antagonism reached such a pitch that a Mormon militia was mobilized. The state's governor intervened, and Smith surrendered to answer charges of inciting a riot. While awaiting trial in a county jail at Carthage, Illinois, he and his brother Hyrum were killed by a mob of locals on June 27, 1844. Two years later, the Mormons were led by Brigham Young to Utah.

Around this same time, North America was in the throes of an anti-Catholic fever, as waves of immigrants, mostly from Ireland and Italy, flooded into the cities. Even prominent men like Samuel F. B. Morse and Presbyterian minister Lyman Beecher fell under the sway of this nativist tide. Morse published *Foreign Conspiracy Against the Liberties of the United States* (1835), claiming the immigrants were part of the Vatican's advance army to take over the world. Beecher published a similarly anti-Catholic polemic, *A Plea for the West* (1835), as did his son, Reverend Edward Beecher, whose diatribe was *The Papal Conspiracy Exposed* (1855).

One of the leaders of this nativist backlash was Reverend William K. Hoyt. Hoyt met a young woman named Maria Monk, who had been kicked out of an asylum for prostitutes in Montreal run by the Catholic Church after it was learned that she was pregnant. Hoyt moved with Monk to New York and began publishing stories about Monk's experiences in a nativist periodical called the *American Protestant Vindicator*. These dispatches, which were fabricated by Hoyt and several other anti-Catholic clerics, were assembled in book form, as *Awful Disclosures of Maria Monk*, and published in 1836. The book purported to describe Monk's conversion to Catholicism, her acceptance as a nun, the debauchery of the priests, the strangulation murders of babies born to nuns, and so on. The book was denounced as a fraud by Protestant and Catholic commentators, and the Montreal asylum was cleared of suspicion. Despite its disreputable origins, *Awful Disclosures of Maria Monk* sold 300,000 copies before the Civil War, tapping in to the tenor of the times, which was embodied by the aptly named Know-Nothing Party. Other anti-Catholic tracts followed, including a sequel (*Further Disclosures of Maria Monk*) and the account of another "fallen" nun *Downfall of Babylon* and Rebecca Reed's perennial selling *Six Months in a Convent* (1835). The Civil War brought much of this nativism to a temporary halt, as Irish and Italian immigrants joined the Union cause.

Meyer Levin versus Anne Frank

Meyer Levin was a central figure in an ongoing battle over the literary legacy of Anne Frank, the Jewish teenager who kept a diary while her family hid from the Nazi occupiers in Amsterdam. He was also an unwitting pawn in the hands of Holocaust deniers. In 1952, already established as a novelist of Jewish life, as well as translator and editor of Jewish literary anthologies, Levin was chosen by Otto Frank, Anne's father, as the U.S. agent for a play version of *The Diary of a Young Girl*. Levin's play adaptation focused on the terrible inescapability of the Holocaust, and was deemed "too Jewish" by many Broadway producers, who chose to pass on the opportunity to stage it. Otto Frank, growing impatient with Levin, turned to screenwriter Lillian Hellman. She produced a more sanitized "inspirational" play, which won the 1955 Pulitzer Prize and became the popular stage adaptation, and later the basis of a popular film. An embittered Levin, claiming to have been plagiarized, sued Otto Frank and was awarded $50,000 in damages. Levin's lawsuit against Otto Frank was the undoing of his literary reputation. It also emboldened those who have, since 1958, insisted that Anne Frank's diary was a hoax, written by a number of people (including Otto Frank and Levin) after the war. The first to air this theory was Lothar Stielan, a Bavarian critic who, for this offense, was charged with "libel, slander, insult, defamation of the memory of a dead person and anti-Semitism"[18]—crimes in the wake of Germany's unconditional surrender at the end of World War II. Three years later, both parties settled out of court, with Otto Frank accepting a public apology and a donation to a foundation set up in his daughter's memory. However, the fact that Otto Frank agreed to settle only encouraged those obsessed with the idea that the diary was a fake. Because it has sold millions of copies in forty countries and is a required text in many schools' curriculum, Anne Frank's diary has great symbolic power for those keeping Holocaust memories alive. As Deborah E. Lipstadt noted, "The diary's popularity and impact, particularly on the young, make discrediting it as important a goal for the deniers as their attack on the gas chambers."[19] The original diary was sent for safekeeping to the Netherlands Institute for War Documentation. Hoping to put the hoax theories to rest, the institute tested every part of the diary and issued a 250-page final report in which it concluded that it was authentic. Nonetheless, detractors still exist.

In a League All Their Own

Racism and right-wing demagoguery were not the sole domain of Christian fundamentalists. Indeed, Meir Kahane, founder of the Jewish Defense League (JDL), and Louis Farrakhan, the leader of the Black Muslims, provoked their own share of scandals through their published works, radio, TV, and public appearances. In the 1960s, Kahane was an editor of the nation's largest Anglo-Jewish weekly, the Brooklyn-based *Jewish Press*. He appeared often on American radio and television. Kahane founded the JDL in 1968, purportedly in response to threats made against Orthodox Jews by members of the Black Panther Party. Fueled by Kahane's rhetoric, the JDL was accused of starting a domestic terrorism campaign from 1970 to 1975. The JDL's main target was Soviet-owned or rented properties; the Union of Soviet Socialist Republics (U.S.S.R.) had incurred the group's wrath for its tight restrictions on emigration of Jews at that same time. In his writings and broadcasts, Kahane used his credentials as an ardent Zionist to exploit the anger and frustration of many Jews, calling for "perpetual war" and "Jewish terrorism" against enemies of Israel, including Palestinians and "Israeli Arabs."[20] Kahane himself was caught making firebombs in 1971; and, for violating his probation in 1975 by planning the kidnapping of a Soviet official and an embassy bombing, he spent a year in a U.S. prison. After he got out of prison, Kahane immigrated to Israel.

In 1985, the Israeli Knesset passed an amendment to Israel's Basic Law, barring "racist" candidates from election, which essentially ended Kahane's ambitions for elective office. In 1990, after giving a speech at a hotel in New York, Kahane was assassinated by El Sayyid Nosair, an Egyptian-American engineer and "jihadist."

Nation of Islam

In June 1934, after the disappearance of Wallace Fard, the founder of the Nation of Islam (a.k.a. Black Muslims), Elijah Muhammad became the "messenger" for the separatist religion. His best-known preacher was the controversial and charismatic Malcolm X, a master at using the media to expound and expand his message. After President Kennedy was assassinated in November 1963, Malcolm set off a media scandal when he told the press, "The chickens have come home to roost ... chickens coming home to roost never did make me sad; they've always made me glad." For these comments, Elijah suspended Malcolm from the Nation of Islam for ninety days. During his suspension, Malcolm's doubts grew over the Nation of Islam and its Messenger, whose lavish lifestyle and six illegitimate children disturbed him. To fan the scandal within his former religion, the March 1964 issue of *Ebony* magazine quote Malcolm as saying the Nation of Islam would have "to kill me. They can't afford to let me live ... I know where the bodies are buried. And if they press me, I'll exhume some." For the remaining eleven months of his life, Malcolm X was a fixture on television and radio shows hosted by, among many others, Mike Wallace (New York), Barry Gray (New York), Bob Kennedy (Boston), and *Kup's Show* (Chicago). As Malcolm X's media presence widened, so did his appeal, and Nation of Islam grew decidedly more hostile. After he formed the Organization of Afro-American Unity in June 1964 as a rival Muslim group, death threats, and attempts on his life, began. In September, the mainstream *Saturday Evening Post* ran excerpts of Malcolm X's autobiography under the title, "I'm Talking to You, White Man." On *Les Crane's Television Show*, in response to the violence, Malcolm X advocated armed self-defense for all black people, a precursor to the message expounded by the Black Panthers two years later.

Filling Malcolm X's shoes after his break with the Nation of Islam was Louis Farrakhan, a former Calypso singer whose stage name was The Charmer. Farrakhan charmed Elijah Muhammad by denouncing Malcolm X as a Judas, using the Nation of Islam's weekly newspaper, *Muhammad Speaks*, as a platform to threaten the former leader. In a December 1964 issue of *Muhammad Speaks*, Farrakhan wrote, "The die is set, and Malcolm shall not escape. Such a man as Malcolm is worthy of death."[21] Malcolm X was assassinated on February 21, 1965. His killers were Black Muslims. One of the shooters said that he was simply doing his duty as a Muslim. (Farrakhan took over Malcolm's former post as minister of the Harlem Mosque No. 7.)

Just before he died in 1975, Elijah named his son, Wallace, as successor, a choice that displeased Farrakhan. Wallace was a former devotee of Malcolm X and had, like Malcolm, converted to Sunni Islam. Wallace set about dismantling the Nation of Islam, and sold off its holdings. Farrakhan split with Wallace and started his own weekly newspaper, *The Final Call*, to keep to the traditions set down by Fard and Elijah Muhammad. In 1984, Farrakhan reached a nationwide audience when he entered the political arena to support Jesse Jackson's presidential campaign. His anti-Semitic slurs, insistence that the national media was controlled by Jews, and off-the-cuff remarks to the press kept him in hot water. Most scandalously, Farrakhan referred to Judaism in a radio broadcast as a "dirty religion."[22] Reverend Jackson's biggest media gaffe of the campaign was to refer to New York City as "Hymie-Town" on a New York radio station.[23] In the wake of these scandals, Jackson's campaign collapsed, but Farrakhan was now a national black leader, and the Nation of Islam enjoyed a revival of its fortunes. His watershed media event was the 1995 nondenominational Million Man March in Washington, D.C.

Holocaust Deniers

Holocaust denial gained international notoriety when French literature professor Robert Faurisson was successfully prosecuted in France for letters that he wrote the editor of a newspaper in 1978 and 1979 that denied the existence of extermination camps. Though initially a European phenomenon, Holocaust denial literature came to America via reactionary groups like the Liberty Lobby and American Nazi Party. The precedent for this literature was set by isolationist American historians like Charles Beard and Harry Elmer Barnes, who opposed U.S. "intervention" in World War II, and organizations like America First, whose most famous member was Charles Lindbergh.

In America, the most powerful financier of Holocaust denial was Willis A. Carto, a millionaire whose Washington, D.C.-based Liberty Lobby published the anti-Semitic newspaper *The Spotlight* (1975–2001) and ran Noontide Press, which specialized in Holocaust denial tracts. Noontide was responsible for the wide-selling *The Myth of the Six Million* (first published anonymously in 1969; later attributed to David Hoggan). In 1978, Carto helped found the Institute of Historical Review (IHR), a California-based group now directed by historian Mark Weber, which critics have labeled a Holocaust denial group. Though the IHR Web site claims that the organization is "devoted to truth and accuracy in history," the group focuses largely on the Holocaust. Many IHR publications state that the Holocaust was a "hoax perpetrated on the world by Zionists and other supporters of the State of Israel" and often minimize the previously published extent of the death and devastation.

Gitta Sereny, noted biographer and historian, wrote, "[Holocaust deniers] are by no means motivated by an ethical or intellectual preoccupation with the historical truth, but rather by precise political aims for the future."[24] In short, it matters little whether their professed "devotion to truth and accuracy in history" attracts a wide audience; the main priority is the anti-Semitic agenda of the present day. Such forays into history, then, are attempts to legitimize their prejudices.

Among the titles that have caused a furor in academic, political, and clerical circles, are *Did Six Million Really Die?* (1974) by Richard Harwood, *The Myth of the Six Million* (1969), as well as "Fred Leuchter's Forensic Examination and Engineering Report on the alleged gassing facilities at Auschwitz, Birkenau, and Majdanek" (a.k.a. *The Leuchter Report*, 1989), the widely debunked "scientific" study that many Holocaust deniers cite as "proof" that extermination camps were a myth. (*The Leuchter Report* was the basis for Errol Morris's 1999 documentary *Mr. Death: The Rise and Fall of Fred A. Leuchter, Jr.*). The Liberty Lobby disbanded in 2001. Noontide Press still publishes.

Fundamentally Christian

The Pilgrim's Progress by John Bunyan, published in 1678 in England, is a staple of evangelist literature. Written as an allegory, Bunyan's book takes the form of a dream in which the main character, Christian, and his family have to flee the City of Destruction and make their way to the Celestial City before the world is burned to a cinder by a wrathful god, to punish the sinners and nonbelievers who remain behind. Translated into more than one hundred languages since its publication, *The Pilgrim's Progress* has served as a template for subsequent apocalyptic literature. Among the most popular American books on this theme was *The Late Great Planet Earth* by Hal Lindsey (1970), an evangelist who proclaimed that the "end times" were upon the world. He predicted that the United States would be severely weakened and that Europe would reunite as the Revived Roman Empire, to be led by the anti-Christ. He also wrote a later book, *The 1980s: Countdown to Armageddon*. Lindsey's writings were rendered irrelevant by many after the Soviet Union fell, as much of his futurist vision was predicated on a permanent Cold War with the Soviets.

The most popular American works in this Christian fundamentalist genre have been the contemporaneous "Left Behind" series of novels by Tim LaHaye and Jerry B. Jenkins. These sixteen novels, and their separate "Left Behind" series for teenagers, graphic novels, and video games, have sold upwards of 65 million copies since 1995. Many argue that they have blurred the line between prophecy and fakery, politics and religion. The plot of the series revolves around a group of born-again Christians who discover that the secretary general of the United Nations is actually the anti-Christ, and that they must prepare the world for the imminent "Tribulation," in which God will "rain down judgment on the world for seven years." Of these books, Jerry Falwell said, "In terms of its impact on Christianity, it's probably greater than that of any other book in modern times, outside the Bible."

One of the criticisms of this series is the same that was leveled at Lindsey— that it has political, not evangelical, motives. LaHaye, cochairman of Jack Kemp's presidential campaign, a founding member of the Moral Majority, and an organizer of the powerful conservative lobbying group the Council for National Policy wielded some influence in the George W. Bush administration, particularly among the neoconservatives who pushed for war in the Middle East. According to some, the ideology expressed in the Left Behind series also provided the impetus for radical shifts in domestic and foreign policy during the Bush era (2001–9). As *Salon*'s Michelle Goldberg noted, "For some of the most powerful people in the world, this stuff isn't melodrama. It's prophecy."[25]

Televangelism: Scandal Gets Religion

The scandals of broadcast evangelism didn't start with Jim and Tammy Bakker. Since the advent of radio, charlatans have exploited the good intentions of those seeking religion's consolations. The stereotype of the televangelist with a 1-800 phone number emblazoned on the television screen while he exhorts viewers to touch the set to receive divine intervention has some basis in reality. Jim and Tammy Bakker were updated versions of revival tent hucksters and faith healers. Evangelists discovered the power of television in the early 1950s, when Fulton Sheen, a Roman Catholic archbishop, segued from his radio pulpit to television, and Protestant evangelicals Billy Graham and Oral Roberts began their own broadcasts, *Hour of Decision* and *Contact!* respectively.

However, the scandals of "televangelism" didn't really explode until the 1980s, when the broadcasts reached millions of people via syndication and cable, with the resultant flow of cash—and its temptations—into the preachers' coffers. These scandals occurred with some regularity, putting the likes of Jimmy Swaggart, Marvin Gorman, Jim Bakker, Jerry Falwell, Pat Robertson, and Ted Haggard on the national stage.

Again, these excesses were nothing that faith healers hadn't done on a smaller scale in the past. However, televangelism's unique power was its ability to extort money from viewers by playing on emotions and "testing" religious faith on a scale heretofore unknown. Though examples of this abound, they are encapsulated by one practitioner: Granville "Oral" Roberts, the Tulsa-based televangelist who began as a tent-revival faith healer before moving on to radio, and then, most lucratively, to television. Roberts was renowned for having "visions" that required money to implement, such as an expansion of the Oral Roberts Evangelistic Association or Oral Roberts University, which he founded in 1963. The biggest scandal Roberts generated involved a 1987 fundraising drive during which he told his TV audience that unless they sent him $8 million by a certain date, God would "call me home"; some believers took this to mean that Roberts was threatening suicide unless they intervened. That same year, he ignited another media storm when his son, also a televangelist, announced that his father had "raised the dead."

Visions of doom to be visited upon Americans have been a popular motif with televangelists. Roberts himself, in 2004, appeared on Kenneth Copeland's *Victory in Jesus* broadcast to announce his vision of New York City surrounded by "a dark cloud," which was a "wake up call" that Christ was soon to return to earth. This, of course, came in the wake of the terror attacks three years before. Those 9/11 attacks generated one of the most divisive media storms in American history, sparked by comments made by televangelists Pat Robertson and Jerry Falwell. Two days after the attacks, Falwell was a guest on Robertson's widely syndicated *700 Club*, on which he blamed the attacks on "pagans, abortionists, feminists, gays, lesbians, the ACLU" and said America got "what we deserve." Robertson responded, "I totally concur." Given that the perpetrators of the attacks were also religious fundamentalists—albeit Muslim, not Christians like Falwell and Robertson—these comments struck millions of Americans as hypocritical and, given the national crisis, inexcusable.

Two years later, Robertson told his TV audience, "What we need is for somebody to place a small nuke at Foggy Bottom," suggesting the State Department be destroyed.[26] Despite the outrage of Secretary of State Colin Powell, Robertson's broadcasting license was not revoked. Two years later on his show, he advocated the assassination of Hugo Chavez, the Venezuelan president; in 2007, he prophesied "mass killings" in the United States from a terrorist attack, possibly with nuclear weapons. Robertson's demagoguery has not been confined to his broadcasts. He has authored many books of apocalyptic prophecies not unlike Lindsey's. Robertson has proclaimed that a "Jewish cabal" has formed a conspiracy to control America's economy and foreign policy, expanding this theory in his bestselling *The New World Order* (1991).

The Curse on *The Satanic Verses*

When Salman Rushdie's novel *The Satanic Verses* was published in 1988, the rift between Islam and the modern (Western) world, which began with the Iran hostage crisis in 1979, widened into an abyss. Though it would be redundant to call Rushdie's novel a work of fiction, Muslims did not make this distinction, as the events depicted were based on the life of the prophet Muhammad. Many Muslims considered the book blasphemous; it was banned in several Muslim countries and India. The Ayatollah Khomeini, spiritual leader of Iran, issued a fatwa that made it the duty of any Muslim in the world to kill Rushdie, a British citizen of Indian descent. Further, the Ayatollah called for the death of "all those involved in [*The Satanic Verses*'] publication." Though Rushdie publicly apologized for any offense the book caused—even briefly converted to Islam—the death sentence remained. As a result of the book's continued availability in the free world, people were killed by fatwa-driven fundamentalists. Among the victims were Hitoshi Igarashi, the Japanese translator of the book, and rioters in Pakistan and India. In Turkey, thirty-seven people participating in a literary festival were killed when their hotel was burned down by anti-Rushdie fanatics. Ettore Capriolo, the book's Italian translator, was stabbed, and William Nygaard, the Norwegian publisher, was attacked.

After the novel was published in the United States in 1989, threats were made against bookstores; Barnes and Noble and Waldenbooks removed the book from the shelves of some stores. Two bookshops in Berkeley, California, were firebombed for selling the book. After the Ayatollah Khomeini died in

June 1989, Rushdie tried to placate the murderous vibe the book had accrued by issuing yet another apology. But, as of 2008, the fatwa has not been officially rescinded. Although Rushdie no longer lives in hiding, he is subject to murder every time he goes in public—all because of a novel, a work of fiction, published nearly twenty-five years ago, and a death sentence issued by a man now dead for nearly as long.

Chapter 3

SEXUALITY AND MORALITY

Two competing threads are woven through the fabric of American history. The Puritan ethic, which many settlers brought with them from Europe, preached a strict and unbending moral code, even as the colonists chafed under the yoke of British repression. Ultimately, the push for freedom won the upper hand. Independence also unleashed a desire for personal freedoms and expanded civil liberties. Though the tension between these two threads has manifested itself in many ways, the threads often intertwined on the third rail of sexuality. When this happened, the puritanical impulse won the upper hand, and efforts to censor, ban, or burn media content deemed immoral or obscene were stepped up. Some great works of world literature were caught in the middle of these battles, including D. H. Lawrence's *Lady Chatterley's Lover*, James Joyce's *Ulysses*, Allen Ginsberg's *Howl*, and Henry Miller's *Tropic of Cancer*.

MUZZLING THE MEDIA

Before the Civil War, the censoring and banning of material in the United States was relatively rare. Obscenity was in the eye of the beholder, and people beheld little to make them squirm. Or, if they did, they censored it individually. (Consider, also, that prior to radio, television, movies, and even photography, print was the only potential conduit of obscene material.) The first case occurred in 1821 when the imported book *Memoirs of a Woman of Pleasure* (a.k.a. *Fanny Hill*) was banned in Massachusetts on the grounds of "obscenity." In 1842, the *Tariff Act* was passed, the first federal law to systematically address imported material; it prohibited the "importation of all indecent and obscene prints, paintings, lithographs, engravings and transparencies." Using this law, in September 1842, U.S. authorities indicted Richard Hobbes and Henry R. Robinson, publishers of "obscene books." Five print shop owners and bookstand operators were also indicted. Among the imported books and prints cited were such titles as *Memoirs of a Woman of Pleasure*; *Memoirs of the Life and Voluptuous Adventures of the Celebrated Courtesan Mademoiselle Celestine of Paris*; *The Curtain Drawn Up, or The Education of Laura*; *The*

Confessions of a Voluptuous Young Lady of High Rank; *The Amorous Songster or Jovial Companion*; *The Lustful Turk*; and *The Auto-Biography of a Footman.*

During the Civil War, soldiers on both sides acquired "great numbers" of erotic pictures, pamphlets, and books. In 1864, Union soldiers—as stipulated in the Post Office Act—were no longer allowed to receive any "obscene book, pamphlet, picture, print, or other publication of vulgar and indecent character" through the U.S. mail.

The Dark Era of Publishing

After the Civil War, Anthony Comstock (1844–1915), a postal inspector, rose to prominence brandishing a weapon called the "Hicklin rule." This legal cudgel stemmed from an 1868 case of English law (*Queen v. Hicklin*), which defined obscenity as "anything that tends to deprave and corrupt those whose minds are susceptible." In 1873, Comstock founded the New York Society for the Suppression of Vice and, using this platform, hectored the U.S. Congress into passing the Comstock Act, which was based on the "Hicklin rule" and banned "obscene, lewd, and/or lascivious" items from being distributed through the U.S. Postal Service. This piece of legislation, an offshoot of which is still on the books, was wide-ranging and severe. Any person who sold or offered:

> to sell, or to lend, or to give away, or in any manner to exhibit, or shall otherwise publish or offer to publish in any manner, or shall have in his possession, for any such purpose or purposes, an obscene book, pamphlet, paper, writing, advertisement, circular, print, picture, drawing or other representation, figure, or image on or of paper or other material, or any cast instrument, or other article of an immoral nature ... shall be deemed guilty of a misdemeanor, and on conviction thereof in any court of the United States, he shall be imprisoned at hard labor in the penitentiary for not less than six months nor more than five years for each offense, or fined not less than one hundred dollars nor more than two thousand dollars.

This law also covered the sale or exhibition of media that championed contraception and abortion, along with "obscene" material.

Joining the federal government, twenty-four states passed further restrictions on the sale or distribution of "obscene, lewd and/or lascivious" material. Collectively, all these statutes were known as Comstock laws. Thus ensued what historian E. R. Hutchison called the "dark era" of book publishing, lasting from 1870 to 1915, the year Comstock died. During this time, manuscripts had to be submitted to Comstock and his minions at the New York Society for the Suppression of Vice for their approval. If they didn't approve, the book wasn't published. In his forty-two-year career, Comstock boasted of destroying fifty tons of books and arresting 3,000 suspects. Of the latter, he claimed to have convicted "enough persons to fill a passenger train of 61 coaches—60 coaches containing 60 passengers and the 61st not quite full."[1] George Bernard Shaw, whose play about prostitution, *Mrs. Warren's Profession*, was the target of censors, coined the term *comstockery* to denote those who are narrow-minded, self-righteous, and censorious.

"Banned in Boston"

Boston had a homegrown Comstock named Richard Sinnott, who used the unofficial title of "city censor" to lead a campaign to eradicate "vice." Sinnott was more zealous than Comstock, lending a certain authenticity to the "Banned in Boston" label slapped on many books and magazines in the early part of the twentieth century. Some movies and plays also suffered similar fates when the censors—who infiltrated audiences—saw something that offended them, and had the power to shut down the show. Movies and plays were often shut down in mid-showing, to groans of protest from paying customers, and theaters were locked down to prevent the continued run of a risqué production. Anything "salacious, inappropriate, or offensive" was subject to the whims of censors.

Aiding Sinnott was the Boston Watch and Ward Society, founded in 1878 to "watch and ward off evildoers" in business, politics, and culture. Although some city officials felt these private citizens had overstepped the law, they dared not intervene for fear of appearing soft on immorality. The power of the Watch and Ward Society was Taliban-like—prodigious and unchecked. They "reviewed" books, plays, and other forms of artistic expression for moral failings. If an item was "obscene," the bookshop owner was given a warning. If the offending item continued to be sold, the police vice squad was alerted, books were confiscated and often burned, and the seller was arrested. Soon enough, Boston—the formerly enlightened epicenter of the American Revolution—was reduced to a cultural backwater. Elsewhere, being "banned in Boston" became a badge of honor, piquing interest in a book, play, or film. Some promoters in other cities even claimed their work was "banned in Boston" when it wasn't, to enhance its appeal.

Enter H. L. Mencken

In addition to being one of the nation's sharpest critics, Baltimore's H. L. Mencken was editor of *American Mercury*, an influential cultural journal. The Watch and Ward Society ruled that the April 1926 issue of *American Mercury* was not fit for public consumption due to its advertisement of an "obscene" book, an essay ("New View of Sex," which suggested that sex was "a pastime for leisure hours"), and a story about a prostitute who plied her trade in graveyards. When Mencken learned that his magazine was "banned in Boston," he sought to test the legality of the censors' campaign. Traveling to Boston with copies of the offending issue of his journal, he met John Chase, head of the

Watch and Ward Society, on the Boston Common. In front of a crowd of press and students, Mencken sold Chase a copy of the April 1926 issue of *American Mercury*. Members of the city's vice squad, also on hand, arrested Mencken. In court, the judge ruled the journal was not obscene and acquitted Mencken. With this ruling, Mencken effectively unmasked the private citizens who had taken the law into their own hands. Not content with the victory, Mencken sued the Watch and Ward Society for "restraint of trade." He won again when a federal judge ruled that it was the responsibility of prosecutors, not private citizens, to censor literature. However, few had the courage to follow Mencken's example, and for the next thirty years Boston led the nation in the number of banned books and magazines.[2]

Despite the judge's ruling, the solicitor of the U.S. Post Office declared that *American Mercury* was obscene and, thus, sending it through the mails was a federal offense. Mencken responded by suing the U.S. Post Office. A month later, the courts dismissed the case on a technicality since the magazine had already been mailed and delivered. The seesaw battle has continued to this day.

Book Banning

Though now considered a classic of literature, *Lady Chatterley's Lover* by D. H. Lawrence was banned in the United States from the time it was first published in 1928 (in the United Kingdom) until 1959, when the U.S. publisher waged a successful lawsuit (*Grove Press v. Christenberry*) to free it for publication. The battle to secure its legal, unexpurgated publication in the United States was a landmark First Amendment success story that opened the door for publication of Henry Miller's *Tropic of Cancer*, which—as a precedent-setting book—in turn loosed the floodgates that had been backed up since the days of Anthony Comstock. The battle began on November 25, 1930, when one of the Watch and Ward Society's minions bought a copy of *Lady Chatterley's Lover* at the Dunster House Book Shop in Cambridge, Massachusetts. James Delancy, the manager, and Joseph Sullivan, his clerk, were both convicted of selling obscene literature, a crime for which Delancy was fined $800 and imprisoned for four months, and Sullivan was fined $200 and imprisoned for two weeks. Striking fear in the hearts of the nation's booksellers, the U.S. Customs Bureau also compiled a list of books to confiscate at 300 U.S. ports of entry if they were found among imported cargo. The U.S. Post Office had the same right to ban the mailing of contraband literature in its more than 40,000 branches in the country.

Such were the risks involved with the sale of literature that was controversial (*Lady Chatterley's Lover*) or even experimental (*Ulysses* by James Joyce) that if a book or journal was ruled obscene, the seller faced prison and fines. Because of this, *Ulysses* embarked on an odyssey through the U.S. legal system. Joyce's groundbreaking/highly praised novel was first excerpted in 1920 in the New York-based journal *The Little Review*. For this excerpt, the journal was deemed obscene in 1921; thus, so was Joyce's book, which was then theoretically banned in the United States. To contest this ruling, Random House, which planned to publish a U.S. edition of *Ulysses* in 1934, imported a copy of the French edition, first published in 1922. When customs officials seized the book, the publisher sued to get it back. The case went to U.S. District Court, where Judge John Woolsey ruled, on December 6, 1933, that the book was "not written for the purpose of exploiting obscenity." The judge even praised the book's technique, saying Joyce "had attempted with astonishing success to show how the screen of consciousness with its ever-shifting kaleidoscopic impressions carries ... not only what is in the focus of each man's observation of the actual things about him, but also in a penumbral zone residual of past impressions."[3] *Ulysses* was "admitted into the United States." Random House published its version of *Ulysses*, as planned, in 1934.

Mailing for Males

In 1946, a case involving *Esquire* magazine loosened postal restrictions on adult material. Prior to this, cheaper second-class mailing rates were guaranteed for newspapers and magazines by the 1879 Classification Act. The reasoning was that this material was "originated and published for the dissemination of the information of a public character, or devoted to literature, the sciences, arts, or some special industry, and having a legitimate list of subscribers." The postmaster general, however, objected to *Esquire*'s bawdy content and revoked its second-class mailing rate permit, stating that *Esquire* was "morally improper and not for the public welfare."[4] *Esquire* contested this arbitrary ruling, insisting that one man should not have the power to decide what should, in effect, be censored (since *Esquire* would not be able to afford to mail its issues out without second-class mailing privileges, the ruling amounted to censorship). The Supreme Court eventually ruled in *Esquire*'s favor, reinforcing the legal precedent that, as long as newspapers and magazines were not deemed "obscene," they were allowed second-class mailing privileges.

The final blow was *Roth v. US*, a 1957 case involving a New York bookseller convicted by a district court of four counts of "mailing obscene circulars." The case, on appeal, went to the U.S. Supreme Court. The high court ruled that the age-old Hicklin rule was "unconstitutional" and that obscenity was not "within the area of speech protected by the First Amendment" and, thus, was allowed when "to the average person, applying contemporary community standards, the dominant theme of the material taken as a whole appeals to the prurient interest." However, the exceptions to this ruling were works "with redeeming social importance."

Harassing Frank

Frank Harris (1856–1931) was an American-born editor and biographer who made his name in England before returning to the United States.

Wherever Harris roamed, scandal followed him like a shadow. In addition to writing biographies of Oscar Wilde and George Bernard Shaw, Harris wrote a four-volume "erotic autobiography," *My Life and Loves* (1922–27)—a fifth volume, of dubious provenance, was published posthumously. *My Life and Loves* contained detailed accounts of his sexual adventures and fabrications about his own accomplishments. Originally printed in Germany, the book had to be smuggled into the United States from Mexico by Esar Levine and Benjamin Rebhuhn. Levine was arrested in New York in 1925 for preparing to publish a second volume of the work, which was deemed obscene. Due to the efforts to suppress and ban it, *My Life and Loves* was Harris's widest-selling book. An unexpurgated edition of the five-volume book was published in 1963 by Grove Press, after the publisher had won its legal cases to publish *Lady Chatterley's Lover* and *Tropic of Cancer*.

How Long Has This Been Going On?

Allen Ginsberg was arguably the best-known postwar poet in America, and his reputation rested largely on his epic work *Howl*. After reading *Howl* in public for the first time in 1955, Ginsberg published the work with the City Lights Books' Pocket Poet Series, an imprint started by poet Lawrence Ferlinghetti. The book was stocked at Ferlinghetti's San Francisco shop, City Lights Books; the first printing quickly sold out. As the notoriety of the poem spread, it came to the attention of Chester MacPhee, Collector of Customs in San Francisco. After reading some of the descriptions of sex, drunkenness, and insanity, Mac-Phee claimed, "The words and the sense of the writing is obscene," and sought to ban the book. Because it had been printed in England, *Howl* had to pass through U.S. Customs to be legally sold in the United States. On March 25, 1957, customs agents seized 520 copies of the second printing, as well as copies of a magazine called *The Miscellaneous Man*, both sold at City Lights Books; proprietors Ferlinghetti and Shigeyoshi Murao were arrested and jailed.

The case went to trial when the ACLU contested the legality of the seizure; Ferlinghetti defended it on the grounds of literary merit, telling reporters, "I consider *Howl* to be the most significant long poem to be published in this country since World War II, perhaps since Eliot's *Four Quartets*." Also coming to the defense of *Howl* were, to paraphrase the poem's now famous opening line, "the best minds of [Ginsberg's] generation." On the other hand, the prosecution called only two witnesses, one of whom suffered from the delusion that she had "rewritten Goethe's *Faust*." Had the judge ruled against *Howl*, and upheld the ban, the police department's Juvenile Bureau had prepared a list of other books it would ban, using *Howl* as a precedent. Thus, in what was a resounding victory, Judge Clayton Horn ruled that the ban violated Ginsberg's First and Fourteenth Amendment rights, as well as the Constitution of the State of California, which says, "Every citizen may freely speak, write, and publish his sentiments on all subjects, being responsible for the abuse of that right; and no law shall be passed to restrain or abridge the liberty of speech or of the press." The judge also cited the "motto" in Latin, *Honi soit qui mal y pense* (Evil to him who evil thinks).[5]

City Lights Books was busted ten years later for selling Lenore Kandel's 1966 collection of erotic verse, *The Love Book*. A clerk at the Psychedelic Shop in Haight Ashbury was arrested for the same offense. After a protest and staged reading of the offending passages by San Francisco State College professors, the charges were dropped.

Artistic Erotica or Pornography?

Another publisher who ran afoul of the censors was Ralph Ginzburg, creator of the magazines *Avant-Garde*, *Fact,* and *Eros*, the latter described as "a quarterly on the joys of love." Ginzburg launched *Eros* on Valentine's Day 1962, saying, "In publishing this magazine we hope to produce an antidote to the cheap and degrading periodicals to which love and sex are generally relegated in this country."[6] The hardbound quarterly, which sold for a whopping ten dollars (a princely sum in 1962), was aimed at a sophisticated audience. He issued a companion newsletter, *Liaison*, and a mail-order treatise called *The Housewife's Handbook on Selective Promiscuity.* However, the censors ruled that *Eros* was "cheap and degrading" pornography. In 1963, Ginzburg was convicted of violating the 1872 law prohibiting the mailing of obscene material. Appealing the ruling to the U.S. Supreme Court, he said *Eros* had "artistic and literary merit," but the Court ruled that it "appealed to prurient interests" and was "utterly without redeeming social value."[7] Ginzburg served eight months of a three-year prison sentence before being paroled.

Tropic of Cancer

The advances of the "sexual revolution" notwithstanding, *Tropic of Cancer*, a novel by the American expatriate Henry Miller, remained banned in the United States in 1961. Barney Rossett, who founded Grove Press, decided to test the ban by publishing a U.S. edition. Rossett had a track record of publishing controversial writers, including the first "legal" U.S. edition of D. H. Lawrence's *Lady Chatterley's Lover*. In 1958, G. P. Putnam published the controversial novel *Lolita* by Vladimir Nabokov. The story of an older man obsessed with an under-aged girl, *Lolita* had created a huge scandal upon publication in England, with all of its copies seized by the Home Office. However, it arrived in U.S. bookshops to little protest, and became the first book since *Gone with the Wind* to sell 100,000 copies in its first three weeks of release. Based on this success, Rossett figured the time was ripe for Henry Miller in his own country.

Henry Miller was the target of censors for two decades for his first novel, *Tropic of Cancer*. In 1947, Miller was living in California but still unable to get his books published in the United States, having to print them by hand. He occupied his time painting and humoring photographers with "surrealistic" acts like snipping petals off a daisy. Courtesy of Library of Congress, Prints and Photographs Division.

When Rossett published a U.S. edition of *Tropic of Cancer* in June 1961, the explicit sex and language, and the author's alleged anti-Americanism, unleashed a scandal that led to the pulling of books from store shelves, dealers were arrested, and copies were burned. The U.S. postmaster refused to allow the book to go through the mail in 1961, but then backed down the following year when the Justice Department warned that, after the lifting of bans on *Lady Chatterley's Lover* and *Ulysses*, the Post Office would lose in court. E. R. Hutchison wrote, "The censorship campaign grew in intensity until Henry Miller became the most controversial literary figure—and *Tropic of Cancer* the most censored novel—in American history."[8] The irony of this controversy was twofold. Nowhere in Miller's book were taboos like sex with under-aged girls (as in *Lolita*) depicted. And, secondly, *Tropic of Cancer* was nearly thirty years old. The novel was originally published in 1934, in English, by Jack Kahane of Obelisk Press; yet it could not be published in Miller's own country due to the efforts to ban it. When a San Francisco book dealer imported the foreign edition in 1948, all copies of the novel were confiscated. To rectify the situation, Rossett vowed to publish all of Miller's banned books, including *Tropic of Cancer*, *Tropic of Capricorn* (first published by Kahane in 1936), and *Black Spring*, as well as the trilogy *The Rosy Crucifixion*. But it was the first one, *Tropic of Cancer*, that turned America's publishing world on its head.

Miller wrote the novel—more memoir than fiction, actually—while an expatriate in Paris, and the events depicted occurred prior to the rise of Hitler in Germany. Miller did himself no favors with the censors by writing, "This is not a book. This is libel, slander, defamation of character. This is not a book, in the ordinary sense of the word. No, this is a prolonged insult, a gob of spit in the face of Art, a kick in the pants to God, Man, Destiny, Time, Love, Beauty...." The battle to keep *Tropic of Cancer* in print cost Grove Press dearly. Rossett was required to pay the legal fees for all of the booksellers against whom lawsuits were filed. Meanwhile, the notoriety drove up sales. Within a week of publication, *Tropic of Cancer* sold 68,000 copies in three printings—unprecedented sales for a twenty-five-year-old book—and it trailed *The Carpetbaggers* by Harold Robbins and Irving Stone's *The Agony and the Ecstasy* on the bestseller list. By July 1962, 100,000 hardcover copies had sold (at $7.50 each). Still, some stores refused to carry it. *Time* magazine called *Tropic of Cancer* "a very dirty book indeed" and *Life* wrote, "*Tropic* will be defended by critics as an explosive corrosive Whitmanesque masterpiece (which it is) and attacked as an unbridled obscenity (which it is)." Massachusetts' Attorney General, calling *Tropic* "filthy" and "rotten," declared it to violate the state's "dirty book" law and refused to allow it to be distributed there. In Dallas, it was banned by state law. Similar cases popped up all over the country, depleting Grove's resources. Also, since legal actions against "obscene" books can be taken at the local level, many cities banned the book.

A paperback edition of *Tropic of Cancer* was published in October 1961. More than 2 million copies were sold despite the fact that only a limited number of booksellers risked selling it. There were, according to the ACLU, sixty cases against *Tropic of Cancer* in twenty-one different states. One of the most contentious was in Milwaukee, where the paperback edition was found to be obscene on June 22, 1962. The judge said the book "corroded and eroded the foundation of the nation's morality." The decision was overturned on appeal. The paperback edition was banned in Massachusetts, Rhode Island, Atlanta, Miami, Los Angeles, Chicago, Philadelphia, Cleveland, Houston, Seattle, Hartford, Wilmington, Indianapolis, Des Moines, St. Louis, Trenton, Buffalo, Phoenix, Oklahoma City, and Birmingham. The only cities where it was openly sold were New York, San Francisco, Washington, D.C., and Minneapolis. Many places, out of fear, chose not to carry it. Some newspapers even excised *Tropic of Cancer* from their bestseller lists.

Oddly, Miller's second novel, *Tropic of Capricorn*, was published by Grove in 1962 and met with little resistance, though it was much more graphically erotic than its predecessor. And, without the notoriety that attended the protracted obscenity charges, the book's sales were only a fraction of those of *Tropic of Cancer*.

Literary Works Regularly Banned from Some School Libraries and Curriculum

The Adventures of Huckleberry Finn by Mark Twain (1885).
Sister Carrie by Theodore Dreiser (1900).
A Farewell to Arms by Ernest Hemingway (1929).
Of Mice and Men by John Steinbeck (1937).
The Grapes of Wrath by John Steinbeck (1939).
For Whom the Bell Tolls by Ernest Hemingway (1943).
The Catcher in the Rye by J. D. Salinger (1951).
Invisible Man by Ralph Ellison (1952).
Lord of the Flies by William Golding (1954).
To Kill a Mockingbird by Harper Lee (1960).
Catch-22 by Joseph Heller (1961).
A Clockwork Orange by Anthony Burgess (1962).
Cat's Cradle by Kurt Vonnegut (1963).
Slaughterhouse Five by Kurt Vonnegut (1969).
Song of Solomon by Toni Morrison (1977).
The Color Purple by Alice Walker (1983).
Beloved by Toni Morrison (1987).
The Satanic Verses by Salman Rushdie (1988).[9]

CHARTING THE SEXUAL REVOLUTION

The so-called *sexual revolution* of the 1960s not only breathed new life into the publishing industry, but also redefined what constituted obscenity and appropriate subject matter for the entire mass media. The tension between old established values and new liberalization was a veritable recipe for scandal. Still, no revolution would have occurred had Americans not been curious about such matters. Indeed, Americans' collective fascination with sexuality, sociologists argued, resulted from the lifting of taboos in a nation originally settled by religious puritans.

The 1960s Were No Overnight Sensation

This sudden embrace of sexual material in the 1960s was a far cry from the reaction to social philosopher Havelock Ellis's classic book, *Studies in the*

Psychology of Sex, copies of which were seized by U.S. Customs when they were imported from England in 1898. When the book was first published in England in 1891, the British publisher was prosecuted for obscenity. Ellis then arranged for his work to be published in the United States. Stanley Kunitz wrote, "In a sense he was the Darwin of sex ... Ellis did more than any other single individual to bring about a change in the general viewpoint on sex and its scientific elucidation in print."[10]

The puritanical impulse to repress discussions of sex did not disappear with the Ellis case, even if Americans continued to harbor a secret fascination with the subject. The advertising industry, which rose to prominence during the time Ellis's book was suppressed, subtly used sex to sell products, and all other media followed suit. Sex caused scandals only when the publishers went too far—that is, when arbiters of public morals like Anthony Comstock and the Watch and Ward Society complained or seized offending copies of books, magazines, and newspapers. The half century after Ellis was marked by nearly continuous litigation over material whose sexual content and graphic language tested the obscenity laws. Many of these were works of literature now considered classics: *Lady Chatterley's Lover* by D. H. Lawrence, *Tropic of Cancer* by Henry Miller, *Howl* by Allen Ginsberg, and others.

Some books, however, did get published and helped eliminate many of the long-held myths and misconceptions about sexuality. Among the groundbreaking novels were Radclyffe Hall's *The Well of Loneliness* (1928), which chronicled a lesbian relationship between a young woman and her older lover. A British judge ruled that the book was "an obscene libel" and ordered all copies destroyed, but an American judge rejected the Society for the Suppression of Vice's bid to ban the book, an early (and rare) victory for censorship foes. Margaret Sanger was another pioneer whose tireless promotion of birth control opened doors, both medical and psychological, for American women. Sanger's most scandalous idea may have been that sex was not just for procreation, which she regularly expounded in a column for the *New York Call* entitled "What Every Girl Should Know." In defiance of the Comstock Law of 1873, which ruled that dissemination of contraceptive information was obscene, Sanger printed and distributed a pamphlet, *Family Limitation*, to poor women. In 1914, she launched *The Woman Rebel*, a newsletter advocating contraception and positing that every woman should "be the absolute mistress of her own body." She was indicted for violating postal obscenity laws in August 1914 and fled to Europe, returning the next year. She published a book version of *What Every Girl Should Know* (1916), followed by *What Every Mother Should Know* (1917). Another birth control advocate, Mary Dennett, was prosecuted under the Comstock Law for her book *The Sex Side of Life* (1928). Her case not only generated scandal, but also led to a precedent-setting ruling in 1936 (*U.S. v. One Package of Japanese Pessaries*) that exempted birth control literature from obscenity laws.

Paging Dr. Kinsey

University of Indiana zoologist Dr. Alfred C. Kinsey's two studies, *Sexual Behavior in the Human Male* (1948) and *Sexual Behavior in the Human Female* (1953), changed the way Americans viewed sexuality. These books were the end result of a fifteen-year survey conducted with 100,000 men and women about their sexual behavior. Kinsey's conclusions created a national sensation; not all of it was positive. Indeed, the loudest voices against Kinsey and his findings—corroborated by follow-up surveys—came from conservatives and clergy. Among Kinsey's findings were that 10 percent of American adults were homosexual and 37 percent of American males had homosexual experiences. Because he used precise scales to rank sexual behavior, critics could not debate Kinsey on the scientific level. Thus, the scandal unloosed by his frank discussions of homosexuality and extramarital sex (he found that half of married men and one-quarter of married women had affairs) led to accusations of "promoting degeneracy." The critics feared that consenting adults, viewing the statistics of infidelity and homosexuality, would have a license to engage in either or both. Some newspapers, including the *New York Times*, refused to take advertising for the first Kinsey report in 1948. As Lawrence Wright noted, "The mirror that Kinsey held up to America showed a country that was frantically lustful but also confused, ashamed, incompetent, and astoundingly ignorant. Despite the evidence of the diversity and frequency of sexual activity, this was a time in America when sexual matters were practically never discussed, not even by doctors."[11] Kinsey's sting has lingered. In 2000, *Human Events* ranked Kinsey's *Sexual Behavior in the Human Male* as Number 4 on its "Ten Most Harmful Books of the Nineteenth and Twentieth Centuries."

More esoteric was Wilhelm Reich's *The Function of the Orgasm*. Originally published in German in 1927, the book became a cult classic in English translation. Though Reich died in 1957, his ideas had a profound effect on events of the 1960s. In this book, Reich posited a link between sex and neurosis, and theorized that people who had potent orgasms led healthier lives. The subject of orgasm—taking pleasure in the sex act—was controversial enough, but Reich claimed to have discovered a form of energy (orgone) that was in all living matter. He prescribed his "orgone accumulators" to patients, who sat inside them to collect more orgone energy. The scandal still rages today over whether Reich was a madman or a genius. Regardless, his and Kinsey's writings opened the Pandora's box of the sexual revolution.

Gurley Girls

It could be argued that the first pitch in the "liberation" ballgame was thrown by Helen Gurley Brown, whose 1962 "guidebook" *Sex and the Single Girl* topped the bestseller list. Her take on womanhood—that women could "have it all," meaning "love, sex and money"—predated most of the tracts written by modern feminists and was summed up in the book's subtitle: "The Unmarried Woman's Guide to Men, Careers, the Apartment, Diet, Fashion, Money and Men." Among her advice was this scandalous tidbit: It was "complete lunacy" for a girl "not to have slept with the man you're going to marry." Brown continued to mine this topic in her follow-up book, *Sex and the Office* (1965), and then as *Cosmopolitan*'s editor-in-chief. During her three decades at the helm of this influential magazine, Brown created a mythical liberated woman known as "Cosmo Girl."[12]

Running parallel to Brown was another feminist-turned-magazine editor, Gloria Steinem, who went "undercover" for one month at New York's Playboy Club to examine that scene in a widely anthologized two-part article for *Esquire* in 1963, "A Bunny's Tale." Steinem went on to found the groundbreaking magazine *Ms.* in 1972. More substantive was Betty Friedan's *The Feminine Mystique* (1963), which was also a bestseller. Friedan is credited with jumpstarting feminism with this book. Its core thesis was that American women had been brainwashed into living in a "comfortable concentration camp." Sexual roles were also challenged, to much scandal, by feminist classics like *The Female Eunuch* by Germaine Greer, *Sexual Politics* by Kate Millet, *The Dialectic of Sex: The Case for Feminist Revolution* by Shulamith Firestone, and *Sisterhood Is Powerful: An Anthology of Writings from the Women's Liberation Movement* edited by Robin Morgan. Included in the latter volume was "The SCUM (Society for Cutting up Men) Manifesto" by Valerie Solanis, who later shot and nearly killed artist Andy Warhol.

Because the subject was now out of the box, even a technical tome like *Human Sexual Response* by clinicians William H. Masters and Virginia E. Johnson (1966) was a bestseller. Based on a decade of research at the Reproductive Biology Research Foundation in St. Louis, *Human Sexual Response* was the first book to offer a graphic scientific description of orgasm. Meanwhile, the self-help books guided readers toward orgasm in the bedroom. Among the most popular were *Everything You Ever Wanted to Know About Sex but Were Afraid to Ask* by David Reuben and *The Sensuous Woman* by "J" (subtitled: "The First How-To Book for the Female Who Yearns to Be All Woman"), published in 1969, followed closely by *The Joy of Sex* by Alex Comfort (1972), an illustrated instructional manual or, as the subtitle put it, "A Gourmet Guide to Love Making." They were all runaway bestsellers. Reuben's book, in paperback, sold nearly 3 million copies in the first eight days of publication, making it the second-fastest-selling paperback in U.S. history (to *The Godfather*).[13] Comfort's book was the third biggest selling hardback for 1972, and then sold 3 million more copies in paperback in 1975. *The Sensuous Woman* spent a year on the *New York Times* bestseller list; "J" was Terry Garrity, who used her real name on all subsequent editions. Reuben's and Comfort's updated guides are still in print today.

So insatiable were American readers for books with sexual themes that even reissued classics of erotica, like *The Story of O* by Pauline Reage and *Memoirs of a Woman of Pleasure* by John Cleland (better known as *Fanny Hill*), were bestsellers. Published in 1749, *Fanny Hill* was known as "the first deliberately dirty novel in English," though it would not be cleared of obscenity charges in the United States until 1966. For those not content with homegrown techniques offered by Reuben and Comfort, the ancient Hindu sex manual *Kama Sutra* was reissued as a bestselling paperback.

Valley of the Dolls

To sate pop fiction readers, Jacqueline Susann followed her popular *Valley of the Dolls* (1966) with the sequels *The Love Machine* (1969) and *Once Is Not Enough* (1973). Even "respectable" authors like Philip Roth (*Portnoy's Complaint*), Gore Vidal (*Myra Breckinridge*), and John Updike (*Rabbit Run* and *Couples*) couldn't resist the urge to flaunt their knowledge of sexual perversity in books that pandered to the bestseller list and provoked "rallies for decency" around the country. The godfathers of this trend toward sexual scandal in works of literary merit were *Lady Chatterley's Lover* by D. H. Lawrence, *Tropic of Cancer* by Henry Miller, and *Lolita* by Vladimir Nabokov.

Sexy Novels: Scandal Magnets

The following novels, published in post-World War II America, created controversy for their sexual themes and descriptions:

I Jan Cremer, Candy, and *City of Night* were three novels of the 1960s denounced as obscene and banned from some libraries. They are widely read as classics of postwar literature today. Courtesy of Tom Hearn.

Lolita by Vladimir Nabokov (1947).

A Spy in the House of Love by Anais Nin (1954).

The Story of O by Pauline Reage (1954).

The Ginger Man by J. P. Donleavy (1955).

Peyton Place by Grace Metalious (1956).

Lucky Jim by Kingsley Amis (1957).

A Walk on the Wild Side by Nelson Algren (1957).

Stranger in a Strange Land by Robert A. Heinlein (1961).

One Hundred Dollar Misunderstanding by Robert Gover (1962).

City of Night by John Rechy (1963).

Candy by Terry Southern and Mason Hoffenberg (1964).

Cotton Comes to Harlem by Chester Himes (1965).

I Jan Cremer by Jan Cremer (1965).

I Am the Beautiful Stranger by Rosalyn Drexler (1966).

An American Dream by Norman Mailer (1967).

The Harrad Experiment by Robert H. Rimmer (1967).

Myra Breckinridge by Gore Vidal (1968).

Portnoy's Complaint by Philip Roth (1969).

Blue Movie by Terry Southern (1970).

Fear of Flying by Erica Jong (1973).

The Backlash against Feminism

By the late 1970s, the pendulum had swung back against feminism, a backlash largely led by men. First out of the gate was author George Gilder, whose shtick was to bill himself as "the nation's number-one male chauvinist." Gilder blamed the women's movement for "emasculating" men and being a "menace" to "the freedoms at the very heart of free enterprise itself."[14] While his *Naked Nomads: Unmarried Men in America* (1974) and *Men and Marriage* (1986) began to sell briskly, Gilder attracted the notice of the Republican Party, which transformed him into, wrote Susan Faludi, "the intellectual darling of the Reagan administration." Gilder seemed to open the floodgate to feminist-bashers.

Other men whose books unleashed fusillades at the women's movement were Allan Bloom, whose 1987 bestseller *The Closing of the American Mind* was ostensibly about the failing education system, but was really a relentless anti-feminist polemic; and Roger Kimball, whose *Tenured Radicals* issued the same veiled attacks on feminism, while ostensibly discussing the state of modern scholarship. He claimed feminist scholars were "intimidating" universities and "their object is nothing less than the destruction of the values, methods, and goals of traditional humanistic study."[15] Needless to add, the opinions of both Gilder and Bloom caused a storm of protest from many educated women.

Even so, some women contributed to the backlash. Surprisingly, Betty Friedan, a pioneering feminist, turned against the women's movement with her

1981 book, *The Second Stage*, alienating many of the women who'd seen her as something of an intellectual deity. Friedan decried the "confrontational" tone feminism had taken and expressed regret over the movement's "blind spot about the family." Likewise, feminist icon Germaine Greer—whose 1970 *The Female Eunuch* was a required liberationist tract—published *Sex and Destiny* (1984), in which she called for "an attack upon the ideology of sexual freedom." The formerly flamboyant champion of unbridled sexuality now touted the virtues of chastity and abstinence. But the most vitriolic of the anti-feminists was literary scholar Camille Paglia, whose *Sexual Personae: Art and Decadence from Nefertiti to Emily Dickinson* (1990) was a touchstone for heated debate. Among Paglia's many scandalous riffs—for many feminists, it was scandal enough that a woman would attack other women—were "If civilization had been left in female hands, we would still be living in grass huts" and "Feminist scholars can't think their way out of a wet paper bag." She also called date rape "feminist nonsense." Faludi, in her equally controversial *Backlash* (1991), insisted that Paglia's motive for her attacks was "simple spite"— that is, "rival literary scholars who were feminists ... had grabbed all the 'acclaim' and failed to be 'respectful' of her prodigious talents."[16]

Captain Bly and Science Fiction

Feminism was also met with a countervailing "men's movement." Previously a marginalized offshoot of New Age spirituality, the "masculinity" quest was given new life when the acclaimed poet Robert Bly published *Iron John* (1990). The book, the central image for which was taken from a Grimm Brothers fairy tale, encouraged men to "take back the power he has given to his mother" and recover "the wild man within." The book spawned all-male drum circles and primitive weekend retreats around the country, while Bly fanned the flames of gender enmity by urging men to be "warriors" and "hit back" (verbally, he later insisted) at those women who dismiss their feelings. The he said/she said debate continues to this day, with subsequent bestsellers like Deborah Tannen's *You Just Don't Understand* (1990), John Gray's *Men Are from Mars, Women Are from Venus* (1992), and *Why Mars and Venus Collide* (2008), further widening the rift between the genders.

Science fiction touched on sexual themes, though more subtly, and, thus, was under the radars of censorious officials. Indeed, the veteran writer Robert A. Heinlein may have done more for "free love" than any "hippie" author, with his 1961 novel *Stranger in a Strange Land*. In it, an Earthling orphaned as a child on Mars (Michael Valentine Smith) is brought back to Earth twenty years later, after being raised within Martian culture. The gentle and naïve Smith is slowly indoctrinated into human ways and means, including sexuality. Smith attracts a following of devotees, to whom he advocates a form of "free love," a concept that would attract a hippie readership and turn the book into a cult novel. The publisher (Putnam) felt that some of Heinlein's more extreme sexual theorizing was too scandalous for 1961, so he was asked to trim 60,000 words from the original manuscript. After Heinlein died in 1988, the full version of the novel was restored, and is the edition in print today. Aldous Huxley was another visionary writer who served as an avatar for the counterculture of the 1960s. Huxley's love note to psychedelic drugs took the form of his two short works, *The Doors of Perception/Heaven and Hell*, which were published together in 1956.

"YA" Titles

Even literature aimed at adolescents—now given "young adult" ("YA") designation in libraries—sparked scandal. Early examples of this now thriving genre—titles like *Anne of Green Gables* (1908), *The Secret Garden* (1909), the Nancy Drew series for girls (starting 1930), the Tom Swift (starting 1910) and Hardy Boys (starting 1927) series—were tame enough not to cause parental distress. However, once the adult literature of the 1960s began questioning authority and tackling "relevant" social issues, YA titles followed suit, straying onto the third rail of sex. The most prolific author of "serious" young adult books was Judy Blume, who did not flinch from issues like menstruation (*Are You There God? It's Me, Margaret*) and divorce (*It's Not the End of the World*). Though each of these titles was the target of protests from parents and school boards, their receptions were tame compared to that which greeted her 1975 YA title, *Forever*. This book, which frankly and maturely dealt with a teenage couple's grappling with sexual urges, was Blume's most popular novel, selling 4 million copies worldwide. Thousands of American teenagers felt that *Forever* spoke to their own confusions and anxieties. The book has been banned from hundreds of U.S. school districts. The American Library Association ranked *Forever* by Judy Blume as Number 8 on their list, "100 Most Frequently Challenged Books." Blume was also number 2 on the "Top Ten Challenged Authors 1990 to 2004" list (number 1 was Alvin Schwartz, author of the Scary Stories series; number 3 was Robert Cormier, author of *The Chocolate War*; and number 4 was J. K. Rowling, author of the Harry Potter series).

Daddy's Little Girls

In the wake of the "repressed memory" debates of the 1990s—wherein women and men who were sexually abused as children had, in therapy, recalled these long suppressed traumas—a book was published that made previous scandals pale by comparison. Not only did Kathryn Harrison claim in her 1997 memoir, *The Kiss*, to have had sexual relations with her father, but she willingly engaged in them for four years as an adult—that is, she reconnected with her father, a Protestant minister who'd been estranged from her family since she was ten years old, when she was twenty. They began a torrid affair. For the next four years, Harrison met her father for trysts "where no one will recognize us." The book provoked a firestorm of angry reviews and editorials. *The Washington Post* called it "slimy, repellent, meretricious, cynical." Harrison, on the other hand, fueled the scandal by her blunt refusal to play "victim." In 1998, Harrison told Marilyn Yalom, a senior scholar at Stanford's Institute for Research on Women and Gender, "I was committed to not glossing it over, and I was committed to not portraying myself as a victim because I think there is this very insidious aspect to our culture right now in which victimhood is almost equated with identity. People begin to think of themselves as children of alcoholics or whatever. Within that understanding of the self is a sort of slipping away from taking responsibility in a situation."[17] Phoebe Gloeckner handled a similar theme of incest differently. Her medium was the "graphic novel," part-memoir, part-cartoon strip, part-diary entries for a fictional girl (Minnie Goetze) who is her stand in. The resulting books, *A Child's Life* (2000) and *The Diary of a Teenage Girl* (2002), created a sensation, not just for the taboo subject of incest, but for Gloeckner's extraordinary artistic talent—she is a professional medical illustrator—showcased in her graphic depictions of the sordid things done to her as a girl by her stepfather. Gloeckner opened the possibilities of the graphic novel genre; Debbie Drechsler pushed the boundaries of her own repressed incest memories in *Daddy's Girl* (1996) and *The Summer of Love* (2003).

Playboy and Her Imitators

When Hugh Hefner started publishing *Playboy* in December 1953, the magazine had a circulation of 53,991. Though the formula Hefner applied—large dollops of cheesecake (but no nudity, at the start) and well-written articles and stories—was a winning one, he still had to contend with a publishing climate that had banned literature like *Lady Chatterley's Lover* and *Tropic of Cancer*. How did he walk that fine line between generating enough titillation to attract readers, but not too much to attract censors? *Playboy's* debut centerfold was the beloved Marilyn Monroe; though she was scantily clad, she was not completely nude. The photograph of her was no more risqué than the pinup girls found in magazines distributed to soldiers by the U.S. military. Thus, the magazine snuck under the radar of the censors. By 1954, *Playboy's* circulation was 175,000; by 1955, it was 350,000. By 1965, it regularly hit 3 million in sales, and then peaked at 7.1 million in November 1972. *Playboy* was, in short, a raving success, popular with a mainstream male audience ages eighteen to thirty-five. Soon enough, Playboy "Key" Clubs sprang up around the country, where members could see the sort of pulchritude depicted on the magazine's pages in the flesh.

This is not to say that *Playboy* did not cause scandal. Citizens groups occasionally brought lawsuits against stores for selling *Playboy*, on charges of "obscenity." One of the most powerful of the groups, Citizens for Decent Literature

(CDL), was led by Clarence Keating, who wrote in May 1960 that book dealers and newsstand owners who sold "dirty books" like *Tropic of Cancer* or magazines like *Playboy* were part of a "vociferous minority whose position is not only opposed to the basic Judeo-Christian morality of the nation, but actually seems to violently advocate its overthrow."[18] From 1986 to 2003, the 7-Eleven chain stopped selling *Playboy* and other "skin" magazines because of the content. Even in places where the magazine is sold, copies are shrink-wrapped and placed high on the shelves, so as not to fall into the hands of minors. Foreign editions of *Playboy* have also been banned in much of Asia and in Muslim countries.

Miss America Caught in the Act

Oddly, *Playboy* has generated more scandal for its left-leaning politics and Hefner's impassioned defense of First Amendment rights than for its nudity. This is largely due to the arrival of *Penthouse* magazine in 1969. Until then, *Playboy* had, unlike *Penthouse*, refused to depict graphic hardcore nudity and was thus considered a bit more "tame" than its competition. Indeed, Bob Guccione at *Penthouse* and Larry Flynt at *Hustler* (started in 1974) pushed the envelope on what could be shown in the way of nudity and sexual proclivities. For example, *Penthouse*'s most popular issue (September 1984) featured nude shots of Vanessa Lynn Williams engaged in simulated lesbian sex acts with another nude model; the scandal erupted because Williams had just been selected Miss America. In the same issue, the featured centerfold was future porn film star Traci Lords, who was later found to have been only fifteen years old when she posed for *Penthouse,* thus making copies of this issue illegal under child pornography laws.

No magazine publisher could hold a candle to Larry Flynt in matters of scandal. The former strip club owner began *Hustler* with the express purpose of outdoing other magazines for outrageous and sexually graphic content. He succeeded. From the outset, *Hustler* was known for its "raunch" factor, showing explicit full nudity and covering sexual issues previously considered off limits. While this initially generated a large audience (peaking at 3 million), Flynt's formula ran dry and circulation figures plummeted. Today, Flynt is best known for the scandals created by his magazine's libertarianism, conspiracy theories, and attacks on religious fundamentalists like Pat Robertson and Jerry Falwell. It was his satire on Falwell—a parody ad that depicted a drunken Falwell encountering his mother in an outhouse—that led to one of the landmark free speech decisions in American history. Eventually, the U.S. Supreme Court heard Falwell's libel case (*Hustler Magazine v. Falwell*) and ruled in Flynt's favor. For many years, Flynt mailed free, unsolicited copies of *Hustler* to every member of the U.S. Congress. His reason: "I felt that they should be informed with what's going on in the rest of the world." Flynt's saga was portrayed in the film *The People vs. Larry Flynt* (1996), which starred an equally scandal-ridden actress and singer, Courtney Love.

Part II

MEDIA AS INDUSTRY

Chapter 4

BOOK PUBLISHING

Before the advent of radio, television, and the Internet, the written word was the lone carrier, and therefore cause, of media scandals in America. Books, magazines, and newspapers were constantly in conflict with the recurrent themes covered in the first part of this book. (*See also* Chapter 5, "Newspapers and Magazines.")

THE PROTOCOLS OF THE ELDERS OF ZION

One of the most destructive publishing hoaxes in history was first perpetrated in the 1890s by the Russian secret police, and spread to the United States in the 1920s. The resulting publication—which had several titles, the most commonly used being *The Protocols of the Elders of Zion*—was an anti-Semitic forgery later used by everyone from Hitler to Osama bin Laden to justify hatred of Jews. (*See also* Chapter 5, "Newspapers and Magazines.") *The Protocols* purports to be a manual for new members of the "Elders," a cabal of Jewish leaders with their eyes on the prize of world control. They will—or so the forgery insisted—gain this control by taking over all media and financial markets and undermining established social order. Among the twenty-four strategies (or "protocols") for accomplishing this nefarious goal are alcoholism, Darwinism, Marxism, media manipulation, materialism, world wars, world government, and destruction of Christianity through atheism, followed ultimately by the establishment of a Jewish king. Not only did Hitler cite the fictional *Protocols* as historical fact in *Mein Kampf*, he also required German schoolchildren to read it. Historian Nora Levin noted, "Hitler used the *Protocols* as a manual in his war to exterminate the Jews."[1]

This hoax was first debunked as fiction in 1921 by both the *Times* (of London) and the *New York Times*, and has since been conclusively proven a plagiarism of a number of satirical works—most notably a French pamphlet by Maurice Joly, called *Dialogue in Hell between Machiavelli and Montesquieu*. Joly's work, published in 1864, did not mention Jews or Judaism; it was, in fact, a satire about Napoleon III's plans for world domination. Nonetheless,

The Protocols has refused to die and continues to be published today, and interpreted as fact, especially in the Islamic world.

The Protocols of the Elders of Zion came to the United States in 1920. First published by Small, Maynard and Co. in Boston, a separate printing of 500,000 copies of this edition was underwritten by car maker Henry Ford, who was convinced of *The Protocols'* authenticity. Between 1920 and 1927, according to Tom Burnam, Ford "mounted a series of anti-Semitic attacks unparalleled in American history" in the pages of his weekly newspaper *The Dearborn Independent* (Michigan), touching off a newspaper scandal separate from the one generated by the book itself. (*See also* Chapter 5, "Newspapers and Magazines.") The newspaper series, written by William J. Cameron, was titled "The International Jew: The World's Foremost Problem" and was based in part on *The Protocols*. Ford biographer Keith Sward noted that Cameron "improved on the forgery so skillfully that, in modern dress, it became one of the foremost existing brochures on anti-Semitism."[2] Vincent Curcio wrote that Ford's publications "were widely distributed and had great influence, particularly in Nazi Germany, where no less a personage than Adolf Hitler read and admired them." In homage, Hitler hung Ford's photograph on his wall and cited Ford as an inspiration in *Mein Kampf.* Ford's edition of *The Protocols* was expanded in 1934 with "text and commentary," much of it thought to be Cameron's, resulting in a 300-page volume that still circulates in reprints today, as well as on the Internet.

Hoaxes for Laughs

American book publishing has long been susceptible to hoaxes. Some were created with the willful intent to deceive for profit or propagandistic purposes; others were more like elaborate practical jokes. Among the latter camp were the following examples.

I, Libertine by Jean Shepherd

This book began as a radio hoax by the humorist Jean Shepherd. On his broadcasts in the early 1950s, he often cited a long-suppressed "erotic classic" called *I, Libertine*, which did not exist. As a published writer, Shepherd was frustrated at how bestseller lists were compiled, not just from sales of books, but from requests at bookshops. Thus, he repeatedly told his listeners about *I, Libertine*, so they would request it at bookshops and the nonexistent book would enter the bestseller list without ever selling a copy. Because the response to this hoax was so overwhelming, Shepherd felt duty-bound to write the "classic." Under the assumed name of Frederick R. Ewing, Shepherd created an outline of the novel's plot, and then the publisher Ian Ballantine hired science fiction writer Theodore Sturgeon to write the book from Shepherd's outline. The result was *I, Libertine*, published by Ballantine Books in 1956 in both hardcover and paperback simultaneously. It came with authentic-sounding blurbs ("here's a saucy bawd!") and back cover copy that said of the author, "Mr. Ewing, an Oxford graduate, was known prior to World War II for his many scholarly contributions to British publication and for his well-remembered series of broadcasts for the BBC on 'Erotica of the 18th Century.' During the war Mr. Ewing served with the Royal Navy and was retired in 1948 with the rank of Commander. He saw much action with the North Atlantic Fleet, serving aboard several minesweepers. He resumed his career as a civil servant, and while stationed in Rhodesia, Ewing completed work on *I, Libertine*."[3] The hoax was exposed by the press weeks after the book's publication. By then, it had entered the bestseller list.

Naked Came the Stranger by Penelope Ashe

To satirize the trend toward sexually-explicit pop fiction and test the gullibility of American book buyers, a group of writers at *Newsday*, Long Island's largest daily newspaper, banded together in 1969 to produce their own soft-core pornographic potboiler. Led by columnist Mike McGrady, twenty-five *Newsday* staffers each wrote one chapter. The only requirement was that each chapter must contain at least two sexual encounters. Parodying the breathless titles of contemporary fiction, their fictional concoction was *Naked Came the Stranger*. Its author was "Penelope Ashe." When it was published in 1969, the publisher, Lyle Stuart Books, was inundated with requests for author interviews. McGrady convinced his sister-in-law to pose as Ashe. Sporting sexy clothes and spouting clichés about free love, she fooled reporters, and the book crept up the bestseller list. Finally, the collaborators confessed to the hoax. A mock "scandal" ensued when parodies of the original parody were created, such as *Naked Came the Manatee* and *Naked Came the Sasquatch*, the latter playing on the popularity of books purporting to have spotted Bigfoot or the Loch Ness Monster.

Amazons by Cleo Birdwell

This book, published in 1980, was, according to the subtitle, "an intimate memoir by the first woman ever to play in the National Hockey League." It was anything but that, of course. This should have been obvious from the start. The premise was absurd on its face: a woman playing arguably the most brutal professional sport in the world, and, judging from the photograph on the dust jacket, "Cleo" was a beautiful blonde bombshell with full red lips and a "come hither" smile, even swaddled in her bulky New York Rangers uniform. Yet, despite it being a completely fabricated "pro sports" memoir, enough people believed in Cleo's authenticity to make this the biggest selling book by its real author, Don DeLillo. Prior to *Amazons*—and in every book since—DeLillo tackled serious themes and, though critically acclaimed, has always been an acquired taste. *Amazons* was a collaboration with Sue Buck, though neither name appeared anywhere on it. After the book was published to good reviews and brisk sales, DeLillo refused to allow it to be reprinted and has disavowed any connection to it.

Steal This Book by Abbie Hoffman

Hoffman compiled this "Handbook of Survival and Warfare for the Citizens of Woodstock Nation" after two controversial bestsellers with traditional publishers: *Revolution for the Hell of It* (under the pen name "Free") and *Woodstock Nation*. In a press release sent out with *Steal This Book*, Hoffman said he had "decided to write a book no one would dare publish." He was right. After completing the book in 1970, thirty publishers rejected the manuscript. One rejection included the comment, "This book will end free speech!" (a quote Hoffman later used as a blurb on the published edition). In 1971, Hoffman paid for the printing himself and released a "Pirate Edition," distributed by Grove Press. Much of *Steal This Book* was culled from other sources by Hoffman and "coconspirator" Izack Haber. Some writers, in fact, accused Hoffman of stealing their work. Hoffman gave the underground press permission to reprint any portion of the book for free. Any royalties realized from the book, he said, went to WPAX, a worldwide antiwar radio network. Many bookshops refused to carry *Steal This Book*, for fear of shoplifting, and for its incendiary contents. Hoffman called his "a manual of survival in the prison that is Amerika." *Steal This Book* contained chapters on useful skills like furniture- and clothes-making, low-cost housing, growing food, hitch-hiking, starting communes, obtaining free medical care, and finding political asylum, as well as "how to identify police agents, steal a car, run day-care centers, conduct your own trial, organize a G.I. coffee house, start a rock and roll band and make neat clothes." These were scandalous enough, but Hoffman upped the ante by offering advice on shoplifting, street-fighting, bomb-making (stink bombs, smoke bombs, pipe bombs, Molotov cocktails), and obtaining guns. Hoffman's ultimate ambition, he said, was to "destroy" the "system," and rid "Amerika" of "sterile machines of corporate death and the robots that guard them." It's not clear how many people actually took Hoffman up on his title's offer, because 200,000 copies of the book were sold, and it was a paperback bestseller. A twenty-fifth anniversary edition of the book was published in 1996; it's still in print. Royalties now go to the Abbie Hoffman Activist Foundation (Hoffman died in 1989).

Overdosing on Fraud

Before James Frey, the fakery of the "drug experience" during the 1960s was a recurrent ploy; journalists posed as drugged-out hippies to get insider looks at the scene. But no book had quite the impact as *Go Ask Alice* (1971), whose author was listed as Anonymous. The book purported to be the diary of a teenage drug addict who died of an overdose, but the sophisticated language and dry, clinical descriptions of the physiological effects of drug use led some critics to believe it was written by an adult. Beatrice Sparks, a Mormon youth counselor, was listed as editor of *Go Ask Alice*, which was a runaway bestseller and is still in print. Sparks eventually admitted that she embellished the diary of one of her clients, who did not actually die of an overdose, as Alice did in the book. Further suspicion about Sparks emerged over the years as she became arguably the most prolific Anonymous author in publishing. She followed *Go Ask Alice* with *Jay's Journal*, about a young man driven to suicide by his involvement with a cult. Four more Anonymous diaries followed, with Sparks listed as editor or preparer. The dubious provenance of *Go Ask Alice* notwithstanding, the book has been banned from many school libraries because of its controversial subject matters (drugs, premarital sex, and suicide). Similarly, in the 1993 "memoir" by Anthony Godby Johnson, *Rock and a Hard Place*, a fourteen-year-old HIV-positive boy claimed to have been ritually abused by adults. The "author," however, refused to be interviewed except over the phone and never appeared in public. Johnson's voice was suspiciously similar to his adult caretaker, Vicki Fraginals. Armistad Maupin was taken in by the ruse and later wrote a novel based on his experience and gullibility, *The Night Listener* (2000).

Overdosing on Freud

Janet Malcolm has been at the center of two book publishing scandals. The first resulted from her book *Inside the Freud Archives* (1991), the subject of which was Jeffrey Moussaieff Masson, former director of the Sigmund Freud archives. Malcolm depicted Masson as having used his position to coax more than 1,000 women into having sex with him, then boasting about it to her. Masson also, she said, called himself "after Freud, the greatest analyst that ever lived." Masson filed a $10 million libel lawsuit against Malcolm and *The New Yorker*, which published an excerpt prior to the book's publication. Masson claimed that Malcolm's quotes were fabrications and that they'd inflicted emotional and financial harm. The case, *Masson v. New Yorker*, went before the U.S. Supreme Court, who sent it back for a retrial; in 1994, a jury acquitted Malcolm. Malcolm's second publishing scandal resulted from her book *The Journalist and the Murderer* (also expanded from a 1990 *New Yorker* article). She criticized Joe McGinnis for his book *Fatal Vision* (1983), about U.S Army Captain Jeffrey MacDonald, a Green Beret surgeon eventually convicted of murdering his pregnant wife and two daughters at Fort Bragg in California. McGinnis and MacDonald reached an agreement before the latter's murder trial to work together on a book that would prove his innocence. In exchange, MacDonald allowed McGinnis access to his legal team and private life, and the two agreed to share the book royalties. MacDonald was convicted in 1984 of the murders, and then again on appeal in 1985. McGinnis's book, *Fatal Vision*, violated the agreement between himself and MacDonald. Malcolm accused McGinnis of "morally indefensible" behavior for conning MacDonald into believing that he thought he was innocent, stringing him along to get material for his book. MacDonald sued McGinnis for breach of contract and "distortion"; McGinnis settled out of court for $325,000.

A Million Little Lies, and Some Plagiarisms

Among the less amusing hoaxes were those that played on the sympathies of readers. One of the biggest scandals of this sort to rock contemporary publishing resulted from *A Million Little Pieces* by James Frey. Marketed as a memoir about the troubles of a young addict and criminal, the book was a bestseller in hardcover in 2003. It was not until 2005, when the book was released in paperback, that Frey sparked a scandal. The paperback memoir was championed by Oprah Winfrey. The respected television talk show host was so moved by the book that she made what she called a "radical departure" and picked it for her book club; previously, the club had been devoted entirely to works of fiction. In a way, then, her selection wasn't a radical departure, because Frey's book turned out to be nearly a complete fraud. After a six-week probe, the Web site The Smoking Gun revealed that Frey had exaggerated his criminal past, turning a night in jail into several stints behind bars, and

Abbie Hoffman, Cleo Birdwell, and James Frey each hatched a literary hoax. The title of *Steal This Book* was seldom acted on, *Amazons* was tongue-in-cheek satire, and *A Million Little Pieces* was fiction masquerading as the truth. Courtesy of Tom Hearn.

claimed to have suffered gruesome tortures and humiliations and even to being "wanted in three states." None of this was true. He had, indeed, been an alcoholic and drug addict, but much of the rest of the material was fabricated. Rather than address the charges, Frey hired a lawyer who threatened a lawsuit against the Web site. When the latter did not retract its claims of Frey's fakery, the author confessed to the hoax. Frey wasn't entirely to blame for the scandal. He had tried to get the book published as a novel, but it had been rejected by seventeen publishers before interesting Nan Talese/Doubleday. However, Talese "declined to publish it as such," and suggested Frey excise the fiction and publish it as a memoir. The temptation of money was too great. Due to Winfrey's endorsement, Frey's paperback edition sold 1.77 million copies in 2005, second only to a Harry Potter novel. When the scandal broke, Oprah was aghast. Hers was one of the most respected names in American media; to be affiliated with the tainted memoir was an attack on her credibility. She invited Frey on her show in January 2006 and expressed shock at how easily she had been duped. Unlike other tainted works, Frey's book has remained in print and, in fact, was still selling briskly years later.

Published and Perished

In 2005, a Harvard student named Kaavya Viswanathan signed a two-book contract with renowned Boston publisher Little, Brown for $500,000. She also sold the movie rights to her first novel, *How Opal Mehta Got Kissed, Got Wild and Got a Life*. However, as soon as the novel was published, the *Harvard Crimson* revealed that the book bore "striking similarities" to two novels by Megan McCafferty, *Sloppy Firsts* and *Second Helpings*. Alerted to this suspicion, McCafferty's publisher, Random House, found forty separate instances of verbatim plagiarism in Viswanathan's novel. Other publishers began to report that Viswanathan had plagiarized their authors, as well. Little, Brown initially denied the allegations, calling any similarities "unconscious" on the author's part.[4] But when charges of plagiarism went beyond McCafferty, they recalled all copies and ended relations with Viswanathan. In another case of plagiarism so blatant that it was likened by Thomas Mallon to "literary suicide," Jacob Epstein lifted fifty-three passages from Martin Amis's *The Rachel Papers* (1973) for his novel *Wild Oats* (1979). Epstein claimed that he'd done so "out of admiration" for Amis's writing and asked Little, Brown to delete the offending passages for the 1980 U.S. edition. Amis, after reading the latter, told the *New York Times*, "How do you rewrite a novel and leave word-for-word passages?"[5] The book is long out of print, as is Epstein's writing career. In 2008, Cassie Edwards, author of more than one hundred romance novels, published under her own byline uncredited chunks of text from historical works and articles. Edwards's publisher, Signet, defended her at first by insisting that "copyright fair-use doctrine permits reasonable borrowing and paraphrasing of another author's words."[6] However, Edwards's constituted an unreasonable amount of "borrowing," bordering on plagiarism. Margaret B. Jones "borrowed" in a different way for her memoir, *Love and Consequences* (Riverhead, 2008). In the book, Jones purported to be a half-white, half-Native American who grew up a foster child in South-Central Los Angeles among the youth gangs. She told of running drugs for gang members, buying a gun and burial plot, how her foster brother was shot in front of her, and how "Big Mom," her black foster mother, carried on amidst the violence. Jones, however, turned out to be Margaret Seltzer, a white girl who grew up in an intact family in upscale San Fernando Valley. None of the events happened to her, though she claimed to have met many gang members and then borrowed their stories as her own. When the hoax was revealed, the publisher recalled all the copies of the book and canceled Seltzer's book tour.[7]

Even Historians Get the Cribs

Stephen Ambrose and Doris Kearns Goodwin were among the nation's most popular historians when they were both, almost simultaneously, charged with plagiarism in 2002. The charges against Ambrose, author of several books about World War II, including the bestsellers *Citizen Soldiers* and *Band of Brothers*, were the more serious and wide-ranging. Known for his breezy style and astonishing productivity—eight books in five years—Ambrose had established himself as the one historian Americans associated with the "greatest generation." However, his prolific output was his Achilles' heel, drawing suspicion from other writers. In January 2002, Fred Barnes reported in the *Weekly Standard* that he'd found numerous passages in Ambrose's *The Wild Blue*, a book about World War II bombers, that had been lifted verbatim from Thomas Childers's book, *The Wings of Morning*. A *Forbes* reporter, Mark Lewis, then investigated other books by Ambrose and found a pattern of lifted words, poor citations, inaccurate attributions, and sloppy documentation, even in what is generally regarded as his best work, *Citizen Soldiers*.[8] Asked about the charges, Ambrose defiantly told a *New York Times* reporter, "I am not out there stealing other people's writings. If I am writing up a passage and it is a story I want to tell and this story fits and a part of it is from other people's writing, I just type it up that way and put it in a footnote." David Plotz at *Slate* wrote, "Ambrose's assertion that he's not a thief is ludicrous. One plagiarism is careless. Two is a pattern. Four, five, or more is pathology." Ambrose died not long after these revelations and many of his books remain, uncorrected, in print.

Goodwin's case, though not as serious, was more shocking. She was not only a respected, Pulitzer Prize-winning historian and biographer—who sat on the board of directors at Harvard—but a regular commentator on the PBS *NewsHour*. The pattern of plagiarism, reported again by the *Weekly Standard*, dated back to her 1987 bestseller, *The Fitzgeralds and the Kennedys*; the *Standard* found that "dozens" of her passages were similar to those in other books, including one by Lynne McTaggert, who settled out of court with Goodwin after threatening to sue the historian for "copyright infringement." Goodwin told a PBS reporter that she was not guilty of plagiarism and the verbatim passages in her work were "simply a mistake in technique." As a result of the scandal, Goodwin resigned from *PBS NewsHour*. Later editions of *The Fitzgeralds and the Kennedys* contain corrected passages.

Even Woodward Can Go Wayward

The acclaimed investigative reporter and editor for the *Washington Post*, Bob Woodward—best known for his and Carl Bernstein's dogged Watergate coverage—has been at the heart of many scandals. Even the vaunted Watergate reportage was marred by its reliance on a government official code-named "Deep Throat." This unnamed source provided information that almost too neatly tied up the case against President Nixon. Because Woodward said he would never reveal the identity of Deep Throat, many critics doubted the existence of such a person. Finally, in 2005, former FBI official Mark Felt admitted to being Deep Throat. However, the revelation seemed self-serving; Felt had published a memoir he wanted to promote. In *Wired: The Short Life and Fast Times of John Belushi* (1984), Woodward was accused by the comedian's widow, Judy Belushi, of distorting the truth by exaggerating the drug use in order to sensationalize his story. She and many of Belushi's friends and colleagues accused Woodward of ignoring the comedian's accomplishments and talent. In *Veil: The Secret Wars of the CIA* (1987), Woodward claimed to have talked with former CIA Director William Casey on his deathbed. This chat can't be corroborated and, to some, is highly suspect given the security detail guarding Casey and the fact that no one else saw Woodward in the hospital room. Conveniently, Casey died soon thereafter.

In *Shadow: Five Presidents and the Legacy of Watergate* (1999), Woodward built his narrative around the enduring scandal of Watergate. Using this lens, he studied the five presidents who had occupied the White House since 1974, when Nixon resigned. The book, though a bestseller, was widely decried by many of the people Woodward either quoted or about whom he wrote. President Clinton's lawyer, Robert Bennett, was extensively quoted in the book, but he claimed not to have had the recounted conversations with the author. Another White House lawyer, Jane Sherburne, claimed Woodward simply made up conversations between her and First Lady Hillary Clinton. Even Steven Brill, who claimed to be a friend of Woodward's, questioned the author's liberal use of phrases like "knowledgeable sources" and "high ranking official" while never actually naming who made various claims and statements in the book. Brill noted, "This book is not the Woodward of Woodward and

Bernstein … This is more the novelization, or even the Hollywoodization, of Woodstein—the triumph of a Hollywood story line over ambiguity."[9] With *Bush at War* (2002) and *Plan of Attack* (2004), Woodward was accused of being "court stenographer" and "war propagandist" for George W. Bush. Those who admired Woodward for his tenacious pursuit of Richard Nixon could not understand how he would so willingly "spin" the Iraq war for a president many believe to be far more deceptive. Woodward's reputation took another blow in 2005 when it was reported that in mid-June 2003 Woodward learned that Joseph C. Wilson IV's wife was CIA employee Valerie Plame, a fact that he didn't share with his bosses at the *Washington Post*. He was put in the hot seat by special prosecutor Patrick Fitzgerald, who later convicted Lewis Libby of a felony in this case.

The O. J. Simpson Industry

The murder of Nicole Brown Simpson and Ronald Goldman in June 1994, the resulting 1995 trial of O. J. Simpson for their murders, and Simpson's subsequent legal troubles have launched more scandals than any event in modern American history. Tabloid newspapers and "tabloid television" were sucked into the vortex of this racially tinged tale of celebrity mayhem and police bungling, and the publishing industry stayed solvent just with spin-off books by the defendant, his legal team, the prosecution team, police detectives, expert witnesses, courtroom visitors, friends and family of the victims, and ex-girlfriends of the accused murderer. One scandal erupted over the defendant himself: Did Simpson have the right to profit from this tragedy? This became a legal issue when Ronald Goldman's parents successfully sued Simpson in civil court after he was acquitted of the murders in criminal court, a jury decision that divided the nation along racial lines. In 1997, Simpson was found guilty in the "wrongful death" of Goldman and was ruled to be financially liable for damages of $33.5 million. Though Simpson's football pension could not be docked, any royalties from the sale of books he might publish would be fair game. This entailed a not insubstantial amount of money from Simpson's *I Want to Tell You* (1995), a book cobbled together from letters he'd received during the course of the trial.

However, the biggest scandal took place more than a decade later and involved a book by O. J. Simpson that was not published. It was entitled *If I Did It*, and the cash-strapped Simpson had brokered a deal with Judith Regan to publish it under her HarperCollins/Regan Books imprint in 2006. Regan was a figure of scandal herself, due to the books she'd published (porn star memoirs, celebrity tell-alls, books by Rush Limbaugh and Howard Stern), and for her public persona (she would, in fact, be fired from HarperCollins a month after the *If I Did It* scandal broke, for alleged anti-Semitic remarks). In what would be her swan song at HarperCollins, Regan signed two books guaranteed to raise hackles. The first was a "fictional biography" based on the life of revered New York Yankees' superstar Mickey Mantle, *7: The Mickey Mantle Novel* by Peter Golenbock. The Mantle family threatened a suit over the license the author takes (e.g., an affair with Marilyn Monroe that can't be corroborated). The second was *If I Did It*, by O. J. Simpson.

According to a Fox News statement, *If I Did It* would tell how Simpson would have committed the crimes if he were indeed guilty. To jumpstart the media buzz for this publishing gaffe, Regan had taped a lengthy interview with Simpson that was scheduled to air in two segments in late November 2006 on Fox News. The scandal generated by this announcement was swift and unprecedented. Not only was Regan vilified by the Goldman family, but HarperCollins and Fox News, by association, were criticized. Fred Goldman, Ronald's father, told the press that television had hit "an all-time low."

Rupert Murdoch, owner of HarperCollins and Fox News, canceled the television interview and the book's publication, and released a statement apologizing for any pain it may have caused the victims' families. All 400,000 copies of the book that had been released were recalled and allegedly pulped, though some were available at online auction sites like eBay. By June 2007, the entire contents of the book were available for free at various Internet Web sites, as were leaked copies of Regan's interview with Simpson. Due perhaps to the new availability of the material, the Goldman family bought the rights to the book and published an expanded version of *If I Did It*, with "commentary," under the title *Confessions of the Killer*. The book was published in September 2007 by Beaufort Books; 90 percent of the royalties go to the Goldman family. The entire saga was revisited by the American media, whose collective hunger for scandal, or at least this scandal, seemed insatiable.

Books by Crooks—Prison Publishing

Any prisoner who achieves fame or money for work done while incarcerated—or, like O. J. Simpson, facing a murder trial—is bound to cause a scandal. The questions raised by prison authors are philosophical—Should society allow "criminals" to profit while being punished?—and legal—Do prisoners "own" the work they create in prison or do the taxpayers who provide room and board own it? Looked at in a slightly different way, however, prison authors have been with us since the nation's birth. Many Americans now regarded as icons spent time inside prison cells, including Francis Scott Key, whose "The Star-Spangled Banner" was written while an unwilling guest of the British in 1814. Other Americans whose work behind bars proved important are Thomas Paine, Henry David Thoreau (his essay "Civil Disobedience" was inspired by a night in jail), Martin Luther King Jr. (whose "Letter from a Birmingham Jail" inspired the Civil Rights Movement), Eugene V. Debs, Malcolm X, and even musicians like Merle Haggard, Joe Hill, Roky Erickson, and

David Allan Coe. Likewise, many figures of political scandal have used prison time to fashion work designed to rehabilitate images, or to justify or explain criminal behavior: G. Gordon Liddy, Charles Colson, John Ehrlichman, Timothy Leary, Abbie Hoffman, Michael Milkin, and Leona Helmsley.

The controversial practice of rehabilitating prisoners through writing was credited to Herman Spector, librarian at San Quentin State Prison, California, from 1947 to 1968. During that time, Spector established a new treatment: bibliotherapy. He held "Great Books" classes and conducted group discussions about the great authors. He expanded the prison library, calling it "a hospital for the mind," and allowed prisoners to visit the library once a week. Spector also directed a series of creative writing classes that, according to Joseph Hallinan, turned San Quentin into "a writer's colony, a criminal version of Yaddo." In 1947, for example, his classes produced 395 manuscript submissions for publication. By 1961, the number was 1,989. According to Eldridge Cleaver, then a San Quentin inmate, Spector was aided by Chris Lovdjieff, a tireless teacher of history and philosophy who was so beloved and respected by the inmates that Cleaver dubbed him "The Christ."[10]

Due in part to Spector's and Lovdjieff's efforts, San Quentin had a legacy of prison authors. In 1953, Spector published a booklet called "San Quentiniana," an annotated list of "books published by officials and inmates of San Quentin." The roster of inmate authors was impressive, including Jack Black, whose *You Can't Win* (1926) is still in print; Ernest G. Booth, best known for his novel *With Sirens Screaming* (1945); Richard J. Krebs, who wrote under the pen name Jan Valtin, and whose *Out of the Night* (1951) was a memoir of the author's experience as a member of the resistance movement against the Nazis during World War II; David Lamson, whose *We Who Are about to Die* (1935) details his year on Death Row at San Quentin, before his murder conviction of his wife was overturned; and Robert J. Tasker, whose account of prison life in *Grimhaven* (1928) has few rivals for authenticity. Each of these published books created a new scandal. To the state's legislators and taxpayers, Spector had created a prison population of self-made lawyers and wannabe Hemingways. However, among enlightened penologists, bibliotherapy was admired and emulated in prisons around the country. Even after Spector compiled his list, San Quentin continued to spawn writers, including Caryl Chessman, Bill Sands, Eldridge Cleaver, George Jackson, and Malcolm Braly.

Chessman was arguably the most notorious prison writer in American history. During his twelve years as a condemned man (1948–60)—at the time, the longest such stay on Death Row in American history—he wrote and published three bestselling memoirs (*Cell 2455 Death Row*, 1954; *Trial by Ordeal*, 1955; and *The Face of Justice*, 1957) and one novel *The Kid Was a Killer*, 1960), as well as a slew of articles for national magazines. He used the money he made to fund his legal case and pay investigators to prove his innocence of the "red light bandit" crimes for which he received two death sentences. Each publication unleashed a wave of scandal. By the time Chessman was executed (for crimes in which no one was killed), his books had been translated into a dozen languages, one was made into a Hollywood movie, and his face adorned the cover of *Time* magazine in 1960. He was Topic A on radio and TV chat shows, and fodder for gossip columns. His case was championed by Pope John, Albert Schweitzer, Bishop James A. Pike, Steve Allen, Shirley MacLaine, Marlon Brando, Aldous Huxley, and Eleanor Roosevelt.

Live from the Beast's Belly

Jack Henry Abbott, who spent nearly his entire adult life in prison, was another literary cause célèbre. His case came to the world's attention through Norman Mailer, whose controversial "true life novel," *The Executioner's Song* (1979), recreated the life and firing-squad death of murderer Gary Gilmore. Abbott, then in prison, contacted Mailer in 1977 after reading about the Gilmore novel, then a work in progress. Mailer arranged for some of Abbott's prison letters to be printed in the June 26, 1980, issue of the *New York Review of Books*. On the strength of the letters, Random House offered Abbott a contract. The resultant book, *In the Belly of the Beast* (1981), contained an introduction by Mailer. The scandal wasn't just the publication of Abbott's book, which became a bestseller (there were precedents of prisoners publishing books). The scandal was that, largely on the strength of his book, Abbott was paroled on June 5, 1981, and placed under the guardianship of Mailer, whose offer to hire him as a researcher was enough to convince prison officials that Abbott would be gainfully employed. On July 19, 1981, Abbott stabbed to death a waiter outside a New York City restaurant. To the public at large, Mailer and all the other celebrities who petitioned for Abbott's parole were held as accountable for the murder as Abbott was. Abbott was sent back to prison, where he died of an apparent suicide in 2002.

Among prison writers still alive (as of 2008), the case of Mumia Abu-Jamal has generated the most scandal. Mumia, born Wesley Cook in 1954, a former Black Panther Party member and taxi cab driver, was convicted of murdering a Philadelphia police officer in 1981. Since his incarceration, Mumia has published a bestselling book, *Live from Death Row*, hosted radio broadcasts, and even made commencement addresses. His writings have inspired an international outcry of support, even while critics have steadfastly maintained that he is guilty and his execution should be carried out by the state of Pennsylvania.

Drinks, Drugs, and Writers

Before the present-day inundation of self-help books and twelve-step programs to combat cravings for drink, drugs, food, gambling, sex, the Internet, pornography, and nearly every other conceivable vice, the subject of addiction was taboo. For radio and television broadcasters, the fear of losing one's license from the Federal Communications Commission for airing controversial subject matter was enough, until the 1960s, to play it safe by avoiding addiction and sexual matters altogether. After the obscenity battles over *Tropic of Cancer* and *Howl* were resolved in 1964, book publishers were more open to testing the waters. Of all the terrible vices to which addicts are drawn, only alcohol was ever mentioned. However, if alcoholism was portrayed at all, it was often a source of humor, like Crazy Guggenheim, the "lovable drunk" on *The Jackie Gleason Show* (1952–70) or the sweet-tempered Otis Campbell on *The Andy Griffith Show* (1960–68), who used the Mayberry jail as his own personal detox unit. The hesitance to address this all-too-common disease was especially surprising given how many American writers suffered from it. Tom Dardis noted, "Of the seven native-born Americans awarded the Nobel Prize in literature, five were alcoholic [Sinclair Lewis, Eugene O'Neill, William Faulkner, Ernest Hemingway, and John Steinbeck].... The list of other twentieth-century American writers similarly afflicted is very long; only a few of the creative talents have been spared."[11]

So many American writers battled the bottle, but so few wrote about their struggles. The first to unflinchingly tackle the subject was Jack London, in his 1913 autobiographical chronicle *John Barleycorn* (1913), but the book hardly made a splash. This may have been due to the author's socialist tendencies, on scandalous display in his other books (*People of the Abyss* and *The Iron Heel*). The book that broached the taboo most sensationally, freeing it as a subject for future authors, was *The Lost Weekend* (1944) by Charles Jackson. This novel, based on Jackson's firsthand experience, was a note-perfect chronicle of a five-day drinking binge, filled to the brim with memorable bits of drinkers' wisdom, like "One's too many and a hundred's not enough." The book created such a media storm that it spawned an equally sensational film that earned Oscars for director Billy Wilder and actor Ray Milland. Though Jackson became a champion for the fledgling Alcoholics Anonymous, founded in 1935 by the alcoholic Bill W., he still could not defeat his addictions, and he committed suicide in New York City in 1968.

Many other writers followed Jackson's lead, pursuing not just alcoholic themes, but also drug addiction and recreational drug use. The following are among the most notable American "Books by Alcoholics."

"Books by Alcoholics"

Alcoholics Anonymous by Bill W. (William Wilson, 1939). This book, a.k.a. "The Big Book," was the forerunner of the now ubiquitous twelve-step programs and self-help movements. For its impact on the lives of millions of people, this book was a revolutionary act and, thus, not without its legion of detractors.

Under the Volcano by Malcolm Lowry (1947). This recounting of a drunk's inner and outer life was Lowry's only major work, due to his own alcoholism.

Revolutionary Road by Richard Yates (1961). This novel, set in Connecticut, is about the dissolution of a married couple due in part to alcohol. The book was seen as an indictment of the 1950s' desperation to conform. Yates, in a 1972 interview, said, "I meant the title to suggest that the revolutionary road of 1776 had come to something very much like a dead end in the Fifties."

Big Sur by Jack Kerouac (1962). By the time Kerouac wrote this underappreciated novel, he was dubbed "King of the Beats," a title he neither sought nor wanted. This book offers a sobering look at the cost of Kerouac's drinking, and when he died in 1969 of alcohol-related health problems, this book was cited as the cry for help that was never answered.

A Fan's Notes by Frederick Exley (1968). This "fictional memoir" about a New York Giants football fan lost in delusions of grandeur is now a cult classic. At the time it was published, however, the author's obsession with Frank Gifford brought that great athlete unwanted notoriety.

Drinking: A Love Story by Carolyn Knapp (1996). This is considered the best book by a contemporary author on alcohol's terrible price tag. The book created some scandal for the author's inability to take full responsibility for her actions regarding her deeper-seated issues with food and sexual relations, as she seemed to blame alcohol for most of her woes.

Drug-fueled Writers

In a nation like America, which was built upon the Protestant work ethic, many viewed drugs as a sign of dissipation, perhaps even of genetic inferiority. British writers like Thomas De Quincey (*Confessions of an English Opium-Eater*; 1822), Samuel Taylor Coleridge ("Kublai Kahn"), Percy Bysshe Shelley, Lord Byron, John Keats, and William Wordsworth were known to have written about, and be under the influence of, laudanum and opium; Arthur Conan Doyle implies that perhaps Sherlock Holmes was a morphine addict. French poets Charles Baudelaire (*Flowers of Evil*), Arthur Rimbaud, and Theophile Gautier formed what was known as the Hashish Club in the later 1800s. Despite the fact that "laughing gas" (ether and nitrous oxide, used as an anesthetic by physicians) was a staple at parties thrown by college-aged Americans in the mid 1800s, the subject was only touched on in the stories of Edgar Allan Poe.[12] It took the transplanted European Aldous Huxley to bring the subject to a general American audience with *The Doors of Perception* (1956). Huxley had a lifelong interest in "visionary experience," and this book chronicled his experiments with hallucinogenic substances. Because a distinguished person like Huxley praised the controlled use of such drugs, *The Doors of Perception* slipped past any censorious government officials to become

Prison writings and books about substance abuse have a long and controversial legacy in America. Caryl Chessman and Eldridge Cleaver were both inmates at San Quentin State Prison and bestselling authors. Jack Kerouac, William Burroughs, and Allen Ginsberg were affiliated with the "Beat Generation," and with drinking and drugging. Courtesy of Tom Hearn.

hugely influential with young people. One devotee, Jim Morrison, named his band, the Doors, after the book.

Other American writers, with Huxley having paved the way, moved into the territory of drug consciousness, both heralding and reflecting the new counterculture of the late 1960s. Among the books published in this controversial wave were:

> *Junky* by William Lee (pseudonym of William S. Burroughs, 1953) and *The Naked Lunch* (1959). Burroughs would go on to write scandalous, and suppressed, novels about homosexual subcultures (*The Ticket That Exploded, Nova Express,* and *Soft Boys*), but these were his earliest works, both being fairly straightforward accounts of heroin addiction through the eyes of an addict, as he had been.
>
> *Speed* by William S. Burroughs Jr. (1970). This is the chronicle of a meth-amphetamine addict, who happened also to be the son of a drug-fueled

writer, William S. Burroughs. Adding to the scandal of the book's graphic depiction of drug abuse was the fact that the author died at age 33 in 1981.

The Yage Letters by William Burroughs and Allen Ginsberg. This lively correspondence between these two "Beat Generation" writers detailed their travels through South America in 1953 and 1960 in search of hallucinogenic plants. Because of its controversial content, the book wasn't published until 1963.

The Teachings of Don Juan: A Yaqui Way of Knowledge by Carlos Castaneda (1968). Don Juan was a sage whom anthropology student Castaneda met in Mexico. The book chronicles Castaneda's initiation into psychedelic consciousness by Don Juan (and copious amounts of peyote and psilocybin mushrooms).

The Electric Kool-Aid Acid Test by Tom Wolfe (1968). "New Journalist" Wolfe's documentation of an LSD-fueled bus trip with Ken Kesey and his Merry Pranksters.

Fear and Loathing in Las Vegas by Hunter S. Thompson (1971). Thompson was sent to cover a convention in Las Vegas but, instead, stared into the abyss of the American soul, with the help of a trunk load of chemicals.

Debunking Sports

The modern "tell all" sports memoir began with *Long Season* (1960) and *Pennant Race* (1962) by Jim Brosnan, a talented relief pitcher for the Cincinnati Reds who also had a talent for writing. These two books were his candid chronicles of two baseball seasons, 1959 and 1961, respectively. Though the books weren't scandalous, per se, they opened a window on the game that took some of the mystique away and engendered criticism from old-timers like Joe Garagiola. But nothing punched the national pastime, or professional sports, as hard as Jim Bouton's *Ball Four* (1970). After having a short, but stellar, career as a starting pitcher with the New York Yankees (1962–67), Bouton found himself with a sore arm and a knuckleball, the latter his only hope for staying in the Major Leagues. In 1969, while hanging on as a relief pitcher with an expansion team, the Seattle Pilots, Bouton began keeping a diary of the day-in, day-out life in professional sports. With the help of journalist Leonard Schecter, Bouton shaped the diary into *Ball Four*, the most honest account of professional sports up to that time. It detailed the drug use (amphetamines), drinking, and skirt-chasing of the players, their eccentricities and foibles, as well as the camaraderie and high jinks. Bouton did not spare himself in his account, detailing how badly he pitched or how obnoxious he was to management—they, in fact, traded him to the Houston Astros at midseason in 1969. Though it was a truthful, humane, and entertaining account, *Ball Four* deflated the myth of sports superheroes that had existed up to that

time. Among the icons who were debunked was his former Yankee teammate
Mickey Mantle, whose drinking Bouton blamed for "the Mick's" chronic injuries. Baseball commissioner Bowie Kuhn was outraged by *Ball Four.*

Unable to stop the book's publication, Kuhn demanded Bouton sign a
waiver saying it was "completely fictional."[13] Bouton stood behind every word
in his book, which made him persona non grata to some baseball players,
including Pete Rose, who heckled him with obscenities when he pitched
against the Reds. Many fans, particularly those of the New York Yankees, were
incensed. Bouton, on the other hand, is one of the game's antiheroes, his
maverick writings ushering in waves of "tell all" sports memoirs. Bouton wrote
a sequel about the scandal his book unleashed, *I'm Glad You Didn't Take It
Personally* (1971).

Though many candid memoirs have since been published, the only one to
cause as great a stir as Bouton's was Jose Canseco's *Juiced* (2005). Canseco, an
All-Star slugger, was, in his own words appended to his book's dust jacket,
"the godfather of steroids in baseball." In his book, he admitted to, and even
endorsed, the use of anabolic steroids and human growth hormones, while also
naming other players whom he personally saw use them, and with whom he
often discussed their effects, including Mark McGwire, Rafael Palmeiro, Jason
Giambi, and Ivan Rodriguez. *Juiced* hit Major League Baseball like a line drive,
particularly after the game had initiated a drug-testing program to eradicate
such abuse. *Juiced*, and the subsequent "outing" of Giambi, Palmeiro, and
Barry Bonds for steroid use, put into doubt nearly every statistic the game has
produced in recent years. Two months after breaking Hank Aaron's career home
run record, Bonds was indicted by a federal grand jury, his career ended,
and achievements—like Pete Rose's, for his gambling—permanently tainted.
Canseco went one step further in a follow-up book, *Vindicated: Big Names, Big
Liars and the Battle to Save Baseball* (2008), in which he claimed to have introduced Alex Rodriguez, the game's reigning superstar in the wake of Bonds's
departure, to a steroid supplier.

Other professional sports weren't spared scrutiny from insiders. In 1971,
Dave Meggyesy published *Out of Their League*, a book that did for professional football what Bouton had done a year earlier for baseball. Meggyesy, a
linebacker with the St. Louis Cardinals for seven years before he quit, opened
a door to let in some much-needed air. The book, published at the height of
the Vietnam War, detailed all of the abuses of America's most violent game:
the racism, drug abuse, and even the gambling. The sports world was shocked
by what Meggyesy revealed, though the book is now a sports classic. Another
professional football player turned writer, Peter Gent, blew the lid off the
game in the 1970s, turning his critical eye on the game via a thinly-veiled fiction called *North Dallas Forty* (1973). Gent, a receiver for the iconic Dallas
Cowboys under the legendary Tom Landry, did not flinch from describing the
brutalizing aspects of the game, use of painkillers to keep seriously injured

players in the games, racism, and ignorance of many of the players and coaches.

Pseudo Science

Book publishing has long been home to a genre of works that purport to be nonfiction or scientific, and yet many include unsubstantiated claims. Debunkers like James Randi and Robert Todd Carroll have coined the term *pseudoscience* to describe this material.

The biggest selling of all pseudoscience books may be *Dianetics: The Modern Science of Mental Health* (1950), later the cornerstone of the Church of Scientology. The book, written by science-fiction writer L. Ron Hubbard and first published by a psychiatry textbook publisher, Hermitage House, claimed to offer techniques that could bring relief from mental and physical health problems. Hubbard posited that almost all illness was the result of an aberration in the "reactive mind," a deep-seated repository of bad memory traces, or "engrams." The reactive mind, he wrote, "can give a man arthritis, bursitis, asthma, allergies, sinusitis, coronary trouble, high blood pressure, and so on down the whole catalogue of psycho-somatic ills, adding a few more which were never specifically classified as psycho-somatic, such as the common cold." These Dianetics techniques, Hubbard said, could treat "all inorganic mental ills and all organic psycho-somatic ills, with assurance of complete cure."[14] The book sold 150,000 copies the first year and inspired the formation of Dianetics clubs. As sales continued, so did criticism from scientists and psychiatric experts. Carroll sums these up: "What Hubbard touts as a science of mind lacks one key element that is expected of a science: empirical testing of claims. The key elements of Hubbard's so-called science don't seem testable, yet he repeatedly claims that he is asserting only scientific facts and data from many experiments ... Such speculation is appropriate in fiction, but not in science."[15]

Sales figures of the book are hard to gauge since later printings, and its many sequels, were published by Bridge Publications, a subsidiary of the Church of Scientology. Thus, their claims of "20 million" sales of the book are doubted by media experts. The Nielsen BookScan figures, a publishing industry standard, indicated that only 52,000 copies were sold between 2001 and 2005.[16] Nonetheless, Scientology has continued to keep a high media profile because major celebrities like Tom Cruise and John Travolta are members of, and advocates for, the church.

Edgar Cayce

Edgar Cayce (1877–1945) was the foremost psychic in American history, as well as a forerunner of the modern holistic health movement. His work became widely known only toward the end of his life, and posthumously through the books of Gina Cerminara (*Many Mansions*; 1950) and Jess Stearn, a journalist whose two worshipful Cayce biographies were bestsellers, *The Sleeping Prophet: The Life and Work of Edgar Cayce* (1968) and *A Prophet in His Own Country* (1974). While working on these biographies, Stearn, a *Newsweek* editor, became convinced that Cayce did possess prophetic powers. These powers came to Cayce, wrote Stearn, while in a self-induced trance during which he channeled answers to long-vexing questions of health and spirituality that his adherents took as divinely inspired. For forty-three years, Cayce claimed he was able to lie on a couch, close his eyes, fold his hands over his stomach, and, through meditation, discern the "secrets of the universe." The son of a Kentucky tobacco farmer with a ninth-grade education, Cayce was not a charlatan; he believed that he was a channel for "the Source," and he offered "readings" to thousands of ill people around the world, and seemed to help many. Among those reportedly helped by Cayce's readings were Woodrow Wilson and Thomas Edison.

Cayce was a devout, though eccentric, Christian, believing in reincarnation and the lost continent of Atlantis. Nonetheless, Cayce's critics say that the evidence for his alleged powers comes from testimonials by his devotees, and they question the efficacy of his alternative medical cures. They also point to the amount of money his organization makes on its myriad products, many of which utilize Cayce's "secrets" and have not been properly tested by consumer advocacy groups. On the other hand, some of Cayce's medical formulae and vitamin- and mineral-based regimens have proven effective and have fueled a worldwide movement of the Virginia Beach-based Association for Research and Enlightenment. The work is underwritten by proceeds from the sales of Edgar Cayce Health Care Products.

Von Daniken's Chariots

On the wings of a 1960s UFO craze, in 1968 Erich von Daniken published *Chariots of the Gods?: Unsolved Mysteries of the Past*, which posited that extraterrestrials supplied ancient civilizations with early forms of technology. He followed that book with three others that expanded on the claims—*Gods from Outer Space* (1970), *The Gold of the Gods* (1972), and *In Search of Ancient Gods* (1973)—which collectively sold 36 million copies in 35 languages. He presented evidence that archeologists had found artifacts that were far too advanced to have been created by primitive civilizations. They were, he wrote, created by advanced civilizations from other solar systems. Among the advanced technologies he cited were the pyramids in Egypt, Stonehenge, Easter Island monoliths, and a "landing strip" in Peru for extraterrestrial vehicles. Also, some ancient art depicts what resembled space travelers, and some religious writings indicate familiarity with outer space, including an Old Testament revelation by Ezekiel. He proposed that humans had mated with extraterrestrials and, thus, evolved beyond all the other earth-bound creatures. James Randi offered a detailed critique of some of the more outlandish theories. "The only facts in his four books that I depend on are the page numbers," Randi wrote.

Rama (a.k.a. Frederick Lenz)

If Hubbard's *Dianetics*, von Daniken's "chariots," and Cayce's "readings" can be dubbed *pseudoscience*, then bestselling books by Frederick Lenz and Carlos Castaneda could be dubbed *pseudometaphysics*. While Lenz claimed to be the Zen master "Rama," Lenz had earned a doctorate in English literature and, with money from his successful computer business (Advanced Systems, Inc.), pursued his interest in Hinduism and Buddhism, eventually claiming he was Rama, the final incarnation of the Hindu god Vishnu. Undeterred by Lenz's lack of credentials, people flocked to his Malibu seminars, paying $5,000 to receive enlightenment at his feet during the 1990s. Lenz/Rama told attractive female clients that if they had sex with him, their karma would become more evolved. He pulled his teachings together in his bestselling book *Surfing the Himalayas: A Spiritual Adventure* (1997). Though obviously a piece of fantasy, and roundly debunked by critics and Eastern philosophy scholars, the book was deceptively marketed as a self-help primer. Soon after publishing a second book of spiritual musings, *Snowboarding to Nirvana*, Lenz drowned off Long Island. The Suffolk County Medical Examiner's office ruled that he had taken enough Valium to kill himself before plunging into Conscience Bay.

Bridey Murphy

In 1952, a Colorado hobbyist named Morey Bernstein hypnotized twenty-nine-year-old Virginia Tighe at a cocktail party. She immediately went into a deep trance, recalling distant childhood memories and speaking in a child's voice. Because of Tighe's receptiveness to hypnotism, Bernstein convinced her to help him with an experiment in past-life regression. A few days later, Bernstein hypnotized Tighe and took her back to a time before her birth. She began to assume the brogue voice of a long-dead Irish woman named Bridey Murphy. Bernstein hypnotized Tighe six times over the next year, coaxed her into singing Irish songs and telling Irish stories, and transcribed the recordings. The amateurish case created a national scandal when Bernstein published the results of his hypnosis as *The Search for Bridey Murphy* (1956). (To protect Tighe's privacy, he referred to her as Ruth Simmons in the book.) Because of the book's runaway success, and the seeming authenticity and detail of Tighe's Irish memories, many Americans began to believe in reincarnation. Newspapers assigned reporters to try to verify the existence of Bridey Murphy in nineteenth-century Ireland; in 1957 *The Denver Post* concluded that Bernstein and Tighe were credible, while the Hearst newspapers set out to expose them as frauds. Soon enough, the "real" Bridey Murphy was found in Wisconsin, where Tighe grew up. She was Bridie Murphy Corkell, who had lived across the street from Tighe's family. The hypnotic state had, apparently, unleashed some of Tighe's childhood memories that were colored by fantasy and confusion. Tighe had no recollection of her hypnotic revelations and did not profit from her notoriety. Bernstein, for his part, was not perpetrating a hoax; he trusted the revelations of the hypnosis sessions and printed them out for all to see, to avoid accusations of deception. Nonetheless, the scandal he unleashed was as large as the sales for his book.

Jeanne Dixon

The 1965 book *A Gift of Prophecy: The Phenomenal Jeanne Dixon* by Ruth Montgomery sold 3 million copies and brought its subject into the national limelight. Dixon's claim to fame was that in 1956, in *Parade Magazine,* she had predicted that the 1960 presidential election would be won by a Democrat, who would "be assassinated or die in office though not necessarily in his first term." She did not mention John F. Kennedy by name, but she was, nonetheless, widely credited, long after the fact, with predicting the assassination of President Kennedy. Dixon's critics pointed out that in her widely syndicated daily horoscope column, she made thousands of predictions over the course of her career, only a handful of which actually proved true, and that her self-professed "prophet" title was more accurately "profit." She also wrote a series of books, including *My Life and Prophecies* (1968), that selectively showcased the prophecies that were even marginally true. John Allen Paulos, a Temple University mathematician, dubbed the "Jeanne Dixon effect" to cover the discrepancy between the huge numbers of predictions and the few that actually come true. As Robert Todd Carroll later wrote, "When one makes as many predictions as Dixon did, you are bound to be correct or sort of correct some of the time." Nonetheless, President Richard Nixon was so impressed with her alleged powers that when she predicted a terrorist attack in his first term, he ordered the nation put on military alert. (No terrorist attack occurred.) Likewise, President Ronald Reagan's wife, Nancy, had astrological consultations with Dixon.

Not Safe for Truth Tellers

In a book called *The Psychic Mafia* (1976), the former self-proclaimed spirit medium Lamarr Keene decided to "go straight" by confessing to the numerous scams and con games he'd pulled. Among the secretive circle of "spiritualists," Keene's revelations were tantamount to ratting on a Mafia boss. He was subjected to death threats by phone and mail, as his former colleagues vowed to get even. For his own safety, he changed his name and opened an import business, but his enemies discovered his whereabouts. While leaving his shop one day in 1981, Keene was gunned down on the sidewalk; he survived the attack, moved to another state, and disappeared.

A similar reaction greeted Paulette Cooper after her book, *The Scandal of Scientology* (1971), was published. Threatened with a $15 million lawsuit by the Church of Scientology, the publisher pulled the book from store shelves. According to James Randi, the church initiated a campaign to discredit and harass Cooper, which continued for years and resulted in nineteen different lawsuits that nearly bankrupted the journalist. In 1977, after several members of the Church of Scientology were arrested and convicted of conspiracy for breaking into government offices and destroying public records, church memos surfaced that detailed the campaign against Cooper, who then sued the Church of Scientology for $15.4 million. It was also learned at this time that L. Ron Hubbard, Scientology's founder, had implemented a "fair game" policy to target anyone who left the church. Though the church settled out of court with Cooper in 1985, the fair game policy was still in effect. A critical biography of Hubbard, *Bare-faced Messiah* by Russell Miller, was published in the United States by Henry Holt in 1988, and then withdrawn within a month due to the cost of litigation. As Miller later wrote, "I had barely started researching the bizarre life and times of L. Ron Hubbard before the first of many lawyers' letters arrived, advising me to desist and threatening dire consequences if I persisted ... I was followed for several days in Los Angeles. I was told my house was under constant surveillance, my mail was being intercepted, and my telephone was tapped. I became aware that teams of private detectives were trawling my friends and associates."[17]

Diet Pills

Two of the most lucrative publishing genres are cookbooks and diet books, clear indications of how Americans are tugged in opposite directions by their hungers and regrets. Annually, or sometimes more often, a new book is published, offering a "revolutionary" new diet that is actually a variation on the hundreds of revolutionary diets preceding it. In some cases, these books have proven more harmful than beneficial, as Americans leaped into dramatic dietary changes without consulting medical experts. *Calories Don't Count* (1961) by Dr. Herman Taller was the first diet book that was not only denounced by nutritionists, but nearly 2,000 copies were seized by the Food and Drug Administration in January 1962 for legal violations. Taller advised obese and overweight people to completely cut out carbohydrates and increase intake of polyunsaturated fats. By the time the FDA seized copies, the book had already sold 300,000 copies in nine printings. Physicians charged Taller with putting people's lives in peril, while the Federal Trade Commission accused him of making false claims and conning people into buying safflower oil capsules from a vitamin company in which he had a financial stake. Taller, his vitamin company, and his publisher (Simon and Schuster) all faced civil lawsuits. Eventually, Taller was convicted of mail fraud, conspiracy, and breaking the FDA law.[18]

Beware Little Old Ladies Bearing Stock Tips

Almost as popular as cookbooks and diet books are books that offer financial advice. Landfills are littered with failed investment guides, starting with innocuous staples like Dale Carnegie's *How to Win Friends and Influence People* (1936) and *Think and Grow Rich* by Napoleon Hill (1937). Most of these books have never caused a scandal. However, nothing compared to the scandal unleashed by a group of retired women from Beardstown, Illinois, who started an investment club and claimed to earn 23.4 percent annual returns, three times the rate of professional money managers. Attracted by this whopping statistic and the seemingly innocent aura of a bunch of little old ladies, Disney gave the women a multimedia contract. The resultant bestsellers, *The Beardstown Ladies' Commonsense Investment Guide* and *The Beardstown Ladies' Little Book of Investment Wisdom*, and videos like *The Beardstown Ladies: Cookin' up Profits on Wall Street* (1993), staked their credibility on this 23.4 percent statistic. However, *Chicago* magazine and the *Wall Street Journal* both investigated the ladies' track record and discovered the statistic was either a hoax or the result of faulty math. The bottom line was, in fact, the bottom line: At best, the ladies achieved an annual return of 9 percent and, overall, fell far behind the Standard and Poor's 500 Index, a standard yardstick by which investments are measured. Not only were buyers of these products shocked to be deceived by the old ladies, but Disney refused to remove the fraudulent 23.4 percent statistic from the jackets of books and videos. Finally, a California lawyer filed a civil suit against the corporation for false advertising. As Steven Brill wrote, "Much of the media we consume today is sold to us by large public corporations. Their highest priority is profit. That's not a criticism; it's an acknowledgment of their duty to shareholders. And one way they maximize profit is to claim as much as they can get away with claiming about their products. Indeed, we live not only in the Information Age but in the age of hype."[19]

How Weird Hughes

One of the most brazen publishing hoaxes in history was pulled off by journalist Clifford Irving. Irving, who had previously written three novels and a bestselling book about an art forger (*Fake!*), was living on the Mediterranean island of Ibiza in 1970 when he convinced the respected publishing house McGraw Hill that he was collaborating on an autobiography of Howard Hughes, with the full cooperation of the legendarily reclusive billionaire. From the outset, Irving knew he had no access to Hughes, but he also knew that a book purporting to be an "authorized" autobiography of one of America's richest and most mysterious men would be a bestseller. Previous attempts to write books about Hughes were suppressed by the billionaire, who simply paid the writers not to write them. Not only did Irving convince McGraw Hill of the legitimacy of the project—and was given a $765,000 advance, $655,000 of which was supposed to go to Hughes—he also contracted with *Life* magazine to run excerpts from said tome. Irving then proceeded as though everything were on the level. With Richard Suskind doing the research and sharing writing duties, Irving concentrated on forging supposedly authentic documents, including handwritten letters by Hughes (used to con the McGraw Hill editors). By early 1972, he produced a manuscript that was partly fiction, and partly lifted from Time-Life files and a work-in-progress about Hughes by another author that Irving managed to illegally photocopy. McGraw Hill planned to publish the alleged Hughes autobiography in March 1972. Despite countless avowals that the book was a fake, Irving fooled the publisher and handwriting experts, and even survived an interview with Mike Wallace on *60 Minutes*. However, the façade crumbled when Hughes filed a lawsuit against the publisher and Irving. Irving soon confessed to the hoax, and he, his wife, and Suskind were convicted of fraud and given prison sentences (Irving served fourteen months). Irving later wrote a bestseller about the ordeal, *The Hoax* (1981), on which the 2007 film starring Richard Gere was based (though Irving denounced the film).

One equally scandalous sidelight to this hoax was its connection to the Nixon White House and the Watergate break-in. One of the revelations in Irving's fake Hughes autobiography—a manuscript copy of which President Nixon was illegally supplied by FBI Director J. Edgar Hoover—concerned a $400,000 loan that Hughes had given Nixon's brother in 1956 that was, essentially, a bribe. Not long after the money was paid, the IRS called off an investigation of a subsidiary of the Hughes corporate empire. Nixon, who was vice president in 1956, was so paranoid about this revelation even sixteen years later that he, according to the Senate Watergate Committee report, sent associates E. Howard Hunt and G. Gordon Liddy to break into the National Democratic Headquarters office at the Watergate complex, specifically to find out what dirt Irving may have supplied Democratic Chairman Lawrence O'Brien. Thus, in a roundabout way, Irving's publishing hoax brought down a U.S. president.

Chapter 5

NEWSPAPERS AND MAGAZINES

P rior to the advent of the radio and dating back to antiquity, the print medium was the primary means by which Americans, or almost everyone in the Western world, conveyed information. Journalism professor Melvin Mencher notes, "What we read, see and hear today is not much different from the material in the daily [handwritten] bulletins posted in the Roman forum."[1] Julius Caesar's realization that Roman citizens needed to be informed may indeed have served as a vital foundation on which the need for free and unfettered information, and, by association, journalism, was built. Though what we have come to think of as traditional print journalism—newspapers and magazines—eventually sought to fulfill that need, these genres were also, at least in democratic societies like America, private enterprises, not state-run propaganda organs. Thus, in addition to informing readers, American newspapers and magazines aimed to entertain them enough to keep them buying their "product." Often this resulted in media scandals. Some scandals were by design, such as those fomented by grocery store tabloids and modern packs of paparazzi to increase sales and shock value. Others were by accident, such as the printed plagiarism and falsehoods that have rocked even the most venerable American newspapers and magazines. There were also those scandals that resulted from touching such "third rail" American topics as politics, race, religion, sex, and morality. (*See also* chapters in Part I.)

SETTING THE AGENDA FOR SCANDAL

A Penny per Peep

The daily newspaper was not a staple of the big city scene in the early nineteenth century. Most papers were published less frequently, and those that were printed daily were dismissively called *penny papers* (they initially cost one cent). In 1833, the *New York Sun* began printing daily compendiums of short and sensational stories; some were paid notices disguised to look like "news." The *Sun* was soon the first successful daily paper in America and a forerunner of the tabloid press. Loren Ghiglione credits the *Sun's* police reporter, George

Wisner, for covering "everyday dramas" and using "colloquial language" that resulted in "some 20 to 30" libel suits in 1834 alone.

But it was a hoax that the *Sun* perpetrated the next year that really made the newspaper a household name. By mid 1835, the *Sun's* circulation topped 15,000, unprecedented for an American daily at the time. Wanting to build on this success, publisher Benjamin H. Day hired acclaimed reporter Richard Adams Locke from the rival *Courier and Enquirer*. The Cambridge-educated Locke began running a satiric series purporting that life existed on the moon. As his source, Locke used John Herschel, an actual astronomer based in South Africa, and, thus, safely out of reach for verification of this outlandish proposition. On August 25, 1835, and for the next four days, Locke printed articles about lunar vegetation, birds, unicorns, beavers that walked upright on two legs, "continuous herds of brown quadrupeds, having all the external characteristics of the bison," and a human-like creature that could fly whose face was described as having "a yellowish flesh-color, a slight improvement upon that of the large orangutan, being more open and intelligent in expression, and having a much greater expanse of forehead. The mouth, however, was very prominent, though somewhat relieved by a thick beard upon the lower jaw, and by lips far more human than those of any species of the Semia genus." This final installment, about the flying humanoids, sold 19,360 copies, the most of any daily paper in the world, beating the *Times* of London (which sold 17,000). Not content with creating a hoax, Locke took the *Sun's* installments, hired a lithographer, and produced an illustrated booklet that sold another 60,000 copies. After scholars insisted on some corroborative proof of his theories about lunar life-forms, Locke admitted it was a hoax, claiming that he was satirizing scientific speculations. He also proudly boasted that he'd performed a valuable public service by "diverting the public mind, for a while, from that bitter discord, the abolition of slavery." Like many editors who would follow in his footsteps, Locke thought that the means justified the ends.

The Storey of Scandal

Wilber F. Storey was owner and editor of the *Chicago Times*, which he bought in 1861. During the Civil War, Storey's paper regularly attacked the Republican Party, the Lincoln administration, and the war itself. He instructed his war correspondents to "Telegraph fully all news and when there is no news send rumors." Such violation of wartime news-gathering protocol provoked General Ambrose Burnside into shutting down the paper's operations for "sedition" while one reporter (Warren Isham) was court-martialed and imprisoned "for the duration of the war." After the war, Storey pushed the boundaries farther, running the sorts of headlines later found in grocery store tabloids; for instance, he used "JERKED TO JESUS" atop a story about the public hangings of four convicted murderers. Storey's professed motto was "print the news and raise hell." For doing this, he was horsewhipped on a Chicago street by the subject of one of his paper's sensational stories, and, according to Ghighlione, "at one time, Storey faced twenty-four libel suits."[2] Through the 1870s, this paper was the widest-circulating daily in Chicago. Storey died from a combination of insanity and syphilis before he could become a national newspaper icon like William Randolph Hearst. But Hearst may not have taken some inspiration from Storey's efforts, or from Charles Chapin, city editor of the *New York Evening World*, who was notorious for overworking his staff. When columnist Irvin Cobb found out Chapin had been stricken by illness, he reportedly quipped, "I hope it's nothing trivial." Chapin created his own scandal in 1918, when he shot and killed his bedridden wife, for which he was sent to Sing Sing Prison, where he died in 1930.[3]

Nickel-plated Scandal

A high-society scandal is not always a media scandal, but sometimes it can mutate into one, depending on how the press covers it. Take the case of Ruth Snyder, a well-to-do Queens, New York, housewife who murdered her sleeping husband on March 20, 1927. Her partner in crime was her lover, a corset and bra salesman named Judd Gray.[4] The scandal of the murder shocked polite New York society, and the ensuing arrests and murder trials were the talk of the town and nation for weeks. The city's newspapers went into a frenzy over the story. The ensuing mad dash for the sensational was the pinnacle in what became known as "the war of the tabs." That is, the city's three "tabs," or tabloid newspapers—*Daily Mirror*, owned by William Randolph Hearst; *Daily News*, owned by Joseph Patterson; and *Daily Graphic*, owned by Bernarr Macfadden—vied for whose coverage could be most sensational. The tabs were essentially the same as the penny papers, though half a century later they cost a nickel. The *Daily Mirror* even hired a phrenologist to study photographs of Snyder to determine her character. He concluded that she had "the character of a shallow-brained pleasure-seeker, accustomed to unlimited self-indulgence, which at last ends in an orgy of murderous passion and lust, seemingly without a parallel in the criminal history of modern times." The more respectable dailies, like the *Herald Tribune* and the *Times*, saw the murder as a harbinger of civilization's end, the predictable end result of Jazz Age hedonism. The *Herald Tribune* attributed the murder to "psychopathia suburbis," and said it heralded a "pale yellow dawn of a new decadence."[5]

Historian Ann Jones wrote that the print media "turned the Snyder case into one of the top media events of the decade and its most important morality play ... The tabloids increased their circulations by reporting every little kink in the Snyder-Gray love affair, so that every reader could indulge vicariously in the forbidden." If the murder was the crime of the year in New York,

This 1927 trial of Ruth Snyder for the murder of her husband set a tone for tabloid journalism that has still not abated. Courtesy of Library of Congress, Prints and Photographs Division.

the trial itself was a major social event, with celebrities flocking to the Queens courtroom to see and be seen, a veritable orgy of scandal. After Snyder and Gray were both found guilty, they were sent "up the river" to Sing Sing State Prison, in Ossining, New York. While awaiting execution on death row, Snyder sold her story to the *Daily Mirror*, but it brought little sympathy. By the time of her scheduled execution, Snyder was suffering from epileptic spasms and hysteria, and her blonde hair had turned gray. She had to be carried to and lifted onto the electric chair. The coda on this scandal came from the *Chicago Tribune*, which sent a photographer with a concealed camera to the execution, where he surreptitiously snapped a photograph of Snyder at the moment 2,000 volts of electricity were sent through the helmet strapped to her head. The photograph, purchased from the *Tribune*, ran on the front page of the *Daily News* the next day under the banner headline, "DEAD!" For once, a sensational caption matched an image: "This is perhaps the most remarkable exclusive picture in the history of criminology." It is for photographs like this that cameras have been forbidden on death rows and at executions, or even inside courtrooms. It could be argued that the real scandal in this murder case was how New York's media responded to it. It could also be argued, conversely, that the photograph in the *Daily News*—and the decision to run it (two different issues)—provided a public service, as the deterrent to capital crime that the death penalty is purported by its proponents to be. Indeed, it begs the question, should the American media be allowed to film and broadcast executions?

Hearst and Yellow Journalism

After being expelled from Harvard, William Randolph Hearst inherited the *San Francisco Examiner* in 1887, one of the holdings of his father, who'd made his fortune with the Comstock Lode, a silver mine. Young Hearst made the underperforming newspaper a success by the mass appeal of its sensationalistic coverage and by dropping the price from one nickel to one cent, to increase readership and undercut competition. He bought the *New York Morning Journal* in 1895 and did the same thing, initiating a circulation war with Joseph Pulitzer at the *New York World*. Hearst printed news about crime and sex, spiced with sports, society, and—his innovation—color comic strips. His formula worked, boosting circulation. His best-known strip, Richard Felton "R. F." Outcault's "Yellow Kid," inspired the term *yellow journalism*, referring to Hearst's type of sensational and often suspect reporting, which his arch rival Joseph Pulitzer was soon forced to emulate. The "Yellow Kid" first appeared in Outcault's single-panel "Hogan's Alley" cartoon in Pulitzer's *World*. Hearst lured Outcault away to the *Journal* and expanded the format to a series of panels with characters speaking inside "speech balloons"; the comic strip and yellow journalism were born. Pulitzer outbid Hearst again for Outcault's services, and the Sunday color comics supplement became the hottest ticket in town. The sensationalist approach spread to all sections of the newspaper, including the headlines, which served as prototypes for grocery store tabloids (e.g., "Why Young Girls Kill Themselves").

Not content with his circulation war, Hearst wanted a real war to make America a world power. To promote this agenda, he pushed for war with Spain—in Cuba, by using his influential newspaper chain to depict a small colonial insurgency into a threat to the security of the United States. In 1895, Cubans revolted against the Spanish colonial rulers. Hearst's correspondent, Richard Harding Davis, filed story after story about the brave Cuban freedom fighters. Stoked by such dispatches and a jingoistic military led by Teddy Roosevelt, who let his friend Davis tag along with his "Rough Riders," readers supported U.S. intervention. Hearst's "spin" convinced Americans it was a battle for freedom from oppression, like the American Revolution. Hoping to up the ante, Hearst sent artist Frederic Remington, according to Philip Knightly, "to convey visually what Davis had done with words." Remington was unenthusiastic about the prospects, reportedly wiring Hearst, "Everything is quiet. There is no trouble here. There will be no war. I wish to return." Hearst responded, "Please remain. You furnish pictures. I will furnish war."[6] And, indeed, he did. When, in February 1898, the battleship USS *Maine* was blown up in Havana harbor (killing 266), Hearst refused to air the distinct possibility that it might have been an accident (the cause of the explosion has still not been conclusively established). Instead, Knightly wrote, "Hearst, without a particle of proof, attributed it to 'an enemy's secret infernal machine,' and in the wave of patriotic fervor that swept the United States ('Remember the Maine!') he was finally able to furnish his correspondents with a war."[7]

Hearst papers' circulation skyrocketed, and other papers, to compete, climbed on the saber-rattling bandwagon. A typically humble Hearst headline was "How Do You Like the Journal's War?"—the smug implication being that his newspaper was an ad hoc wing of the U.S. Army. The ensuing conflict, which Hearst's propaganda helped start, was called by Secretary of State John Hay, a "splendid little war," one that allowed the United States to annex Cuba and Puerto Rico in the Caribbean and the Philippines and Guam in the Pacific. Though Cuba gained independence, President William McKinley deemed it our duty "to civilize and Christianize" the Philippines (a country that was already Catholic).[8] After the smoke cleared, Hearst's jingoism was roundly criticized, and the pejorative "yellow journalism" came into common use to denote biased, provocative, and untrue reportage. It was not intended as a compliment.

The "Great Bathtub Hoax"

On December 28, 1917, H. L. Mencken published a column in the *New York Evening Mail*, entitled "A Neglected Anniversary." In it, he purported to give the history of the bathtub. For example, he claimed that the novelty was introduced in England in 1828, and that the first bathtub in America was built by a Mr. Thompson of Cincinnati in 1842. Millard Fillmore, said Mencken, was the first U.S. president to install a bathtub in the White House, while the first prison bathtub in the United States was installed in 1870. All of these confidently stated "facts" were revealed by other members of the press as complete fabrications. Mencken's motive, he said, was "to relieve the strain of war days" as World War I dragged on, calling his column "a tissue of absurdities, all of them deliberate and most of them obvious."[9] Mencken, it should be noted, had fallen out of favor during the war for his pro-German isolationism, and had turned his hand to satire to avoid politically controversial topics. Nonetheless, people took the column seriously, and for years thereafter his "facts" about bathtubs continued to be reported. Mencken himself noted, in a later article, "I began to encounter my preposterous 'facts' in the writings of other men ... They got into learned journals. They were alluded to on the floor of Congress." Even President Harry Truman told visitors to the White House the history of the bathtub, based on Mencken's fiction. This became known as the "Great Bathtub Hoax" and has since been echoed in other similar media "story lines," like the WMDs in Iraq, and the lie that Al Gore claimed to have "invented the Internet." Though things like this are not true, they are treated as conventional wisdom.

Winchelled, Parsoned, and Hoppered

Yellow journalism, to appeal to the masses, required more than comic strips. It needed real-life cartoons. Enter Walter Winchell, Louella Parsons, and Hedda Hopper, the trinity of nationwide syndicated gossip columnists. They wielded tremendous power for promotion as well as for scandal. Parsons honed her poison pen in the birthplace of yellow journalism—Hearst's Universal News Service—where beginning in 1926 she was the self-proclaimed "czarina of Hollywood." She sniffed out dirt on stars like Rudolf Valentino and Douglas Fairbanks. Hopper, a failed actress, was Parsons's main competition. Known for her wild hats that, Ghiglione noted, "sometimes looked like Dagwood sandwiches," Hopper was vicious to any celebrity who snubbed her, reporting things like a gay liaison between Cary Grant and Noel Coward, for which she had no evidence other than unnamed gossipers, and attacks on Charlie Chaplin for his "Communism." Parsons destroyed the career of Sidney Skolsky, a Broadway columnist who was also syndicated by Hearst. She told Hearst that Skolsky was a Communist; he wasn't, but he had beaten her to a scoop and needed punishing.[10] Hopper described her Beverly Hills mansion (replete with maid, cook, and chauffeur) as "the house that fear built." Parsons and Hopper, occasionally seen at the same soirees, were in vicious competition. Biographer Neal Gabler noted, "However much they loathed each other, Parsons and Hopper were really very much alike ... both conservative, prudish, narrow-minded small-town women in an essentially conservative and prudish community."[11]

Of the three gossip columnists, Winchell was by far the most powerful. He didn't just take on Hollywood; he took on the world—celebrities as well as socialites and politicians. His gossip columns were known to provoke divorces, feuds, and criminal indictments. So loathed was Winchell by legitimate journalists that one of the latter, Emile Gauvreau, published a novel called *The Scandal Mirror* (1932), whose main character Roddy Ratcliffe was modeled on Winchell. Gauvreau called gossip mongers like Winchell "glorified Peeping Toms who are terrorizing the metropolis. To feed the insatiable appetite for scandal they do not hesitate to break up homes, blast reputations, wreck men and women's lives." Gauvreau's novel about scandal provoked a scandal of its own, for one simple reason: he was the managing editor for the *New York*

Mirror, Winchell's home paper. Winchell threatened to quit the *Mirror* over the book. He reconsidered when he realized that the book had given him new-found notoriety. Indeed, several Hollywood films were made with characters modeled on Winchell; he even played himself in *Love and Hisses* (1938).

Ford Family Values

America's best known industrialist, Henry Ford, held many controversial political views, which included an open admiration for Adolf Hitler. Ford's primary media organ to propound his views was a weekly newspaper, the *Dearborn Independent*, which was published from 1920 to 1927. During that time, Ford ran excerpts from the anti-Semitic hoax *Protocols of the Learned Elders of Zion* in the *Independent*, which reached 700,000 readers. (*See also* "Publishing Hoaxes.") Articles from the *Independent* were published in a four-volume set as *The International Jew: The World's Foremost Problem*, which was translated into German and became a favorite of the Nazi leadership. (Ford would later be given the Grand Cross of the German Eagle, the highest award the Nazis gave to foreigners.) The Anti-Defamation League and President Woodrow Wilson denounced the *Independent* and its offshoot publications. In 1927, San Francisco lawyer Aaron Sapiro filed a libel lawsuit against the *Dearborn Independent*. This suit, coupled with a boycott of Ford products, prompted Ford to cease publishing his scandalous weekly.

Truman Gets the Last Laugh

Among headlines that have appeared in American newspapers, few have achieved the blatant inaccuracy of the one that appeared in the *Chicago Tribune* on November 7, 1948: "Dewey Defeats Truman." The nation's political pundits had been assuring voters for weeks that the incumbent president was going be defeated by New York Governor Thomas E. Dewey. In the issue of *Newsweek* published the week before the election, fifty of America's "leading political writers" predicted a landslide victory for Dewey. After reading the issue of *Newsweek*, Truman told his assistant Clark Clifford, "I know every one of these fifty fellows. There isn't one of them who has sense to pound sand in a rat hole."[12] Because of the widespread "conventional wisdom" that Dewey was assured a victory, the *Tribune*—embroiled in a workers strike and, thus, understaffed—printed its infamous edition early in the afternoon. By late that evening, it was official: Truman won by 4.4 percent of the vote, taking 303 electoral votes to Dewey's 189. That issue of the *Tribune* became a collector's item.

Publishing the Unabomber

On September 18, 1995, the *Washington Post* and the *New York Times* simultaneously published a 35,000-word manifesto called "Industrial Society and Its Future," setting off a heated national debate. The manifesto was written by an unnamed, unknown writer who had waged a campaign of terror for seventeen years, sending mail bombs to university staff, airline officials, and government officials. In that time, the mail bombs killed three people and injured twenty-three. The FBI called this the UNABOM case, and the press had taken to referring to the perpetrator as the Unabomber; "Industrial Society and Its Future" came to be called the "Unabomber Manifesto." Among its assertions were that "The Industrial Revolution and its consequences have been a disaster for the human race.... They have ... destabilized society ... led to widespread psychological suffering ... and inflicted severe damage on the natural world." The Unabomber scorned both political extremes, calling leftists "crazies" and conservatives "fools." While some truths echoed through the manifesto, they were undermined by the fact that the writer was a murderer.

The *Post* and *Times* were both widely criticized for publishing "Industrial Society and Its Future." The newspapers defended the publication by insisting that it was not done impulsively, that they had been discussing it for months with federal government officials, including Attorney General Janet Reno. "Neither paper would have printed this document for journalistic reasons," wrote *Post* publisher Donald E. Graham in a note accompanying the manifesto. *Times* publisher Arthur O. Sulzberger said, "You print it and he doesn't kill anyone else; that's a pretty good deal. You print it and he continues to kill people. What have you lost? The cost of newsprint."

Nonetheless, experts debated the publication, saying that it essentially held the media hostage and surrendered to the demands of the kidnappers. It also, critics said, emboldened future terrorists to make similar demands. However, the so-called Unabomber did not mail any more bombs, and the prime suspect, fifty-three-year-old Ted Kaczynski, was arrested on April 3, 1996. Kaczynski, a Harvard graduate with a doctorate from the University of Michigan, was tried, found guilty, and sentenced to life in prison in May 1998. Nine years later, Kaczynski sparked another scandal when he challenged the government's plan to auction 40,000 pages of his writings to raise funds for victims of his bombs. He said the auction violated his First Amendment rights, while others said the writings would teach terrorists about how to make mail bombs.

Despite media experts' denunciation of the *Post's* and *Times's* printing of Kaczynski's "Unabomber Manifesto," his wasn't the first publication by a wanted criminal. During the so-called "Summer of Sam" in 1977, serial killer David "Son of Sam" Berkowitz wrote a series of taunting letters that were printed in the *New York Post*. Another wanted man, "The Mad Bomber," was finally arrested in 1957, after a nine-year terror campaign in which he had left homemade bombs in public places in and around New York City. He was captured because one of his letters was published in the *New York Journal-American*, and a former coworker recognized the phrasing of a disgruntled Consolidated Edison employee, George Metesky.

Other "manifestos" have been publicly circulated through the media, including the Left-Wing Manifesto, Port Huron Statement, and Black Panther Party Platform.

The Left-Wing Manifesto

Benjamin Gitlow and three others were found guilty of "statutory criminal anarchy" for this 1925 publication, which advocated overthrowing the government via "mass strikes and revolutionary mass action" to "progressively foment industrial disturbances" and "overthrow and destroy organized parliamentary government." The publication was said to violate the Anarchy Act of 1902, a ruling upheld by the U.S. Supreme Court. Justice Oliver Wendell Holmes dissented, however, saying that "if the Manifesto, as alleged, was an incitement rather than a theory, so is every idea an incitement."

Port Huron Statement

The radical student group, Students for a Democratic Society (SDS), met for five days in Port Huron, Michigan, June 11–15, 1962, to draft a "living document" that would open "a dialogue with society." The result, known as the *Port Huron Statement*, has generally been credited with radicalizing a generation of college students. In 1964, 20,000 copies of the sixty-three-page document were printed and distributed on campuses nationwide. In 1966, the SDS printed another 25,000 copies. Excerpts were included in bestselling collections of "New Left" writings, including *The New Student Left*, edited by Mitchell Cohen and Dennis Hale, and *The New Radicals*, edited by Paul Jacobs and Saul Landau. The ideas trickled down into conversations taking place on campuses. The *Port Huron Statement* was, noted historian Jim Miller, "one of the pivotal documents in post-war American history," both for "catapulting the SDS to national prominence" and for planting the idea of "participatory democracy" in the university setting, the very hotbed of radical change, where the "New Left" would soon emerge as a force that the government felt compelled to combat. The Port Huron Statement was, in one sense, the gauntlet hurled at the feet of the federal government, the first step in the rebellion known collectively now as "the Sixties."

Black Panther Party Platform

Though the core principles of the Black Panther Party for Self Defense were largely ignored by the mainstream press during the late 1960s, they did exist in a widely-printed and distributed manifesto called The Ten Point Plan. This document quoted from the Declaration of Independence and contained such reasonable demands as "We want full employment for our people," "We want decent housing, fit for the shelter of human beings," and "We want an immediate end to all wars of aggression." However, FBI Director J. Edgar Hoover determined that the Black Panther Party was "the most dangerous radical political party in the United States," and considered it a threat to national security. The FBI's COINTELPRO program was designed to harass and attack the party and its members, even to the point of provoking violence through infiltrators and sabotage. One of the targets of sabotage was the party's media organ, the weekly newspaper called *The Black Panther*. Through this organ, and a network of underground newspapers, the party disseminated their Ten Point Plan.

THE PRESS GOES UNDERGROUND

Prior to the 1960s, many publications flaunted the prevailing mores (*Evergreen Review, Nugget, Cavalier,* and *Playboy*). Some pushed the envelope on graphic art (EC Comics, *MAD, Wild,* and syndicated comic strips *Pogo* and *Krazy Kat*). Toss in more literary, artistic, and spirit-seeking journals like *Contact, Psychedelic Review, Yugen, Kulchur, Big Table, New Directions, Horizon,* and *View,* and you'd have to say the foundation was laid for a new type of underground journalism. Arguably the first underground magazine that tried to make the leap into the 1960s was *The Realist,* a monthly started by Paul Krassner in 1958. Krassner was determined to create what he called "a *Mad* for grownups." The emphasis was on outrageous satire, taboo-trashing, and borderline libel. His most scandalous sketch was a 1963 fantasy of Lyndon Johnson desecrating the corpse of President Kennedy on the plane trip from Dallas after the assassination. "Irreverence is the only sacred cow," said Krassner, who found himself in hot water with the FBI.[13]

This same boundary-pushing spirit was found in the newsrooms of the underground press. Among the first and best of the underground papers that appeared regularly were the *L.A. Free Press* (begun in 1964), New York's *East Village Other,* and the *Berkeley Barb.* The *Free Press* (or "Freep") was founded and edited by Art Kunkin, who ran it like a professional operation. Moreover, Kunkin ran reliable news (local and national) and the forthright views of Harlan Ellison, film critic Gene Youngblood, Lawrence Lipton, and cartoonist Ron Cobb, arguably the underground press's most talented graphic artist. The *Barb,* forged in the flames of the Free Speech Movement at the University of California at Berkeley, was as cantankerous as its founder, Max Scherr, a labor activist determined to produce a "people's paper." The *Barb* set precedents that were followed by other papers: shoestring budgets and street-level reporting and vending. The *Seed* in Chicago combined superb graphic art with professional investigative journalism. Typical of the scandals sparked by underground newspapers was one that involved the *Seed.* Gifted staff artist Karl-Heinz Meschbach created a piece of subtle but erotic-themed art that the *Seed* used on its cover. Because the art contained sexually suggestive art near a drawing of Chicago's powerful mayor, Richard Daley, all copies of that issue were confiscated, and the *Seed* editor Abe Peck and one of the street vendors were prosecuted for obscenity charges. The charges were eventually dropped, and Peck went on to become head of the Medill School of Journalism at Northwestern University.[14]

The true essence of the countercultural spirit was found in the *Oracle*, which grew out of the Haight-Ashbury neighborhood in San Francisco that is purported to be the birthplace of the "hippie." Though it lasted only twelve issues, the *Oracle*'s influence was huge, primarily because it so perfectly captured the utopian but utterly apolitical mind-set of the so-called "flower people." Its content was driven by the explosion of art that had begun appearing on rock posters. The modus operandi said it all: "designed to aid people on their trips." That an American newspaper would be inspired by psychedelic drugs was enough to find it roundly denounced by the mainstream press.

Similar messages were disseminated by and similar denunciations were leveled at many of the following underground publications: *Argus* (Ann Arbor), *Avatar* (Boston), Big Fat (Ann Arbor), *Connections* (Madison, Wisconsin), *Crocodile* (Gainesville, Florida), *East Village Other* (New York), *Fifth Estate* (Detroit), *Free Press* (Washington), *Good Times* (San Francisco), *Graffiti* (Philadelphia), *Great Speckled Bird* (Atlanta), *Guerrilla* (Detroit), *Helix* (Seattle), *Kaleidoscope* (Milwaukee), *Kudzu* (Jackson, Mississippi), *Open City* (Los Angeles), *Sage* (Santa Fe), *The Paper* (East Lansing, Michigan), *The Rag* (Austin), *The Rat* (New York), *The Seed* (Chicago), and *View from the Bottom* (New Haven). Of these papers, only *Fifth Estate* is still in print. Other kindred-spirited publications—including zines and blogs—have risen in the ensuing years. (*See also* Chapter 7, "Internet Scandals.") Scandal did not just arise from these papers' alternative political slant, but from the explicit language, the erotic graphics, the personal classifieds, and the advertisements for head shops, marijuana paraphernalia, and adult entertainment.

Comic Books as Villain, *MAD* as Hero

Comic books were a phenomenon that grew out of the daily newspapers' comic strips. The first real comic book, *Famous Funnies*, was, in fact, a collection of newspaper strips in book form, published in 1934 by Max Gaines. By 1941, there were thirty comic book publishers in the United States, with 150 different titles and 15 million sales per month, and an estimated 60 million readers, an astonishing audience in a nation of 200 million people. Anything that became this popular this fast among the nation's young was, like rock 'n' roll, going to attract parental concern. Indeed, citizens groups, editorialists, and articles began drawing parallels between comic book readership and juvenile delinquency. By 1943, 25 million comic books were being sold per month.

While there was a "code" as early as 1946, it wasn't really enforced. Self-policing was the name of the game. Max Gaines tried to use his imprint Educational Comics (EC) to do what their name suggested—enlighten, uplift, and educate the young readers. Among his work were titles like "Picture Stories from the Bible." After Max Gaines died in a boating accident in 1947, his son Bill took over EC. Bill Gaines began a series of horror and science fiction titles. By 1952, he'd turned a profit with popular titles like *The Crypt of Terror* and *The Vault of Horror*. The graphically drawn stories tackled controversial topics like race, anti-Semitism, and war. Teen readers flocked to EC. By 1953, three of their titles sold 400,000 per month; others sold upwards of 250,000.

Ladies Home Journal was compelled to address the scandal of EC's themes and pictures, excerpting Frederic Wertham's *Seduction of the Innocent* in their November 1953 issue. Wertham, director of mental hygiene at Bellevue Hospital, had spent seven years researching the book, and he concluded that comic books had a deleterious impact on young minds, leading to crime and degeneracy. They were, he wrote in the *Saturday Review*, "the marijuana of the nursery," and he cited a 50 percent rise in the juvenile crime rate as proof of his pudding. He also charged that Superman was a symbol of "violent race superiority," Batman and Robin were "a wish dream of two homosexuals living together," and Wonder Woman was a lesbian. As a result of Wertham's book, EC was decried by angry parents, who staged comics-burning rallies. Gaines, with editor Al Feldstein, started a humor comic book called *Panic*, which only exacerbated their woes. *Panic* created a scandal by mocking Santa Claus and was banned in Massachusetts. In fact, the very first issue of *Panic* provided the test case for Wertham's views when EC's business manager, Lyle Stuart, was arrested for selling a copy of it to an undercover policeman. The case was later tossed out, but not before costing EC some legal fees.

Comic books were burned, Senate Judiciary hearings were convened, and venerable witnesses like Walt "Pogo" Kelly and Milton "Steve Canyon" Caniff spoke against the horror and crime genres. Gaines offered an eloquent defense of the First Amendment in his opening statement. Senator Estes Kefauver, the chairman, went through issues of Gaines's EC crime titles. The following exchange occurred:

EK: This seems to be a man with a bloody ax holding a woman's head up which has been severed from her body. Do you think that is in good taste?

BG: Yes sir, I do, for the cover of a horror comic. A cover in bad taste, for example, might be defined as holding the head a little higher so that the neck could be seen dripping blood from it and moving the body over a little further so that the neck of the body could be seen to be bloody.

EK: This is the July one. It seems to be a man with a woman in a boat and
    he is choking her to death here with a crowbar. Is that in good taste?
BG: I think so.[15]

On September 16, 1954, due mainly to Wertham's influence, a Comics Code
Authority was adopted, covering 90 percent of all comic book titles. No torture,
gore, or disrespect for authority was allowed. All comic books had to carry the
code's seal on their cover or risk not being distributed. Even though young readers were buying EC in record numbers, Gaines suspended the horror and crime
titles; the cost of private distribution and threat of lawsuits against retail outlets
were prohibitive. Even the "clean" comic book titles that EC produced (*Aces
High*, *Impact*, *Piracy*, and *Valor*) were seized by censors and had their contents
bowdlerized. The last straw occurred when the Comics Code censors objected
to the presence of a black astronaut with sweat on his forehead. The sweat was
deemed "offensive." At first, Gaines threatened to sue the code, then abandoned
it, and turned his comic books into magazines to circumvent the censors.

    Though he was nearly bankrupted from fighting the code, Gaines ultimately
got a measure of consolation. Without gore, and without the Comics Code
Authority sanction, Gaines circumvented the comic book genre by starting a
new humor title in 1952, called *Tales Calculated to Drive You Mad* (shortened
to *MAD* in 1954). Edited at first by Harvey Kurtzmann, and featuring the
work of gifted artists like Wally Wood, Will Elder, and Jack Davis, as well as
the writing of Ernie Kovacs, Orson Bean, Roger Price, and even Andy Griffith,
MAD was filled with such sophisticated satire and subtle intelligence that it
began to attract a new audience. Lyle Stuart was hired in 1953, after his own
muckraking tabloid *Exposé* had created its own share of scandal. Kurtzmann's
eclectic menu attracted loyal fans as well as competitors that tried to (less successfully) imitate its formula: *Whack*, *Unsane*, *Bughouse*, *Crazy*, *Eh!* and *Nuts*.
By 1954, *MAD* was no longer a "comic book," and thus avoided the Comics
Code Authority rules. When Kurtzmann left in 1956, Al Feldstein took over
the magazine. The only other scandals it generated were from those who were
satirized—proof that they'd hit their targets. In one landmark case, *MAD* was
sued for copyright infringement by Irving Berlin for using his songs in their
musical parody feature, "Sing Along with MAD." Judge Irving R. Kaufman
ruled against Berlin and, in his March 13, 1964, opinion, set an important
precedent for future humor publications: "We believe that parody and satire are
deserving of substantial freedom—both as entertainment and as a form of social
and literary criticism."[16] *MAD* is still in business more than half a century later.

Underground Comix Rewrite the Rules

Marvel Comics, started in 1939, was a mainstream publisher that produced
predictably plotted comic books until 1961, when a young street-smart

publisher named Stan Lee launched two new titles (with artwork by Jack Kirby) that found a ready audience: *The Fantastic Four* and *Amazing Adventures*. While continuing to adhere to the Comics Code rule that good must prevail over evil, Lee allowed artists and writers to mine their imaginations for new twists on old formulas. New "super-hero" characters appeared, as complex and troubled as their times, including Spider-Man, Hulk, Silver Surfer, and Thor. Rather than pander to the old audience of adolescent boys, these comic books clicked with college students. A 1965 *Esquire* article proclaimed Spider-Man to be more popular among radicals than Che Guevera, the charismatic Latin American revolutionary. As a result, Marvel came under tighter scrutiny from the censors. (Besides the characters, a dramatic change was evident in Marvel artwork. To circumvent any scandal that might accrue from themes like sex and drugs and the continued censorious campaign of Frederic Wertham, the artists turned their rebellion on to the graphics themselves. Panels were expanded, graphics and ink overlapped into kaleidoscopic patterns, and landscapes were more otherworldly than they'd been since the glory days of George Herriman's *Krazy Kat* comic strip, a masterfully surrealistic cat and mouse saga that ran from 1914 to 1944. The greatest of the envelope-pushing comic book artistry could be found in *Strange Tales*, starring Dr. Strange, beginning around the tenth issue (July 1963). As depicted by artist Steve Ditko, *Strange Tales* was a visual feast, and the character of Dr. Strange was, well, unusual. "Unlike the other *Marvel* heroes," writes Les Daniels in *Comix: A History of Comic Books in America*, "he never punched anyone. Instead he cast spells and entered weird dimensions.... There can be little doubt that much of the psychedelic art that was to emerge from the West Coast two years later owed something to the vistas explored in the *Dr. Strange* pages."

Mr. Natural Cometh

The one person who tore down the wall on which the comics code sat was Robert Crumb, or "R. Crumb." Though steeped in comic book tradition, Crumb had no interest in adhering to any code of censorship. Lacking outlets for his work, he nonetheless pressed on, hanging out in the fledgling community developing in San Francisco's Haight Ashbury neighborhood in the mid-1960s. He came into contact with psychedelic drugs. The combination of hallucinatory visions and his own unmistakably eccentric graphic style led to his remarkable artistry (Robert Hughes called him "the Brueghel of the second half of the 20th century"). Other comic artists followed his lead, and "in a matter of weeks," said Crumb, an underground comix revolution was born. Among the artists who entered this new, uncharted, and unregulated territory—the "x" in comix was not just a semantic affectation—were Gilbert Shelton, creator of the *Fabulous Furry Freak Brothers* and *Wonder Warthog*; Spain Rodrigues, *Trashman*; Victor Moscoso and Rick Griffin, both of whom also made rock posters; Frank Stack, a.k.a. Foolbert Sturgeon, who flirted with sacrilege in his *Adventures of Jesus Christ* strip; and Vaughan Bode, Kim Deitch, Skip Williamson, S. Clay Wilson, Bill Griffith, and Art Spiegelman. These artists, in turn, inspired the renaissance of sophisticated comic book art we see today, ushered in by the seminal *RAW* magazine in the 1980s (created by Spiegelman), but now completely running wild and on its own speed. This entire cultural revolution occurred "underground"—that is, shops that sold these wares, and the artists who created them, were subject to obscenity laws and harassment from overzealous vice squads in cities where they were found. The work itself was seldom available at any acceptable outlets (newsstands, or book shops). Rather, they were sold on the street and in head shops and music stores, earning the art, music, and literature the term *countercultural.*

New and Gonzo Journalism

The 1960s underground press spawned a new type of engaged journalism that one of its practitioners, Tom Wolfe, famously dubbed "new journalism." The *Wall Street Journal*, in a review of Wolfe's work, defined new journalism as "a style incorporating slang and contemporary speech patterns, stream of consciousness and abrupt switches in perspective ... he was free to select from the novelist's whole bag of tricks." Wolfe helpfully delineated the four elements of new journalism as: (1) Tell the story through scenes rather than traditional techniques; (2) Give the full flood and flavor of conversation, including accents and speech patterns; (3) First-person writing is encouraged; (4) Present as many details of every setting, to put the scene in cultural or social context.

Predictably, this new style raised hackles within the profession and for those about whom new journalism stories were written. For one thing, the style blurred the line between fact and fancy, leaving readers to determine these essentials of journalism for themselves. And, for another, most journalists did not (still do not) have the talent that Wolfe possessed. Thus, the style unleashed a deluge of imitators who were big on style but lacking in content. In fact, the best practitioners of the style were also novelists, like Truman Capote (whose novelistic "true account" *In Cold Blood* was a pioneering effort), Norman Mailer (whose account of an antiwar march in Washington, D.C., *Armies of the Night*, was arguably the finest example of new journalism), Joan Didion, and Terry Southern. Some of the mainstream journalists who switched to this style were Gay Talese, music critics Lester Bangs, Richard Meltzer, and Nick Tosches, and George Plimpton, who brought new meaning to the term "participatory journalism" in books like *Out of Their League* and *Paper Lion*. The scandal arose not from the style's readability, but from its reliability. The writers were entertaining, but were they telling the truth?

Arguably, the new journalist who pushed the boundaries furthest was Hunter S. Thompson. His work went so far into the realm of participation and sensory derangement that a new term was required: *Gonzo journalism*. Kurt Vonnegut called Thompson "the most creatively crazy and vulnerable of the New Journalists. His ideas are brilliant and honorable and valuable ... the literary equivalent of Cubism: all rules are broken." Thompson began his career as a traditional print journalist after a stint in the U.S. Air Force. His first published work, *Hell's Angels*, sparked a scandal as it purported to have infiltrated the infamous motorcycle gang, eventually earning the author a severe beating at their hands. After this, he dove into the burgeoning counter-culture, becoming inextricably linked to *Rolling Stone* magazine, where (with Ralph Steadman's brilliant artwork) his "gonzo" style thrived. His best work was his political reportage, collected in several volumes, most notably, *Fear and Loathing on the Campaign Trail*.

ALL THE NEWS THAT'S FIT TO FAKE

In the past two decades, some top names in print journalism—the *Washington Post, New York Times, Boston Globe, USA Today, New Republic*—have been rocked by scandals involving members of their own staffs or contributing writers. Though each instance was unique, they had some common elements. One, the writers made stuff up—quotes, sources, events, and credentials. Two, the fabrications were chronic and went undiscovered until damage was done. Three, the writers had good reputations. Four, the publications' reputations were damaged, while the writers went on to other pursuits.

The first blow was to the *Washington Post* in 1980, which was still basking in the glory of its Watergate coverage that hounded a president from office and vaulted reporters Bob Woodward and Carl Bernstein into national prominence. That year, a young reporter named Janet Cooke joined the *Post* staff. Her resume was impressive (Vassar graduate, Sorbonne student, prize-winning journalist). On September 29, 1980, the *Post* published Cooke's article, "Jimmy's World," which depicted the life of an eight-year-old heroin addict in Washington, D.C. The Dickens-like tale of the child's existence moved readers and prompted city officials to locate and help "Jimmy." The problem: "Jimmy" didn't exist. Cooke had cooked him up. Though suspicions were raised, the *Post* defended the story and even nominated it for the Pulitzer Prize, which Cooke won the following spring. The Pulitzer brought new scrutiny to the story and Cooke. It turned out that even her resume was fake. She confessed to all the deception and resigned from the *Post*, and the Pulitzer Prize was rescinded. Even after the scandal, Bob Woodward, at the time the *Post*'s assistant managing editor, claimed, "The decision to nominate the story for a Pulitzer is of minimal consequence. I also think that it won is of little consequence. It is a brilliant story—fake and fraud that it is." Such remorseless defiance did not help the *Post* in the court of public opinion.

Double Trouble at the *Globe*

The *Boston Globe* received a one-two punch in 1998 when two columnists were discovered to have been fabricating their work for years. The first was Patricia Smith, a poet and playwright hired by the *Globe* as a columnist in 1991. By 1994, Smith's column ran twice weekly, but suspicions surfaced when readers questioned the existence of some of her sources. By the time editors began to look into the matter, fifty-two of Smith's columns had raised questions of accuracy. It turned out that Smith regularly invented people, places, events, and even quotations in her human-interest columns. However, *Globe* editors were reluctant to confront her with the allegations, because similar allegations had been made about the *Globe*'s more popular and longer-running columnist, Mike Barnicle. If Smith were fired and Barnicle allowed to stay, the backlash would be furious (Smith was a black woman and Barnicle was a white man). When confronted with the fabrications in 1998, Smith admitted to only four instances; the *Globe* asked for her resignation. Since that time, Smith has become a college instructor, writing workshop leader, and biographer.

More damaging to the paper was the departure of Barnicle, the columnist whose truth-shading dated to 1973. He was successfully sued for libel in 1981 by a merchant to whom Barnicle attributed racist remarks that the man never said. Harvard law professor Alan Dershowitz sued the *Globe* in 1990 over disparaging remarks about Asian women that Barnicle attributed to him, and which he claimed he never said. Famed Chicago columnist Mike Royko accused Barnicle of copying his columns, though he never pressed charges. Royko told the *Washington Post*, "A guy who only works three days a week ought to come up with his own ideas." Barnicle's reign of error came to a head with a column published on August 2, 1998, in which he took material from George Carlin's book *Brain Droppings* and printed them as his own. When confronted, Barnicle claimed to have never seen *Brain Droppings*, though he'd been a guest on a TV show weeks earlier touting the book. The *Globe* asked for his resignation; Barnicle refused. Still, the *Globe* kept him on staff, but suspended him for two months. In the interim, more charges surfaced about his fabrication and plagiarism in past columns, some of which had resulted in lawsuits that were settled out of court. As Tom Mashberg, a former *Globe* colleague, wrote, "Barnicle Mike the Piper, we called him—that rich feller whose quotes and characters seem a little too good to be true, and who gives the impression he's done his reporting in person when he's in fact done it by phone, if at all." Despite the fall from grace, Barnicle soon found work at the *New York Daily News* as a radio and television commentator and business consultant. His return to grace was apparently so triumphant that Barnicle was hired to take over Don Imus's radio show after the latter was suspended for racist remarks in April 2007. (*See also* "Don Imus Is in Mourning.") Imus's show was later canceled, and Barnicle returned to his other lucrative gigs.

The Old Gray Lady Sings the Blues

The biggest "fake news" scandals of recent years involved the *New York Times*, a newspaper so venerated it earned the respectful nickname "The Old Gray Lady." However, two separate scandals tarred that reputation. The first involved a Taiwanese-born U.S. citizen named Wen Ho Lee. Lee was a respected scientist at the Los Alamos National Laboratory until the *Times* published a story in March 1999 that accused him of stealing atomic secrets for the Chinese government. The accusations, contained in stories by the *Times* (followed up with stories by the *Washington Post, Los Angeles Times,* Associated Press, and ABC News), were eventually proven to be without merit. However, Lee spent months in prison awaiting the trial that exonerated him. The *Times* never offered a retraction or correction of the stories, nor did they offer Lee an apology. Lee did, however, receive $1.6 million from the federal government and the aforementioned media venues to settle his lawsuit over the violation of his privacy.

The second scandal involved *Times* reporter Jayson Blair. This one would rock the *Times* newsroom like no other scandal before it, leading to the resignation of top executives, including executive editor Howell Raines, who'd championed the young reporter. Blair came to the paper as a college intern in 1998, and was hired as an intermediate reporter in 1999 and then a full-time staff reporter in January 2001. Despite concerns about Blair's sloppy reporting by his Metro section editors, Blair was promoted the next year to the national desk, where his problems resurfaced when he was assigned to the "Beltway sniper" story. During the weeks that the Washington, D.C., suburbs were terrorized by snipers, Blair filed more than fifty stories. Many of them contained glaring errors and misquotes, and complaints about his work were regularly filed with *Times* editors. Nonetheless, Blair was kept on the beat. However, the ample warnings about Blair were proven true in April 2003, when he was caught plagiarizing large chunks of a story by Macarena Hernandez of the *San Antonio Express-News*. Blair resigned from the *Times* on May 2, 2003. An investigation of the nearly 600 articles he had written for the *Times* discovered many that were "suspect." Specifically, thirty-six of the seventy-three stories he wrote on the national desk contained fabrications and plagiarisms. Also, he filed many stories from out of town, though he seldom left New York. Hoping to forestall further disgrace, the *Times* ran a front-page confession of Blair's "long trail of deception" and referred to it as "a low point in the 152-year history of the newspaper." In a book published the following year, Blair—who is black—blamed racism, drugs, and "bipolar disorder" for his mistakes. Blair implied that he wasn't the only reporter who did what he did, which only further shamed the *Times*, even if it too was a lie. Blair wrote, "I lied about where I had been, I lied about where I found information, I lied about how I wrote the story. And these were no everyday little white lies—they were complete fantasies, embellished down to the tiniest made-up detail ... In the end-justifies-the-means environment I worked in, I had grown accustomed to lying."[17] Blair founded Azure Entertainment in 2003 to "handle a number of publishing projects."

USA Today Low-Jacked

Just weeks after the *New York Times* was rocked by the Jayson Blair scandal, *USA Today* began investigating one of its star reporters, five-time Pulitzer nominee Jack Kelley. Kelley, a foreign correspondent who'd been with the national daily since it was founded in 1982, was accused of embellishing his stories to make them more compelling. As *USA Today* reporter Blake Morrison noted, "Kelley had drawn the enmity of some staffers. His incredible stories from abroad were just that, some groused; not credible. And almost impossible to verify—at least without substantial effort." Indeed, all efforts by an in-house panel to verify some of the more "incredible" of the stories proved impossible; his most famous stories—about a Jerusalem suicide bombing and the drowning of Cuban refugees—turned out to be total fabrications. Of the 720 Kelley-written stories the panel examined, they found that "Kelley fabricated substantial portions of at least eight major stories, lifted nearly two dozen quotes or other material from competing publications, lied in speeches he gave for the newspaper and conspired to mislead those investigating his work." Several other stories raised serious doubts, as well, and Kelley was forced to resign in January 2004. Like the *Times* after the Blair scandal, *USA Today* fired two top executives, printed a front-page apology to its readers, and had its growing reputation for excellence severely harmed.[18]

The Greene-ing of Scandal

Bob Greene had been a popular columnist for the *Chicago Tribune* for twenty-four years when a sex scandal forced his resignation in 2002. The scandal grew out of a column he'd written about a female high school student who had come to interview him at the *Tribune* in 1988. Greene, married with two children, later met the young woman for dinner and then seduced her in a motel room. The indiscretion came to light fourteen years later, and unleashed other unconfirmed instances of similar behavior on his part. Chicago columnist Neil Steinberg told CNN that Greene had been "famous for using his position as a columnist ... to try to get women into bed." The scandal divided the profession, with many journalists insisting that an adult's private life, no matter how tawdry, should have no impact on his employment. Others said that Greene had abused the power of his employment to woo the young woman, and perhaps other young women, under false pretenses. The latter position was the one taken by Greene's employers at the *Tribune*.

Embedded Journalists, or Journalists in Bed?

Armstrong Williams was a syndicated newspaper columnist and TV show host whose opinions were eerily similar to the policies of the Bush White House in 2005—too similar. *USA Today* revealed that Williams had received payments indirectly from the White House to tout Bush administration initiatives. Specifically, he was paid $240,000 by the Department of Education to promote Bush's "No Child Left Behind" policy, widely decried by public school officials and teachers.[19] Williams defended himself by insisting that he never took a position on an issue that he didn't personally believe. And yet, prior to receiving this payoff, he had been a vocal critic of "No Child Left Behind." The scandal did not arise over the fact that writers or broadcasters were paid to take positions; it was the fact that Williams was paid to take the positions with public funds. Taxpayer money cannot legally be used for partisan political, or government propagandistic, purposes. The Tribune New Service dropped Williams's column from its syndication. Soon thereafter, columnists Maggie Gallagher and Michael McManus were also discovered to be receiving public funds to promote Bush policies.

Sports Is Serious Business

Some Americans take sports more seriously than they do politics and even religion. Thus, for newspapers to appear to be partisan, to take sides or judge sports opponents, in their coverage has led to canceled subscriptions, angry phone calls to editors, and, sometimes, much worse. In 1989, in Kentucky, for example, the *Lexington Herald-Leader* ran an expose of the University of Kentucky men's basketball team, members of which were reportedly receiving cash from boosters of the team, a violation of NCAA rules. After the story ran, reporters Michael York and Jeffrey Marx received death threats. The local radio and television stations (including an ABC affiliate) piled on the newspaper, criticizing it for "sensationalism." The reporters later received the Pulitzer Prize for investigative reporting. Similarly, in Arizona, the *Arizona Daily Star* in Phoenix ran an expose of the University of Arizona football program, which led to a backlash from "business leaders, wealthy alumni, the president of the university and other prominent citizens." Advertisers boycotted the paper and the editor's family was threatened. The reporters won a Pulitzer Prize.

Not all newspapers are as responsible as the *Herald-Leader* and the *Daily Star*. Tom Osborne, head coach of the University of Nebraska football team, learned about a story that the *Omaha World-Herald* planned to publish about law-breaking by some of his players. He confronted the editors, telling them that the article would hurt the university's sports programs. The newspaper did not run the story. That, in itself, was a scandal, though it has likely happened more often than the few occasions when newspapers break scandalous news about popular sports programs.

SCANDALS FOUND AT THE GROCERY STORE

Tabloids filled with scandals are now a staple of the grocery store checkout counter and many other places. Though now plentiful, scandal tabs are a relatively recent development in print journalism. They grew out of the aforementioned penny-and-nickel press. The publication that created the biggest sensation was a magazine called *Confidential*.

Confidential Magazine: The Real School for Scandal

Gossip correspondent Jeannette Walls has estimated that 400 full-time reporters plied their trade on the Hollywood beat by the 1950s. Not all were newspaper gossip columnists like Walter Winchell, Hedda Hopper, and Louella Parsons, though this trio paved the way for the deluge of scandal. Many reporters came at the behest of celebrity magazines, a publishing subgenre that grew exponentially after World War II. These publications were not bastions of good journalism; critics referred to them as "the gutter press" because the reporters sniffed in every nook, cranny, and gutter for dirt, or were paid informants complicit in the dirt that was reported.

The "dirtiest" of the magazines was *Confidential*, begun in 1952 by publisher Robert Harrison. Harrison grew up admiring Winchell's syndicated column. Nearing the end of a long career in newspapers and radio, Winchell was now trying to break in to the relatively new field of television. When his TV career floundered over some ill-advised comments, Harrison came to Winchell's defense in *Confidential*, which was also floundering, its national circulation a paltry 150,000. Winchell, in gratitude, plugged *Confidential* on his TV gossip show, which was seen by a national audience. The raised profile helped *Confidential*. To meet the new readership demand, Harrison ratcheted up the gossip with the best dirt from Hollywood (though he lived in New York). As Walls notes, "Readers went wild for the exposes: After only five years of publication, *Confidential* was selling nearly four million copies of each issue, making it the best-selling magazine on American newsstands."[20]

What made this a true phenomenon was that the magazine did not offer subscriptions; all sales were from newsstands. Also, unlike other "reputable" magazines, *Confidential* was not printed on slick paper stock. Harrison used an economical "super newsprint," one step up from newspaper stock. This gave *Confidential* the slightly shady feel of a pulp fiction magazine, which added to its "forbidden fruit" allure. *Confidential* proved so popular that it single-handedly created its own sub-sub-genre. As Walls noted, "The scandal magazine was born."

Desperately trying to copy the success of *Confidential*, similar publications popped up like mushrooms after a summer rain: *Top Secret, Rave, Hush-Hush, Inside Story,* and *Exposed*. Harrison himself started a second scandal magazine, called *Whisper*.

Novelist James Ellroy described "scandal rags" and their era this way:

Cheezy covers. Tall print. Clashing color schemes. Jarring shades that agitated the eye. Cheap paper. Typos and misspellings. Back-page ads. X-ray glasses. Sex guides. Home law school.... The rags built the world from photo files and innuendo. Socialites. Film stars. Politicians. Jazz horns and playboys. Mobsters with crossover appeal. The celebrity matrix.... The rags were prophetic. The rags presaged the media age and the age of tabloid TV.[21]

The change in tone, from the days of idle gossip and celebrity worship, was dramatic. Stars were, Walls writes, "suddenly being exposed and ridiculed." Their bedroom habits were discussed, as were their alleged infidelities, scenes of public drunkenness, and, best of all, criminal activity. The change can be seen in the way the press handled film star Rock Hudson's homosexuality. In the past, the gossip columnists chattered about Hudson's dates with lovely actresses. Now, scandal magazines hired private investigators to chart his sexual liaisons with other men, and then bribed Hollywood executives to kill the evidence.

This publishing equivalent of extortion was bound to end in a courtroom. It did, sooner rather than later. The story that broke *Confidential*'s back was "The Real Reason for Marilyn Monroe's Divorce," which ran in the September 1955 issue. The most curious fact about the ensuing scandal over this article was that, at least in this case, Harrison published a true story—that is, Monroe and baseball star Joe DiMaggio were in the process of divorcing. Hoping to catch his estranged wife in an affair, DiMaggio, his friend Frank Sinatra, and a hired private detective broke down the door of an apartment where they thought Monroe might be, presumably consummating an affair with another man or even another woman (the apartment they sought belonged to the actress Sheila Stuart, Monroe's close friend). The problem was that the jealous trio had the wrong apartment. The one they barged into belonged to a perfect stranger, a middle-aged woman named Florence Kotz, who instantly recognized Sinatra and DiMaggio. Kotz went to the police. The police did nothing, in deference to the celebrity stature of the perpetrators of what was, essentially, a breaking and entering crime (and, if the detective was carrying a gun, it was armed robbery). *Confidential*, however, had no qualms about reporting the incident. And, though no one disputed the story, the ensuing scandal put the state of California's legal arm in motion—its target: *Confidential*. The state attorney general, Edmund "Pat" Brown, was sympathetic to the stars. By May 1957, he felt he had enough of a case to indict Harrison on a charge of "conspiracy to commit criminal libel."

Harrison hired an expensive lawyer and a team of private eyes and threatened to dish the biggest platter of dirt ever served in a Los Angeles courtroom. The fear of subpoena was rampant and most of the stars likely to be called as witnesses suddenly found commitments out of town to honor. Death threats, meanwhile, were made on *Confidential*'s staff and potential witnesses. None-theless, the trial proceeded and exploded into delicious scandal when Ronnie Quillan, Hollywood's top madame and a prostitute herself, took the stand to testify that she'd provided *Confidential* a number of hot (and accurate) tips for pay. Other witnesses included Maureen O'Hara and Dorothy Dandridge, both of whom disputed stories that appeared about them in the magazine.

"The trial was turning out to be devastating to the Hollywood image that it was intended to protect," writes Walls. Indeed, rather than kill the scandalous stories that appeared in *Confidential*, witnesses corroborated them, even going further in their description of the hedonistic whims of some of Holly-wood's biggest names. The trial lasted six weeks, and the jury still could not reach a verdict after deliberating two weeks.

Harrison, financially strapped by the trial, agreed to a plea bargain. "The Attorney General would drop the charges if *Confidential* would change its edi-torial policy and publish only flattering stories about movie stars and politi-cians," writes Walls. Further, Harrison was required to put ads in major newspapers announcing that he would "eliminate expose stories on the private lives of celebrities." The pending lawsuits against *Confidential* were dropped, except the one by Liberace, who eventually collected $40,000 for an article "suggesting he was gay." (*Confidential* had said the candelabra-loving pianist's theme song should be "Mad about the Boy.") But, without scandal in its edi-torial sauce, *Confidential* lost customers. The magazine stopped publishing within a decade, but its legacy lives on in the countless grocery store tabloids, the slick "personality" magazines, tabloid TV shows, and even Internet gossip-mongers like Matt Drudge and The Smoking Gun. (*See also* Chapter 7, "Internet Scandals.")

The plight of *Confidential* raises an issue relevant to contemporary media outlets—that is, the magazine was sued, and essentially put out of business, for reporting things that were true: that DiMaggio and Sinatra broke into a stranger's apartment, that Liberace was gay, and so forth. Were the subjects of these stories to file lawsuits today against a magazine, or a tabloid TV show, most judges would toss them out as without merit. The issue is this: Are we better or worse off today because of this? As *Saturday Night Live*'s faux gossip maven Linda Richman (portrayed in drag by Mike "Austin Powers" Myers), hostess of "Coffee Talk," would say, "Discuss amongst yourselves."

King of the Scandal Tabs

The leap from the slick monthly *Confidential* to weekly publications like the *National Enquirer*—a hybrid of newspaper tabloid and celebrity maga-zine—was short, easy, and as natural as the proverbial slippery slope. Indeed, the only real difference was that they cost less at the newsstand, published more often, and were printed on the cheapest paper stock available, newsprint.

The man responsible for the *National Enquirer* was Generoso "Gene" Pope Jr., son of a prominent Italian-American media mogul. Because of his father's success, young Gene grew up in Manhattan's most exclusive social circles, and attended private school with Roy Cohn, later Senator Joe McCarthy's chief counsel. In 1950, at age twenty, Pope inherited the family media empire when his father suddenly died. Young Gene had, however, become friends with members of the Mob in the interim, and the rest of his family severed ties with him. In 1952, with loans from Cohn and Frank Costello—the Mafia boss whom he called "Uncle Frank"—Pope bought the *New York Enquirer*, a failing Sunday afternoon tabloid that was started in 1926. With his connections in government (through Cohn) and in the Mob (through Costello), Pope was privy to some of the most salacious stories of his time. The selling point was scandal, and scandal sold; the *New York Enquirer*'s circulation rose from 17,000 to 250,000 within five years. All sales were in the New York City area.

In 1957, Pope hired Carl Grothman to be editor, the paper's stories became more macabre, and circulation continued to rise. Emboldened by his newsstand sales, as well as the simultaneous success of *Confidential*, Pope distributed his scandal sheet nationwide, giving it a new, soon to be household, name: *National Enquirer*. Craving respect, even while putting out a magazine that ran photographs of mutilated corpses and headlines like "Mom Uses Son's Face as Ashtray," Pope added feel-good stories about ordinary people and celebrities to the mix. As a result, women began buying the *National Enquirer*. The circulation skyrocketed, leaving all of the competition and imitators far behind. But as the number of newsstands in the U.S. declined—the sole distribution point for scandal tabloids, which did not have subscribers—Pope sought other outlets for the *National Enquirer*. By 1969, after Pope had sufficiently cleaned up the content of his publication, fourteen of the nation's largest grocery store chains agreed to place the *National Enquirer* in racks beside the checkout counters. The grocery store tabloid was born.[22]

In 1971, Pope moved his operation from New York to Lantana, Florida, and the paper's circulation rose to 3 million by 1975. The scandal that pushed his circulation worldwide took place in July 1975, when *Enquirer* reporter Jay Gourley was detained in Washington, D.C., outside Secretary of State Henry Kissinger's residence. Gourley had removed garbage bags from the curb and put them in the trunk of his car. After an interview with the Secret Service, Gourley was allowed to leave with the bags because he had broken no federal laws. He found Secret Service documents in the bags. When Kissinger insisted that his privacy had been violated, Pope carried a story in the next issue headlined, "Secret Service Admits: Confidential Documents That *Enquirer* Found in Kissinger's Trash Was a Breach of Security." Advantage *National Enquirer*. Kissinger did not return the serve.

The *National Enquirer* was staffed mostly by well-compensated British, Scottish, and Australian reporters who had cut their teeth in the competitive tabloid industry on London's Fleet Street, traditional home of the British press offices. They also engaged in the controversial practice of paying sources for news tips. On one occasion they staged an alien landing in Texas, outfitting a reporter as a Martian. The reporter was nearly killed; the story never ran. Nonetheless, the freewheeling approach worked. By 1978, circulation hit 5.7 million.[23]

The *National Enquirer's* biggest self-generated scandal involved actress Carol Burnett. It stemmed from a small news item that appeared in the March 2, 1976, issue, claiming that a "boisterous" Burnett had argued with Henry Kissinger at a Washington, D.C., restaurant, then "traipsed around the place." She was said to have "knocked a glass of wine over one diner and started giggling instead of apologizing." Burnett was outraged by being depicted as "being drunk … rude … uncaring … and physically abusive." She had, for years, been a spokesperson for efforts to help alcoholics; both of her parents had died of the disease by age forty-six. Burnett filed a $10 million libel suit against the *Enquirer* and spent $200,000 on legal fees over the next five years. Hers was the first lawsuit against a modern tabloid that made it to a courtroom, and Hollywood waited anxiously for the verdict. Many stars rallied to Burnett's cause, including Johnny Carson, who'd been the subject of many unflattering articles in the scandal press. He denounced the *Enquirer* on the *Tonight Show* for an article about his rocky marriage (though the story was true). Because two of the Burnett jurors had seen the Carson show, the judge nearly declared a mistrial.

Burnett won the suit, and was awarded $1.6 million in damages. The tabloid magazine industry was effectively put on notice. A rash of lawsuits against the *Enquirer* followed. All were either dismissed or fell apart under the weight of events (Carson and his wife did separate; Senator John Warner and Elizabeth Taylor did divorce), and even the award the jury gave Burnett was reduced by an appeals judge.

Nonetheless, after losing the suit to Burnett in 1981, Pope set up a twenty-six-person fact-checking unit. While the tabloid's focus didn't change, the circulation dropped as competitors pushed the envelope to fill the void left by the *Enquirer's* softer approach. Pope died in 1988, and, ironically, by 1994, with the number of scoops the *National Enquirer* managed to unearth in the O. J. Simpson case, the formerly maligned tabloid earned the grudging respect of the *New York Times* and *Columbia Journalism Review*. Once the Simpson trial began, however, the *National Enquirer's* circulation plummeted. Curious readers no longer needed to buy scandal at the grocery store when they got it for free 24/7 on TV.

Pushing the Tabloid Envelope

If the sincerest form of flattery is imitation, *National Enquirer* had many admirers. The novelist Robert Stone began his career working for Countrywide

Publications in New York, a chain that published nearly identical imitations of more successful competitors like the *Enquirer*, including *National Mirror*, for which Stone worked. The idea, he said, "was to try to confuse a distracted and overstimulated public into buying its periodicals by mistake." The emphasis at the *Mirror* was on what Stone called "the freakishly improbable."

Unlike the *Enquirer*, which at least stuck with actual events, the imitators' enterprises were built on fiction. Their ruses included doctored photographs, fake articles that were impossible to verify, gruesome headlines, and often false names for the places where the grim events were alleged to have taken place. For example, Stone wrote a story for the *Mirror* based on nothing more than a doctored photograph from a vampire movie. The art department, trying to blot out the fangs, spilled ink on it. Up against deadline, Stone wrote a story around the resulting "photograph," with the headline "MAD DENTIST REMOVES GIRL'S TONGUE." This served as the cover of the June 16, 1965, edition of the *National Mirror*. Nothing in the story was true. Surprisingly, no readers filed suit against Stone's magazine or any of the other similar tabloids for false reporting; they had perhaps accepted the stories as false and simply enjoyed the relatively inexpensive titillation.

National Enquirer's closest competitor was the *Globe,* founded in 1954 by Joe Azaria. For years, the *Globe*'s circulation was one-third to one-fifth the *Enquirer*'s. The O. J. Simpson case changed that. The *Globe* was willing to go even deeper into the gutter than the Enquirer to get titillating, if implausible, stories, some barely connected to Simpson or the case. The *Globe*'s perspective was also unique; the tabloid insisted Simpson was innocent of the murders of his wife and Ronald Goldman. "WORLD EXCLUSIVE: O. J. WAS FRAMED" claimed one headline. Furthermore, the *Globe* offered $1 million to any person who produced evidence of Simpson's innocence. Close to 200,000 *Globe* readers offered tips about the "real killer." Circulation doubled, to 1.4 million. "It was marketing genius," wrote Walls, "and a journalistic travesty."[24]

The *Globe* was soon embroiled in another big scandal when the paper hired a prostitute to entrap Frank Gifford, in order to report "FRANK CAUGHT CHEATING ON KATHIE LEE WITH BLOND!" Later, the prostitute, Suzen Johnson, admitted to other reporters that she'd been paid $250,000 to approach Gifford. The Giffords never sued the tabloid, though had they done so it's likely the verdict would have awarded them a cash settlement exceeding Carol Burnett's.

One tabloid that stooped lower than the *Globe* was *News Extra*, which had been sued by Rod Stewart for reporting that he was cheating on his wife and by Sylvester Stallone for reporting that he'd been rendered impotent by steroids and had a penile implant. In the wake of these unresolved suits, a desperate *News Extra* ran a story on March 24, 1992, suggesting that Oprah Winfrey's fiancé Stedman Graham had had gay sex with his cousin. Winfrey and Graham sued for $300 million, after having discovered that *News Extra* never even interviewed the cousin and had, in fact, used notes pilfered from the files of the *Globe*. *News Extra* ceased publishing and its publisher never showed up for the trial.[25]

O. J. Simpson: The Tipping Point

The O. J. Simpson saga, which began in 1994 and has continued ever since, was not a media scandal per se. After all, it involved a celebrity accused of murdering his wife and his wife's friend, and the media had no hand in the events, other than as a news outlet to cover them. However, the Simpson story was what might be called a media tipping point. According to Jeannette Walls, it changed "the very nature of the American media." As a result, "tabloid values, tabloid techniques, and tabloid standards would become the values, techniques, and standards accepted by the mainstream media."[26] From the start, with Simpson's flight from justice in his Ford Bronco, seen by 93 million viewers in the United States on live television, the nation was hooked.

Indeed, like an addict, the nation collectively needed its daily fix of the Simpson saga. America's media outlets went into overdrive to provide the fix. One of the many practices that came under fire during the Simpson saga was the paying of sources. *National Enquirer* paid more than $150,000 for various Simpson-related scoops. However, since the *Enquirer* was known for this practice, it caused no scandal. The real scandal was the more than 1,000 journalists from around the world who went to Los Angeles to cover the murder trial; most were television news personnel. The juggernaut of cable television, catapulted into prominence by the Simpson case, was strangling the tabloid print media. Some telling statistics: *National Enquirer*'s circulation dropped from 3.15 million in 1994 to 2.7 million in 1995; revenue dipped from $80.3 million to $73.5 million. The void was picked up by the three major TV network news programs, which ran 1,392 stories on Simpson in 1995, compared to the war in Bosnia, which warranted only 762 stories. CNN's ratings rose 600 percent in just a few months. Cable television was the new home of scandal.[27]

Death of a Princess

Princess Diana's gruesome death on August 31, 1997, and the worldwide outpouring of grief leading up to her funeral, was the ultimate event in tabloid sensationalism. For days, all other stories, in any media outlet (television, radio, or newspapers), were shunted aside by the collective wallowing in the unfolding scandal. Prior to her death, the scandal revolved around trysts with Dodi Al Fayed, playboy son of Mohammed Al Fayed, owner of Harrods department store in London and several luxury hotels, and nephew to Adnan Kashoggi, the shady Saudi arms dealer. Dodi's father had often referred to his son as "useless" and despaired at underwriting his costly lifestyle. And, despite her posthumous image as the inviolable "people's princess," Diana had a hand in the media scandal over her trysts, as she cavorted with Dodi on his yacht and a St. Tropez beach in full view of the paparazzi. On the night of her death, she had earlier briefed the press on her plans to visit the Ritz in Paris, which explains why a floating contingent of them appeared when she and Dodi exited to take their fateful drive. She had essentially asked them to be there.

However, Diana's death was blamed on the press. The pack of paparazzi that gave chase on scooters was said by Diana's brother, Charles Spencer, to "have blood on their hands." No matter how many facts came out about how intoxicated the driver was, how heedless and reckless was his driving, how intimately choreographed this whole media charade had been by Diana herself—and, eventually, how the paparazzi on the scooters were shown to have had no role in the fatal crash—the tabloid press was blamed for her death. Elizabeth Taylor went on *60 Minutes* the night after Diana's death to say, "The world's princess was killed by the greed of the paparazzi."[28]

The irony, in hindsight, is obvious. The so-called mainstream media (read: non-paparazzi) roundly denounced the feeding frenzy of the tabloid press. Even while covering Diana's death and funeral around the clock and reexamining every aspect of her public and private life—especially her love life—the commentators bitterly complained about how "celebrity culture" had killed the princess. Barbara Walters, the queen of tabloid television, told ABC viewers that Diana was "a friend"—a "friendship" based on a single lunch date. *People* magazine—which had put Diana on its cover forty-three times, by far the most of any other person—high-handedly opined, the week after her death, "We work hard to avoid buying pictures taken by so called stalkarazzi photographers who menace their subjects, trespass or operate under false pretenses." Walls noted that this was not true, citing numerous occasions when *People* paid for paparazzi photographs.

As Walls also noted, Diana's death inspired other similarly-hounded celebrities, like Tom Cruise, Donald Trump, Madonna, Stallone, and Michael Jackson, to denounce the tabloids. Even O. J. Simpson went on the record, saying, "I, like Princess Diana, have been hounded by the press. It has gone too far."[29] After Diana's death, the ailing *National Enquirer* and *Globe* were sold.

While the relentless and aggressive pursuit by European paparazzi was initially blamed for the death of Princess Diana—in fact, seven people were arrested and questioned by police after the fatal crash in Paris in August 1997, though none were convicted of any crimes—the profession has also found a home in the United States. Celebrities, particularly troubled ones like Anna Nicole Smith, Lindsay Lohan, Robert Downey Jr., John F. Kennedy Jr., Bobby Brown, and Britney Spears, have been shadowed by veritable armies of videographers and photographers, who then sell their images to press outlets that crave them. Often these press agents stake out celebrity neighborhoods in hopes of catching a celebrity off guard.

Britney Spears is surrounded by Los Angeles police officers, as a throng of media tries to photograph her leaving a Los Angeles court after a hearing to work out custody arrangements with her ex-husband Kevin Federline for their two young sons on October 26, 2007. AP Photo/Kevork Djansezian, file.

Many victims of this sort of media attention have likened such invasions of their privacy to stalking, which is a crime. When this attention crosses that thin line—after all, many of these same celebrities court the attention of the press hordes—the police have had to utilize antiloitering ordinances and traffic laws to clear areas where paparazzi have gone too far. Britney Spears is a case in point. Following her January 2008 hospitalization at Cedars-Sinai Medical Center, Los Angeles police cracked down on the paparazzi, arresting four photographers for blocking the sidewalks outside of the hospital and the salon where Spears had famously shaved her head. Prior to Spears's hospitalization, four other paparazzi were arrested for reckless driving when they nearly ran her car into a ditch while giving chase. *Atlantic Monthly*'s David Samuels claimed that a pack of thirty to forty-five paparazzi routinely pursued Spears on any given night, noting, "History's best-publicized celebrity meltdown has helped fuel dozens of television shows, magazines, and Internet sites, the combined value of whose Britney-related product easily exceeds $100 million a year." However, Samuels also indicated that Spears had courted this pack of photographers as a means to maintain a high celebrity profile.[30] Most of the photographers cited by Samuels worked for the paparazzi agency X17, but other large agencies include JFX, Hollywood.tv, and Finalpixx. Members of these groups often parked along Mulholland Drive near Spears's neighborhood, and then, upon sighting her, pursued the star at high rates of speed through the area's winding backstreets. Two members of this group, according to the Associated Press, made $100,000 per year just from selling their photographs of Britney Spears.[31]

Ravaging JonBenet

The unsolved murder of six-year-old JonBenet Ramsey was not so much media scandal as media madness. The known facts were that on December 26, 1996, the young girl's dead body was found in the basement of her family's home in Boulder, Colorado, eight hours after she was reported missing. A ransom note was allegedly found at the scene; *Vanity Fair* and *Newsweek* magazines published the note in September 1997. On October 13, 1999, the grand jury investigating the crime decided—nearly three years after the murder—that no indictments would be served. Despite the sparse amount of evidence and the silence of the Ramsey family, the media went into a feeding frenzy of fantasy, speculation, and invasion of privacy during these three years. According to *Brill's Content*, nine major network TV shows aired 438 hours of programming devoted to the case; Geraldo Rivera, alone, devoted another 195 segments to it on two different shows. On his nationally syndicated *Geraldo Rivera Show*, the host staged a "mock trial" of John and Patsy Ramsey for the murder of their daughter. Among the witnesses Rivera called to "prove" their guilt were the editor of a grocery store tabloid, a gossip columnist, and a former Miss America.

Compared to the television frenzy, the grocery store tabloids showed relative restraint, with only the *Globe* publishing more than one hundred stories. Mainstream magazines like *Time* and *Newsweek* ran thirty and twenty-five stories, respectively. Local TV "reporters" staked out the Ramsey home, and authors descended on Boulder to cobble together a number of instant books filled with all manner of dubious speculation. One enterprising reporter, Lawrence Schiller, noted that *Brill's Content* "parlayed the story into a big-media trifecta: a book deal, a movie deal, and a contract with NBC News."[32] When a journalist for the *Rocky Mountain News* reported that the police report indicated that there were no footprints in the snow outside the Ramsey house and, thus, the suspect may not have been an intruder, suspicion fell on the girl's parents and even on some of their close friends.

Having apparently learned nothing from the two-year feeding frenzy of the O. J. Simpson case, local police and prosecutors failed to secure the crime scene, to stop press leaks from within its staff, or to protect the family from the voracious, and insatiable, needs of the media. Defamation lawsuits were filed by an attorney for the Ramseys against St. Martin's Press (publisher of two books about the case), Fox News Channel, American Media, Inc., the *Globe*, Court TV, and the *New York Post*. The Ramseys eventually left Boulder.

The case remains unsolved, though briefly resurfaced in August 2006 when a delusional schoolteacher living in Thailand, John Mark Karr, claimed to have murdered the little girl. After DNA tests showed no link to evidence in the case, the case against Karr was dismissed, though not before the requisite weeklong media frenzy had run its course. Karr's sudden media profile and equally sudden obscurity embodied Andy Warhol's pronouncement: "In the future, everybody will be world-famous for 15 minutes."

PRECEDENT SETTING SCANDALS: TRIAL BY THE MEDIA

The media frenzy surrounding the death of JonBenet Ramsey may seem unprecedented, but similar media "wildings"—in which persons were tried and found guilty by the media—had occurred before. One such case was at the trial for the kidnapping and murder of the son of Charles and Anne Morrow Lindbergh. On March 1, 1932, twenty-month-old Charles Jr. was snatched from his crib at the Lindbergh home in Hopewell, New Jersey. Whoever took the baby had climbed a ladder into the second-floor window of his nursery, then climbed back out. The baby was driven five miles away, killed, and buried in a shallow grave in the woods. The kidnapper then hoaxed the distraught parents into thinking the baby was alive and extracted a $50,000 ransom from them. A nationwide manhunt ensued, one of the most intense in U.S. history. The viciousness of the crime shocked the community, and the celebrity of the parents riveted the nation. Even Al Capone, from his cell in Atlanta's federal penitentiary, offered help.

No arrest was made in the Lindbergh case until September 1934, when one of the gold certificate bills from the ransom money turned up at a Bronx service station. The attendant, noting the customer's license plate in case there was trouble with the bank in depositing the bill, passed the information to police. Five days later, they arrested Bruno Richard Hauptmann, a German-American carpenter who lived with his wife and child in the Bronx. The resultant murder and kidnap trial was one of the most press-blanketed in U.S. history. In what was called "trial by newspaper," Hauptmann was convicted of first-degree murder on Valentine's Day, 1935, and executed in the electric chair on April 3, 1936, at New Jersey's state prison.

Another celebrated "trial by newspaper" took place in Ohio in 1954. On July 4, 1954, Marilyn Sheppard, the pregnant wife of a prominent Cleveland osteopath named Samuel H. Sheppard, was beaten to death in her bed while her husband was allegedly sleeping downstairs. Though Dr. Sheppard suffered neck injuries during a fight with a "bushy-haired intruder," he was charged with the crime. Before his case came to trial in October, Sheppard was at the eye of an intense media storm that raged all summer across the nation and harkened back to the Lindbergh case. Cleveland newspapers were, in particular, arrayed against Sheppard. After Sheppard was released on bond, one headline proclaimed, "Why Isn't Sam Sheppard in Jail?" and another pointed "The Finger of Suspicion" at him. The local media all but tried, convicted, and sentenced Sheppard in print long before a jury could. Sheppard's trial, from October to December 1954, played out like a national soap opera—among the trial's revelations was that he'd had a three-year affair with a nurse prior to his wife's murder. In late December, the jury found Sheppard guilty of the murder of his wife and baby. He was spared a death sentence. Sheppard, proclaiming his innocence, was released from prison in 1964, got a new trial in 1966, and was acquitted. A popular TV series, *The Fugitive*, debuted in 1963, using many aspects of the Sheppard case as the basis for the series.

No Jewel in the Media's Crown

The final case of "trial by media" involved Richard Jewell, a security guard who, on the night of July 27, 1996, discovered a pipe bomb at Atlanta's Centennial Olympic Park. Jewell helped to clear the area before the bomb went off thirteen minutes later, killing one and injuring one hundred people. Had Jewell not acted as swiftly as he did, many more would have died, as the park was packed with people attending a free concert. After being hailed as a hero, word leaked out to the press that Jewell might be a suspect in the case. The media reported the story as if Jewell had, in fact, planted the bomb. The *Atlanta Journal-Constitution* called Jewell "an individual with a bizarre employment history and aberrant personality" and said he "fit the profile of a lone bomber."[33] His house was swarmed by media and curiosity seekers, and his and his mother's lives were ruined, their possessions confiscated as "evidence" and their home under twenty-four-hour-a-day surveillance. He was a national butt of jokes, including Jay Leno's referring to him as "the Una-doofus." By October, Jewell was officially "cleared" of suspicion by the U.S. Attorney's office. Jewell then filed lawsuits against NBC News, the *Atlanta Journal-Constitution*, and the *New York Post*. He settled out of court with NBC and the *Post*. The case against the *Journal-Constitution* remained unsettled after Jewell's death, of natural causes, in August 2007. Eric Robert Rudolph, a domestic terrorist, was later convicted of planting the bomb at Centennial Park, as well as the bombing of a gay nightclub and two doctor's offices where abortions were performed.

The Rise of Rupert Murdoch

Rupert Murdoch was Australia's leading media magnate, owner of newspapers, TV stations, magazines, and record companies when he expanded his base to Great Britain in 1968, with the purchase of the *News of the World*, the widest-circulating (6 million) English language newspaper in the world. He also bought the *Sun*, transforming the daily into a popular scandal tabloid, and the *Times*. By the late 1970s, as the most powerful media owner in Australia and England, Murdoch set his eyes on the United States. He got his foot in America's door by purchasing San Antonio's daily *Express-News* in 1973, and then started his lucrative U.S. grocery store tabloid, *Star*. In 1976, he bought the *New York Post* from Dorothy Schiff. At the time, *Time* and *Newsweek* ominously proclaimed "Aussie Takes Gotham." In 1985, partly to nullify charges of being a foreign usurper and to satisfy FCC regulations that U.S. television stations could only be owned by Americans, Murdoch became a naturalized citizen.

Murdoch's chief reporter at the *Star* was Steve Dunleavy who, like Murdoch, was both Australian and an ardent conservative. Dunleavy was named city editor of the *New York Post*. Before his arrival, the *Post* had been losing $50 million a year, and its circulation had dropped to 500,000. Dunleavy turned the *Post* into a daily scandal tabloid, creating a niche in the competitive New York market with simple, sensational headlines (e.g., "Headless Body Found in Topless Bar"). With the "Son of Sam" serial murder spree, the *New York Post* soon turned a profit again. The *Post* and the *Daily News*, another daily tabloid, competed for the most sensational coverage of the growing numbers of murders in the summer of 1977. Both Dunleavy and *Daily News* columnist Jimmy Breslin addressed the killer in their pages. Dunleavy beseeched the killer to surrender personally to him. The pandering worked; *Post* circulation doubled to one million. When David Berkowitz was arrested as the Son of Sam suspect, *Post* reporters snuck into his cell to take photographs. They bought some of his letters and published them under the headline "How I Became a Mass Killer by David Berkowitz." Such a changeover at the *Post* alarmed media critics. Osborn Elliot, dean of Columbia University School of Journalism, wrote of the *Post*, "Here we enter a moral universe in which judgments are of a different order altogether ... For the *New York Post* is no longer merely a journalistic problem. It is a social problem—a force for evil."

Murdoch responded, in a speech to the American Newspaper Publishers Association, "I cannot avoid the temptation of wondering whether there is any other industry in this country which seeks to presume so completely to give the customer what he does not want." However, few of Murdoch's moves elicited quite the response of his August 2007 purchase of the *Wall Street Journal*. With that, he became America's leading media owner. With the trifecta of Australia, England, and the United States, Murdoch's is now the dominant voice in the English-speaking world. Because his conservative politics are an integral part of his media outlets, justifiable concerns were raised about his journalistic impartiality. Though the *Wall Street Journal*'s editorial page is reliably right wing, the news department is one of the most respected in the world, and one of the few with the resources to conduct thorough, international investigative reportage.

As with the wave of media takeovers in the United States over the past two decades, Murdoch's bold bid began with words of conciliation and assurances that news judgment and reportorial freedom would not be compromised. These words have seldom proven to be true in the past, as news staffs have been decimated, reporters hamstrung, and editors chastised by publishers and stockholders for tackling controversial issues. The bottom line here may not even be ideological or political—conservative versus liberal—but rather it may be the bottom line itself. Profits drive the media, above all other considerations. In such a climate, the ensuing "scandals" may swallow the media itself.

Subtle Revenge in Academia

Academia is as rife with intrigue and scandal as Hollywood or Washington, D.C., but it goes unnoticed beyond the intellectual elite circles. Nonetheless, one of the cleverest magazine hoaxes in U.S. publishing warrants a mention. The hoax was printed in the prestigious literary journal *Poetry*. The target of this elaborate ruse was the estimable Nicholas Murray Butler (1862–1947), president of Columbia University and cowinner (with Jane Addams) of the 1931 Nobel Peace Prize. Despite his fame, Butler owned the reputation of a braggart; his 1939 memoir struck many as grandstanding. Rolfe Humphries, a renowned poet and former student of Murray's, was asked to submit a work to *Poetry* soon after Butler's memoir was published. Humphries submitted an acrostic—writing that contains a hidden message—entitled "Draft Ode for a Phi Beta Kappa Occasion." *Poetry*'s editors found it to be of sufficient merit to print in their June 1939 issue. Upon first glance, the thirty-two-line poem appeared to be an accomplished work of classical influence. However, upon closer inspection, one could see that the first letter of each line spelled out a message: "Nicholas Murray Butler Is a Horse's Ass." The editors did not catch this prank. An incensed Butler let his feelings be known. *Poetry* printed a disclaimer in the August 1939 issue that read, in part, "Not being accustomed to hold manuscripts up to the mirror or to test them for cryptograms, the editors recently accepted and printed a poem containing a concealed scurrilous phrase aimed at a well-known person ... The phrase in question is puerile and uninteresting, and would not be referred to except that it is necessary to disclaim editorial responsibility."

Founded in 1912 by Harriett Monroe, *Poetry* was renowned for publishing T. S. Eliot's first major poem, "The Love Song of J. Alfred Prufrock," and as a venue for poets like Ezra Pound, Wallace Stevens, William Carlos Williams, Marianne Moore, and H. D. (Hilda Doolittle). Thus, when such a respected journal perpetrated—albeit inadvertently—a hoax, it reverberated widely through academia. The scandal did not, ultimately, hurt the magazine; it is still one of the leading literary journals in America.

Scholarly Preemptive Strike

Nearly sixty years later, another scholar pulled a similar hoax on a respected journal. The perpetrator was Allan Sokal, a New York University physics professor; the victim was *Social Text*, a leading American journal of cultural studies. Sokal's article, "Transgressing the Boundaries: Towards a Tranformative Hermeneutics of Quantum Gravity," was published in the 1996 Spring/Summer issue of *Social Text*. Sokal said he'd been "troubled by an apparent decline in the standards of intellectual rigor in certain precincts of the American academic humanities." The fake article was intended to expose this decline. It proved his point that a "leading journal" would "publish an article liberally salted with nonsense if (a) it sounded good and (b) it flattered the editors' ideological preconceptions." The article was filled so thickly with academic jargon and pseudo-intellectual prose that it's a wonder no one at the journal suspected a hoax (though many readers later caught on). On its face—that is, judging from the title alone—a perceptive reader should have suspected something amiss, as quantum physics would appear to have nothing to do with psychiatry. Sokal targeted *Social Text* because he believed it was out of touch with the reality beyond academia. Though he called himself a "leftist," Sokal attacked the journal for being a doctrinaire bastion of the "New Left," which created a "self-perpetuating academic subculture that typically ignores (or disdains) reasoned criticism from the outside." The hoax was widely discussed among academics. Some were angry at Sokal; most accepted the humbling lesson—that scholars and laymen alike are often willing to accept uncritically things that confirm political leanings or intellectual and religious beliefs and attack those who challenge such prejudices.

LANDMARK LIBEL CASES

The fear of libel lawsuits has long plagued print media. Libel is, by definition, defamation of character that is published. (When the defamation of character is spoken on radio or television, it is slander.) The libelous writings or illustrations must expose a person to shame, disgrace, or ridicule. They must harm the person's reputation, or create a financial burden by affecting their job or profession. Like the garlic bulbs that ward off vampires, however, libel suits can be deflected if the published material is the truth; if it's part of a public and official proceeding (such as a trial); and, in the case of editorialists and reviewers, if it's fair comment and criticism.

The American press was granted this leeway by one crucial legal decision: *The New York Times Inc. v. Sullivan*. The background to this U.S. Supreme Court ruling was the civil rights movement in the South. In 1963, Medgar Evers, a civil rights activist, was murdered outside his Jackson, Mississippi, home, and four girls were killed when a bomb exploded at a black church in Birmingham, Alabama. Members of the press descended on the South to cover the escalating racial tension. Footage of police dogs attacking unarmed civil rights marchers and fire hoses spraying peaceful protesters began to fill the nation's TV screens. Firsthand accounts of the violence and fear appeared in major newspapers and magazines, accompanied by photographs of black children surrounded by phalanxes of police and troops escorting them to formerly segregated schools. Though the media were depicting these events as they unfolded, white Southerners filed libel and slander lawsuits against various press outlets that, by 1964, totaled $300 million in damages. At the time, libel rulings were made on a state-by-state basis. Thus, the American media was being severely restricted in doing their job.

The *New York Times* found itself the defendant in one of the biggest libel suits, when a group of Alabama officials claimed to have been defamed by an ad that appeared in the newspaper in 1960. The ad, headlined "Heed Their Rising Voices," was intended to raise funds for civil rights activists, and it suggested that black schoolchildren were being harmed by Alabama police officers. L. B. Sullivan, a Montgomery city commissioner, was the lead plaintiff, and the judge and all-white jury ruled in his favor, awarding him $500,000 in damages. The *Times* appealed the case, which was heard by the Supreme Court in 1964. The Supreme Court ruled in favor of the *New York Times*, essentially stripping state courts of libel powers. More importantly, as Justice William J. Brennan wrote in the majority opinion, the right to criticize government is "the central meaning of the First Amendment." The ruling was no blanket immunity. Rather, Brennan wrote, "The Constitutional guarantees require a federal rule that prohibits a public official from recovering damages for a defamatory falsehood relating to his official conduct unless he proves that the state was made with actual malice—that is, with the knowledge that it was false or with reckless disregard to whether it was false or not." This case came to be known as the Times Doctrine.

Another case, *Gertz v. Robert Welch Inc.*, pushed beyond the rights assured by the Times Doctrine. The monthly magazine *American Opinion*, published by the right-wing John Birch Society, referred to a civil rights lawyer from Chicago, Elmer Gertz, as a "Communist-fronter." Gertz sued for defamation of character. While the judge said the magazine hadn't published "recklessly," the jury sided with Gertz and awarded him $50,000 in damages. *American Opinion* appealed. In 1974, the case went to the U.S. Supreme Court, which ruled that Gertz, a private citizen (not a public figure), did not have to show "actual malice" to collect damages; all he had to do was prove that the description was false and the publication was careless or negligent in running it. While this would seem to have been a victory for truth and fairness, free speech advocates saw the ruling as a tightening of First Amendment rights that had been expanded dramatically by the *New York Times Inc. v. Sullivan* ruling.

The Fix That Broke

The *Saturday Evening Post* was an American magazine icon, its prestige deriving from, among other things, 323 cover illustrations painted by Norman Rockwell between 1919 and 1963. That icon was broken in 1963 when the magazine ran a story that claimed the head football coach of the University of Alabama and University of Georgia's athletic director—Paul "Bear" Bryant and Wally Butts—conspired to "fix" their 1962 game, won by Alabama, 35–0. This score surpassed the point spread, so that those who knew ahead of time about the "fix" could bet accordingly. The corroborative evidence for the story was a phone call between the coaches alleged to have been intercepted by an Atlanta insurance salesman named George Burnett, who claimed to overhear Butts detailing all of his strategies to Bryant. The *Post*'s story was woven from this flimsy thread. Bryant and Butts sued the magazine for $10 million, winning the case, with Butts getting $460,000 and Bryant an out-of-court settlement of $300,000. The original award of $3 million in punitive damages (reduced on appeal) was the highest libel judgment ever brought against an American magazine. The case eventually went to the Supreme Court (after the *New York Times Inc. v. Sullivan* victory), but the damage to the magazine's reputation was done, and it limped along until January 1969, when it folded. Another landmark case took place in the same time frame, when the Associated Press (AP) reported that former Army general Edwin Walker had instigated a crowd of angry whites on the University of Mississippi campus to charge federal troops. The troops were sent there by President Kennedy to protect James Meredith, the first black student enrollee. Walker, who was an ardent segregationist and was on the campus with the protestors, sued the AP. He won his case in court, but lost it on appeal to the U.S. Supreme Court. The difference in the two cases was that the AP reporter was under the tight deadline of a breaking news story, whereas the *Saturday Evening Post* editors had plenty of time to check sources and facts.

Progressive Controversy

The United States government sued the left-wing magazine the *Progressive* in 1979 to prevent the monthly from running an article that explained how to build a hydrogen bomb. The article, by antiproliferation activist Howard Morland, was intended to show the ease with which such information could be obtained and, thus, call attention to the runaway "arms race" between the United States and the Soviet Union. The Department of Energy, citing the "born secret" clause of the Atomic Energy Act of 1954, claimed that revealing such information was a breach of national security and would contribute to nuclear proliferation. Much of the information in Morland's article was derived from an entry in the *Encyclopedia Americana*, found in most public school libraries. Morland also conducted follow-up interviews with nuclear engineers instrumental in building the bomb, including Edward Teller and Stan Ulam, who were not prosecuted. A preliminary draft of the article was obtained by a professor who passed it on to the U.S. Department of Energy. The government's case, *United States of America v. Progressive, Inc., Erwin*

Knoll, Samuel Day, Jr., and Howard Morland, temporarily halted the article's publication, but did not prevent it. Ultimately, the article did not explain how to build a bomb; it documented the scientific and technological processes, which were common knowledge to scientists in those countries seeking nuclear bomb capabilities.

New Republicked

The *New Republic* was once among the most respected political magazines in America. But two back-to-back scandals undercut its credibility, and its circulation saw a precipitous drop as a result. The first scandal involved Ruth Shalit, who came to the magazine with impressive credentials (*magna cum laude* Princeton, assignments for the *New York Times Magazine*). In 1995, she wrote an article for the *New Republic* about racial tension in the newsroom at the *Washington Post.* The piece was riddled with what even Shalit admitted were "major errors," and backlash from its publication led *New Republic* editors to examine her other articles. They found a pattern of plagiarism and inaccuracies; Shalit was fired. Since then, she has worked for an advertising agency and freelanced for other magazines. Stephen Glass was another young phenom (age twenty-three) when he began writing for the *New Republic* in 1996. Glass was hardworking, almost too hardworking. He filed forty-one long stories for the magazine in the two years before his fictional ruses were discovered. The prolific Glass not only fabricated quotes, characters, and sources, he was also allowed wide use of anonymous sources. The article that finally shattered Glass was his May 18, 1998, "Hack Heaven" piece about a teenage computer hacker courted as a consultant by the corporation he had once sabotaged. Though none of the basic facts of the article were true, Glass fooled his editors by creating a mock Web site and voice mail for the fake corporation. He too was fired. He has since completed law school and worked as a paralegal and comedy troupe member.

Chapter 6

BROADCAST JOURNALISM

T he arrival of radio in the 1920s and television in the late 1940s both spawned media revolutions. Commercial radio broadcasting in America had only just begun in 1920; the NBC and CBS networks were established in 1926 and 1928, respectively. Radio news and commentary was, at first, just an audio version of newspapers, with announcers reading aloud from the daily paper. But then broadcasting became something else entirely.

RADIO COMES OF AGE

The Radio Priest

Father Charles E. Coughlin set a standard for radio demagoguery that has seldom been matched. Coughlin was pastor of the Shrine of the Little Flower, a Roman Catholic Church in Royal Oak, Michigan. He was given a Sunday afternoon time slot on CBS Radio, from which he offered homilies and inspirational talks about charitable works and patriotism, delivered in a friendly avuncular voice. By the time Coughlin took to the microphone—his first program was on October 3, 1926—Americans were turning to the new medium in droves. As historian Alan Brinkley noted, "Coughlin was exploiting a system of communication whose potential conventional politicians had not yet begun to appreciate. And he was exploiting it at a time when the radio was becoming central to the lives of American families. His success, therefore, was in part simply a result of luck."[1]

Father Coughlin stuck to simple themes and everyday issues and made his remarks accessible to Americans of all faiths and denominations—unusual for a priest in a nation that retained vestiges of prejudice against Roman Catholicism. Then, on January 12, 1930, he abruptly changed the format and attacked "Bolshevism" on the air.

As the Depression began and then widened in the 1930s, Americans turned to radio for solace, news, and entertainment. In 1924, there were 3 million radio sets in the country; by 1935, there were 30 million, or three times the number of telephones. When Coughlin intensified his political rhetoric, he

The Reverend Charles E. Coughlin, a.k.a. "The Radio Priest," was the first American media demagogue. His nativist rhetoric created such a distraction to President Franklin Delano Roosevelt during a time of war preparedness that his license was revoked. Courtesy of Library of Congress, Prints and Photographs Division.

rose to prominence as the "Radio Priest." His Sunday afternoon platform was a venue for preaching politics. At his peak, Coughlin had nearly 40 million listeners; he further disseminated his views through a newspaper, *Social Justice*, which claimed a paid circulation of 1.2 million. He could, literally, make or break politicians or legislation by mobilizing his audience to write letters to Congress or march against whatever bee got stuck in his bonnet that week. Initially, his populist broadcasts were welcomed by an America beset by an intractable Depression, as he denounced "greed" and "the God of Gold," and "the concentration of wealth in the hands of a few," echoing the same vaguely socialist views of Huey Long of Louisiana.

Brinkley wrote, "[Coughlin's] solution lay in a converted effort to redefine the structure and goals of American society at home." Thus, he was a supporter of President Roosevelt's New Deal legislation, which provided a glimmer of hope for millions of hard-hit Americans. By 1936, however, Coughlin turned against Roosevelt, denounced him as a "great betrayer" and "liar," and "soft" on Communism. The priest turned isolationist, preaching against aid to Europe even as Hitler consolidated power.

It wasn't just that the subject of Coughlin's broadcasts was new; rather, it was the hostile tone of his voice and the provocative rhetoric. He regularly called the targets of his wrath "fanatics" and "scoundrels." By comparison to today's partisan airwaves, that may seem tame, but for its day this was heated invective, especially coming from a man of the cloth. Though his attacks on Roosevelt caused the president some problems, Coughlin became a serious political problem when he began expressing on the air admiration for the policies of Adolf Hitler and Benito Mussolini. In Coughlin's view, fascism was an acceptable alternative to Communism. He then began to target Jews in his commentary. He blamed Communism on the Jews and the Depression on "an international conspiracy of Jewish bankers." This echoed the views espoused in *The Protocols of the Elders of Zion*; in fact, Coughlin published excerpts from the *Protocols* in *Social Justice*. In the December 5, 1938, issue of *Social Justice*, Coughlin published an article that was adapted from a speech by Joseph Goebbels, the Nazi propaganda minister. He also blamed the Jewish victims of Kristallnacht—Nazi fomented attacks on Jewish businesses across Germany that began on November 9, 1938—for their own problems, suggesting that it was justifiable retribution for Jewish persecution of Christians.

Some CBS affiliates dropped Coughlin's broadcasts. His shrinking but fanatical fan base led protests against what they saw as violations of Coughlin's First Amendment rights. They also led protests against the proposed asylum laws, which would give Jews fleeing Hitler safe haven in the United States. Some evidence exists that Coughlin was secretly getting funds from the Nazi government. A domestic terrorist group called the Christian Front did get Coughlin's blessing. This group, the FBI discovered, had plans to "murder Jews, communists and a dozen Congressman." Coughlin refused to denounce them. In the name of national security, the Roosevelt administration took action against Coughlin. Attorney General Francis Biddle had the Post Office "suspend" the second-class mailing privileges of *Social Justice* and ordered a federal grand jury probe. They confiscated Coughlin's files, and the Department of Justice considered prosecuting the Radio Priest for sedition in a time of war. Congress also passed legislation that regulated the content of the "limited national resource" (the airwaves) and restricted broadcasting to those broadcasters who received operating permits. Coughlin was denied an operating permit.

A Voice from the Other Side

On the other side of the political spectrum, Hans von Kaltenborn was a Harvard honors graduate who presented a series of "Talks on Current Talks" at the auditorium owned by the *Brooklyn Eagle*, a daily newspaper where he worked as an editor. In 1923, these talks were broadcast on New York radio station WEAF, but his opinionated commentary upset powerful sponsors like AT&T, and he was forced out of his job. By then, he was popular enough to get jobs at bigger venues, first at another New York radio station, WOR, and then at CBS Radio. During the 1930s, Kaltenborn's interviews with Hitler and Mussolini, and live coverage from the front lines of the Spanish Civil War, riveted American listeners. CBS Radio, under pressure from critics for Kaltenborn's leftist views, fired him—even though his warnings about Hitler and Mussolini were proven true. He was hired by rival NBC Radio in 1941, and founded the Association of Radio News Analysts. He was a strong advocate for "the right of news analysts to state their opinions without using such smokescreen phrases as 'It is said …' or 'There are those who believe....'"[2] Kaltenborn's legacy, for better or worse, can be found today at any part of the radio dial.

The Radio "Hoax" That Panicked America

The most famous hoax in U.S. history occurred October 30, 1938, when a twenty-three-year-old actor named Orson Welles presented an hour-long dramatization of H. G. Wells's classic *War of the Worlds*. The adaptation was created for CBS Radio's fledgling "Mercury Theatre on the Air," which had the misfortune to be scheduled in the 8 P.M. time slot opposite the most popular radio show in the country, NBC's *Edgar Bergen and Charlie McCarthy Show*, which routinely attracted 30 million listeners. On this night, which happened to be Halloween, Bergen and his ventriloquist dummies took a break at 8:12 P.M., turning the microphone over to a guest singer for a lengthy segment. Disappointed listeners turned their dials and most ended up at CBS Radio. Thus, they tuned in Welles's dramatization in progress and missed the opening disclaimer: "CBS presents Orson Welles and the Mercury Theatre on the Air in a radio play by Howard Koch suggested by the H. G. Wells novel *The War of the Worlds*." (The show was also interrupted three times to announce that it was a presentation of Mercury Theatre of the Air.) The original novel, published in 1898 by H. G. Wells, was set in England, but events in the radio play were moved to Grover's Mill, New Jersey, a real setting (part of West Windsor Township). During the week of rehearsals prior to the live Sunday night broadcast, the Mercury crew was unhappy with the show. Biographer Simon Callow wrote, "Welles dismissed the script as 'corny,' urging Koch to break it up more and more. Paul Steward devised the sound effects and rehearsed them in careful detail; these might be spectacular enough to distract attention from the thinness of the piece. Even the technicians were unenthusiastic about the show; the secretaries denounced it as silly."

A brilliant stage actor and director fresh from acclaimed productions for the Federal Theatre Project, Welles decided to "play it for all it was worth, and then some more." This was in keeping with his envelope-pushing philosophy. When he signed with the Mercury Theatre, Welles told the press he wanted "to bring to radio the experimental techniques which have proved so successful in another medium (theater), and to treat radio with the intelligence and respect such a beautiful and powerful medium deserves." In 1938, American families owned 27.5 million radio sets. The radio was more commonplace than the telephone, car, newspapers, or magazines. It was the American family's prime medium of information about the world beyond its own towns. Callow wrote, "They were accustomed to trusting it; why should they doubt the familiar voices, describing events in their familiar manner? The nature of radio, whose unique appeal to the audiences' imagination Welles and his collaborators had so brilliantly exploited in their earlier broadcasts, made the Martian broadcast horribly convincing."

For *War of the Worlds*, this included "real"-sounding interruptions of the program for late-breaking bulletins, the panicked sound of the actors, the feigned loss of a signal, with the station replacing the program with dance music. Thus, when listeners joined the broadcast late—which is to say, most of the 6 million listeners—many mistook the program as a newscast about a real Martian invasion of New Jersey. Unlike a true hoax, however, *War of the Worlds* was not intended to deceive, but to give the listeners a sense of heightened drama, in keeping with the Halloween spirit. Nonetheless, the context for the show is what turned it into a hoax. The rise of Hitler in Germany in 1933 produced a steady drumbeat of anxiety about impending war. When fascist Italy invaded Abyssinia (now Ethiopia) in 1935, blitzing unarmed civilians by air, and the Nazis backed the fascist insurgents of General Franco in the Spanish Civil War in 1935–1937, the fears seemed justified. Americans were, said Callow, "daily reminded in the press that they alone of all Western nations had failed to devise a system of civil defense against attack from the air." Three days earlier, CBS had broadcast Archibald MacLeish's radio play, "Air Raid," about the bombing of defenseless civilian targets, based on the devastation wreaked by Nazi-backed fascists in Spain (including the obliteration of the village of Guernica, which Pablo Picasso memorialized in one of his most famous paintings).

Thus, Americans already were fearful. They turned to Sunday night radio programs to forget their worries. Rather than laughing at Bergen's dummies, they found themselves panicked by Welles. Many went to church; some lay down to die. The actual Grover's Mill was evacuated, then filled with members of the press and curiosity seekers. In Times Square, the message was broadcast, "Orson Welles Frightens the Nation." Not everyone leveled their wrath at CBS Radio or Welles. Dorothy Thompson wrote in her *New York Tribune* column, "Far from blaming Mr. Orson Welles, he ought to be given a congressional medal and a national prize for having made the most amazing and important of contributions to the social sciences ... he made the scare to end all scares, the menace to end all menaces, the unreason to end unreason, the perfect demonstration that the menace is not from Mars but from the theatrical demagogues."

Welles was shocked by the reaction. "His only thought as he came off the air was that he hadn't given a very good performance," wrote Callow. His "Halloween joke" backfired terribly. Legal actions were filed against CBS and Mercury, to no avail. Callow said, "Welles was praised for having his finger on the pulse of his times, and for being the conman of the century, able to make anybody believe anything. The truth is that he was more surprised than anyone at what had happened, and extremely irritated by it."[3]

Pounding on Pound

One of Kaltenborn's nemeses was Ezra Pound, the Idaho-born poet who lived as an expatriate in fascist Italy. Kaltenborn had raised Pound's ire for his relentless antifascist radio broadcasts, many of which were also heard in Europe. Pound was enamored of Mussolini, Italy's fascist leader. When World War II began, Pound began making regular broadcasts on Rome Radio. From January 1941 until July 1943, Pound offered commentary ten times each month on the "American Hour." These broadcasts were generally anti-Semitic diatribes that emboldened the Axis audience while enraging Allied soldiers. Typical of the sentiments he expressed to Italian listeners was, "The kike is all out for power. The kike and the unmitigated evil that is centered in London. And every sane act you commit is committed in homage to Mussolini and Hitler." After the war, Pound was arrested and extradited to the United States to stand trial for treason. Because he was deemed mentally incompetent to serve a long prison sentence, Pound was committed to St. Elizabeth's Hospital in Washington, D.C., until April 18, 1958, when a federal judge dismissed the indictment of treason. Pound was released in the custody of his wife. He died in Venice in 1972.

Radio in the War

Armed Services Radio was a lifeline for American troops in combat zones all over the world, broadcasting from Los Angeles. All of the programming was recorded onto "V-disks," so that the far-flung military bases would hear it over their airwaves, as if it were being broadcast live. These broadcasts were "antidotes" to the poison spewed by propagandists like Ezra Pound, Lord Haw Haw, and Tokyo Rose, among other English-speaking broadcasters working for the Axis Powers. In this manner, troops were made to feel, in regular guest Dorothy Lamour's words, "almost as if they were home." The greatest figure in radio broadcasting during the war was Edward R. Murrow, director of European programming for CBS Radio from 1938 to 1945. His regular dispatches from London were indispensable in informing Americans about the progress of the war. Broadcasting live during bombardments, he brought the war home to Americans before Pearl Harbor. During that time, he broke new ground by reporting live from inside a U.S. B-29 bomber above Germany, from a London street during the Blitz (e.g., "a man is pinned under wreckage where a broken gas main sears his arms and face"), and from occupied France. His assistant, William L. Shirer, was one of the great CBS correspondents, whose biggest coups were reporting firsthand on the annexation ("Anschluss") of Austria in March 1938, and the surrender of France from Compeigne in June 1940. Shirer resigned in December 1940, fearing he would be arrested by the Nazis as an undercover agent, and then published *Berlin Diary* in spring 1941, which offered a warning to all Americans about the dangers Nazi Germany presented, a warning heeded only after Pearl Harbor that December. Also on the staff of CBS radio were Eric Sevareid and Walter Cronkite, as well as Marvin Breckinridge Patterson, the first woman to broadcast from Europe. Sevareid, who was renowned for his erudite reportage, braved the most combat, offering firsthand dispatches from the fall of Paris, the battle for North Africa, and the London Blitz. He had a harrowing stint in China and Southeast Asia, during which time he survived an air crash in Burma that killed the copilot.

After Coughlin and Kaltenborn, the Deluge

While Father Coughlin's career came to an unceremonious end, his ability to grab large numbers of listeners did not go unnoticed by other radio personalities who adopted his provocative style but tried to avoid his mistakes. One radio voice that picked up the anti-Communist baton from Coughlin and wielded it throughout the "witch-hunting" days of the Cold War was Fulton Lewis Jr. (1903–66). Lewis, a Washington, D.C.-based conservative, hosted a nightly news roundup (from 7 to 7:15 P.M. EST) on the Mutual Radio Network that reached 16 million listeners on 500 stations. He was sued repeatedly and twice successfully for personal attacks on public figures. Among the legal actions was a $6 million libel suit filed by Drew Pearson, the respected investigative reporter. Lewis admired Senator Joe McCarthy, and his broadcasts served as a counterpoint to those by Edward R. Murrow on CBS Radio. Lewis made no pretense of embracing "social justice." He was ardently pro-business, patriotic, and anti-integration. He claimed to have received death threats and that his vacation home on Maryland's Eastern Shore was burned down by his critics, though neither claim was corroborated by police. After Senator McCarthy's fall from grace, Lewis stayed in the public eye by supporting Richard Nixon, whom he admired and whose career he facilitated in his broadcasts.

Many other radio commentators followed a similar confrontational format, but did not provoke the scandals that Coughlin regularly generated. One of the most vitriolic and entertaining was Joe Pyne, based at KLAC-AM in Los Angeles, who blazed the trail for "talk radio" during the 1950s and 1960s. Unlike Coughlin or Lewis, Pyne did not hide in his studio, make his pronouncements, and sign off. Rather, Pyne encouraged listeners to respond, and he engaged them in heated dialogue, sometimes even shouting matches. For this, his broadcast earned the nickname of an "insult show." Pyne's first show to put this format into practice was "It's Your Nickel" (a pay phone call in 1950 cost five cents); on it, he let callers vent their spleen as readily as he vented his. If things got too heated, he cut the caller off with quips like "Go gargle with razor blades." He told one caller, "Take your false teeth out, put them in backwards and bite yourself in the neck." Pyne's radio persona translated well to television, and by 1954 he had his own TV show in Wilmington, Delaware, *The Joe Pyne Show*. He moved the show to Los Angeles and simultaneously hosted it as a TV and radio program in 1957 (beating Don Imus in this regard by forty years). In 1965, *The Joe Pyne Show* was syndicated nationally. His show was simultaneously aired on 250 radio stations and 85 television stations nationwide. The timing was perfect for scandal. The civil rights and women's movements were in full swing, the Vietnam War was escalating, and rock 'n' roll was "threatening" the values of the nation's young. Pyne was the protector of the "Silent Majority," attacking "hippies," "feminists," and "lefty creeps." However, unlike so-called conservative commentators who would borrow his style after he was gone, Pyne was a supporter of America's workers and decried racial prejudice (though he did once wave a gun in the face of a black militant guest on his show). His confrontations often produced scandals that lasted well beyond his hour-long broadcasts.

Pyne's best-known confrontation was with editor Paul Krassner and folksinger Phil Ochs. Unable to get a rise out of Krassner by attacking his political views—calling his magazine, the *Realist*, "a filthy, avant-garde, left-wing rag"—Pyne asked about the acne scars on his guest's face. Never known for his tact, Krassner said, "If you're going to ask me questions like that, let me ask you, Do you take off your wooden leg when you make love to your wife?" Pyne turned to the audience for support. One by one, Silent Majority-types stepped into Pyne's "Beef Box"—a podium set up not unlike a witness stand in a courtroom, with Pyne as the presiding judge—to denounce Krassner. Finally, Phil Ochs stepped into the box, and Pyne called him "one of the leaders of the hippie revolution." Ochs said, "What Paul Krassner does is in the finest tradition of American journalism." Though he continued to talk, Ochs's message was drowned out by the audience's boos. Pyne had done his part to further widen the "Generation Gap." A similar face-off with Frank Zappa occurred when Pyne greeted the musician, "So I guess your long hair makes you a woman." Zappa responded, "I guess your wooden leg makes you a table."[4] Lesser-known guests also threatened Pyne in the heat of their confrontations. Indeed, it was not unusual for chairs to be flung in his direction, or for insulted guests to simply walk off the show, or be thrown off the set by the host, with his patented salute, "Take a hike." Though Pyne's format is common today, he was the originator of the style, and one of the best at it. He was funny, well-read, articulate, bombastic, and patriotic. His patriotism was well-earned. A former U.S. Marine, he lost his leg in World War II combat.

Pyne would, in all likelihood, have continued his successful run had he not developed lung cancer from his cigarette addiction. He was only forty-four when he died.

Another Coughlin protégé was Morton Downey Jr., who got his start as a radio deejay in California in the 1960s, gaining a regional reputation for his on-air antics. It wasn't until he turned to a radio "talk show" format in the 1980s that he found his niche. The format worked well for his larger-than-life personality. In Sacramento, at KFBK-AM, he honed a uniquely fierce style that gained him a wide reputation. His politics were right-wing, and he was always on the attack, mocking guests or callers who had views contrary to his own and viciously lighting into "liberals." His stint in Sacramento attracted the notice of television executives who hoped to exploit Downey's big-mouthed populism. When he left KFBK for New York in 1984, Downey's replacement at the radio microphone was another itinerant jock looking for his niche, Rush Limbaugh. Limbaugh borrowed much from his predecessor at the start of his own long and controversial career.

Not content with his radio legacy, Downey ratcheted up the rhetoric and antics for his television show, *The Morton Downey Jr. Show,* which by 1986 had attracted a wide national audience in syndication. He shrieked with rage at guests and audience members who heckled him (memorably telling one to "suck my armpit"). His favorite epithet was "pablum-puking liberal." As his initial popularity waned, due largely to his one-note style, Downey created a news scandal by staging a hoax, presumably to get sympathy. He was found beaten in a men's room at the San Francisco International Airport and claimed he had been attacked by neo-Nazis who painted a swastika on his face and shaved part of his head. The police never found evidence to corroborate his story; he later admitted it was a hoax. A chain smoker, Downey was infamous for, literally, blowing smoke in his guests' faces. (He would die of lung cancer in 2001.) His style was widely imitated by those who came in his wake, like Mike Savage (born Michael Alan Weiner), "Doctor" Laura Schlesinger, and Limbaugh, but his imitators could not quite duplicate the staged contempt that Downey exuded. After he left broadcasting, Downey parodied his style by appearing on professional wrestling shows and in Grade B movies. In interviews, he expressed regret for some of his extreme theatrics, saying he had taken things too far.

After this wave hit the shore, more waves followed: Rush Limbaugh, Michael Savage, Laura Ingraham, Don Imus, Bob Grant, and Glenn Beck.

It Wasn't His Faulk

The anti-Communist witch hunts of the 1940s and 1950s had a chilling effect on the radio industry, just as they did on the fledgling television medium. Shouters like Pyne and Downey were acceptable as long as they touted flag and country, but anyone with left-leaning views was suspect. On little more than rumors or innuendo, many talented people were chased from the industry. Radio writers, producers, musicians, and actors lost their jobs when their names appeared on "blacklists" or "Red-lists." The so-named had little recourse short of the long, expensive process of clearing their names of suspicion. One radio star who refused to passively accept a career death sentence was John Henry Faulk, a Texas humorist whose folksy style was compared to Will Rogers's style. In 1957, Faulk lost his job because an organization called AWARE, Inc. declared him a "disloyal" American. AWARE billed itself as "an organization to combat the communist conspiracy in entertainment-communications." For a fee, they ran background checks on people to determine their "loyalty." Those whom AWARE deemed disloyal were given no opportunity to face the accusers or even to see the evidence against them. They were summarily fired, thus terminating their media career. Faulk hired famed lawyer Louis Nizer and brought a libel suit against AWARE. After six years of legal battles that bankrupted his family, and an eleven-week trial, Faulk and Nizer prevailed in 1963. A jury awarded him $3,500,000 in damages. The money wasn't as important to him as the fact that Faulk and Nizer had exposed the inner workings of right-wing vigilante justice.

Killed by Talk Radio

Sometimes those who threaten media figures for their views make good on the threat. One such victim was Alan Berg, a confrontational talk radio personality who debuted at KOA in Denver in February 1981. Berg regularly talked about hot-button issues like gun control and homosexuality. KOA's powerful signal could be heard in more than thirty states. Many listeners tuned in just to hear Berg antagonize his callers. He often upset them to such an extent that they became incoherent, at which point he was known to berate them further. His liberal views were as controversial as his manner, and he received many anonymous death threats. On June 18, 1984, Berg was gunned down in his driveway. A white supremacist group called The Order, which had made several death threats against Berg for his "Zionist" views, was suspected as the perpetrator. Though no one was convicted of the murder, members of The Order were tried and convicted of conspiracy and civil rights violations.[5]

THE NEW WAVE OF ANGRY RADIO

Simultaneous with Rush Limbaugh's ascendancy in the 1990s, a sea change took place on the radio dial. According to *Broadcasting* magazine, the number of talk radio stations in the United States jumped from 238 in 1987 to 875 in 1992. The vast majority of the new shows were politically conservative, reflecting the ideologies of Ronald Reagan and George H. W. Bush. One survey found that 70 percent of the 8,000 talk show hosts—nearly all of whom were white males—described themselves as conservative. Regardless of the politics, radio networks coveted the talk show format because it was cheap to produce and it generated a rabid base of regular, reliable listeners—which, in turn, attracted advertisers.

Even Convicted Felons Get a Show

Among the most controversial of this new wave of radio "talkers" were two convicted felons, G. Gordon Liddy, who served a prison term for his role in the Watergate break-in, and Lieutenant Colonel Oliver North, whose felony conviction for his part in the Iran-Contra scandal was later "vacated." Liddy's was the more controversial and popular of the shows. On August 26, 1994, for example, Liddy told listeners the proper way to kill an agent from the Bureau of Alcohol, Tobacco and Firearms. ("They've got a big target there, ATF. Don't shoot at that because they've got a vest on underneath that. Head shots, head shots.... Kill the sons of bitches.") A complaint was filed with the Federal Communications Commission against Liddy for this breach of radio rules, but he faced no penalty. Liddy has often cited Hitler as one of his boyhood heroes, telling his fans that listening to Hitler on the radio "made me feel a strength inside I had never known before.... Hitler's sheer animal confidence and power of will [entranced me]. He sent an electric current through my body." In 2008, Liddy was still hosting a nationally syndicated radio show. Oliver North learned the ropes of radio talk shows by guest-hosting both Liddy's and Rush Limbaugh's shows.

Granting Bob No License

One radio talk show host pushed the envelope even further than Liddy and Limbaugh. Bob Grant, from 1993 until 1996, had the largest talk show audience in the country, using New York's WABC as his flagship. He also regularly sparked scandals. During New York's Gay Pride march in 1994, for example, Grant fantasized on the air about how much pleasure he would derive from "a few phalanxes of policemen with machine guns" who would "mow them [unarmed homosexuals] down." After two years of complaints, WABC fired Grant when he rejoiced over the death of U.S. Commerce Secretary Ronald Brown in a plane crash in April 1996. Undeterred, Grant soon found a slot at New York's WOR station. Matching Grant for incendiary rhetoric, Colorado-based radio host Chuck Baker broadcast from a gun shop and periodically encouraged "patriots" to engage in "armed revolution" to "cleanse" the government. One of Baker's loyal listeners, Francisco Duran, took him up on the dare. Driving his pickup truck from Colorado to Washington, D.C., Duran fired twenty-nine bullets at the White House on October 29, 1994, before being apprehended. Duran was sentenced to forty years in prison for attempting to assassinate President Clinton. Baker was allowed to continue broadcasting.

Don Imus Is in Mourning

Radio personality Don Imus saw his thirty-nine-year career in broadcasting disappear in the space of ten seconds on April 4, 2007. On his *Imus in the Morning* show on CBS Radio—simulcast on MSNBC TV—he made racial and sexist comments about the Rutgers University women's basketball team, which had just completed an improbable run for the national championship, falling to the heavy favorite University of Tennessee in the finals. He referred to the players as "nappy-headed hos." Imus and his defenders justified his remarks by equating them to the language on hip hop recordings. Despite his public apologies, including meeting with the Rutgers team, Imus saw both his radio and TV shows canceled amid the scandal, which also sparked a national debate on race. Many politicians and entertainers risked public condemnation by defending Imus on the grounds that to fire him, after his apologies, was a violation of free speech. Many of these politicians had appeared on his show, which purported, between bathroom humor and endless ridicule of public figures, to tackle serious political issues. For this reason, *Imus in the Morning* was influential, regular fare for Washington, D.C., power brokers (many of whom, like Bob Dole and Joe Lieberman, were regular guests). Lost in the debate, however, was how this incident was par for the course for Imus. Prior to this incident, Imus had faced lawsuits for similarly offensive commentary about women, blacks, Arabs, Jews, and homosexuals. The scandal unleashed on April 4, 2007, was the tipping point of Imus's career. By December 2007, however, Imus had landed another multimillion-dollar talk radio gig on WABC, flagship for *The Rush Limbaugh Show.*

Rush in Limbo

An entire book could be devoted to the scandals unleashed by radio personality Rush Limbaugh, who has proclaimed his "talent" to be "on loan from God." Since 1984, when he secured his first top radio job at Sacramento's KFBK, Limbaugh has carved a semipermanent niche as the voice of the political right-wing on the radio dial. To secure that perch, Limbaugh has taken the lessons he learned from Morton Downey Jr. to the extreme. His rise was aided by President Ronald Reagan's 1987 repeal of the FCC's Fairness Doctrine, a move that effectively allowed commentary to be aired unchallenged by the opposing view. The *Wall Street Journal* editorialized, "Reagan tore down this wall ... and Rush Limbaugh was the first man to proclaim himself liberated from the East Germany of liberal media domination." Prior to that, Limbaugh's career had floundered. He was an itinerant Top 40 deejay, and even left radio altogether to work as a publicist for the Kansas City Royals baseball club. But, because the Fairness Doctrine no longer presented a barrier to his extremist views, Limbaugh treated his listeners to a vituperative stew of racial insensitivity, feminist-bashing (he coined the term *feminazis*), green-bashing

Radio personality Rush Limbaugh became a wealthy man by pushing the envelope on politically partisan rhetoric. AP Photo/Eric Risberg.

(*tree huggers*), gay-bashing, flag-waving, and saber-rattling. To guarantee that he did not have to face those with opposing views, Limbaugh had his on-air phone calls screened ahead of time and his staff handpick his audiences at public events. Given that his own personal life (three divorces, self-confessed addiction to Oxycontin, draft-dodging, and welfare recipient) was fraught with many of the issues about which he has fulminated on the air, his act was dismissed, or defended, as mere "entertainment," not to be taken any more seriously than professional wrestling. However, along with his wide national stance (his show now broadcasts on 650 stations), Limbaugh also accrued considerable political clout. This was evident in 1994, when Limbaugh helped facilitate the Newt Gingrich-led "Republican Revolution," which secured a majority in Congress and set in place the power base that would hound President Bill Clinton to the brink of impeachment over an extramarital affair. Many of the newly elected Congressmen in 1994 dubbed themselves "the Dittohead Caucus" in homage to Limbaugh, whom they designated "an honorary member of Congress." When Limbaugh married his third wife that year, Supreme Court Justice Clarence Thomas—a leading right-wing voice— performed the ceremony. Limbaugh's self-assessment as "an entertainer" began to ring hollow to his critics and political targets.

For the two decades that Limbaugh has been popular—his weekly radio audience estimated at 20 million—he has ignited numerous scandals, exacerbated when his show was made available on "DittoCam," a Web-only TV broadcast for subscribers, in 2004. Among the most notorious of Limbaugh's DittoCam moments was his October 23, 2006, mockery of actor Michael J. Fox's Parkinson's disease. Fox had appeared in political ads for U.S. Senate candidate Claire McCaskill, praising her support of stem-cell research, research that might lead to a medical breakthrough in treating Parkinson's and other diseases. Limbaugh, while jiggling in mockery of Parkinson's symptoms, said Fox was "exaggerating the effects of the disease. He's moving all around and shaking and it's purely an act.... This is really shameless of Michael J. Fox. Either he didn't take his medication or he's acting." Limbaugh was wrong on both counts, but never apologized.

Race-baiting nearly cost Limbaugh his radio job and did, in fact, cost him a television job. (*See also* "ESPN Gives Limbaugh the Bum's Rush.") As a young disc jockey, Limbaugh told one African American caller to "Take that bone out of your nose and call me back." Later, as a famous entertainer, he opined, "Why should Blacks be heard? They're 12% of the population. Who the hell cares?" and "The NAACP [National Association for the Advancement of Colored People] should have riot rehearsal. They should get a liquor store and practice robberies." He has called those Americans who live in poverty "the biggest piglets at the mother pig and her nipples. The poor feed off the largesse of the government and give nothing back.... I don't have compassion for the poor." And yet, Limbaugh had fed off the largesse himself, filing for unemployment benefits after running up credit card expenses he could not pay. His on-air explanation: "My wife made me file for unemployment."

The Potty Mouths

In 1973, on New York's WBAI-FM station, George Carlin gave a monologue that he called "The Seven Words You Can't Say on Radio and Television." They were all, Carlin said, the words "ordinary people" used all the time and were, thus, neither a threat nor obscene. He repeated the seven words several times on the air. A listener filed a complaint with the FCC, which issued a "declaratory order" that ruled that the seven words were "patently offensive by contemporary community standards ... and are 'indecent' when broadcast by radio or television." The station, put on probation, appealed the ruling. The case (*FCC v. Pacifica*) became a cause célèbre. In 1978, it reached the U.S. Supreme Court, which ruled that radio and television stations do not have the constitutional right to broadcast "indecent words."

The FCC and the Supreme Court never reckoned on Howard Stern.

Getting Stern with Howard

Howard Stern began his radio career in the early 1980s, distracting Philadelphia-area commuters stuck in morning traffic with his iconoclastic banter in between playing rock 'n' roll songs. His stock in trade was the on-air parody, which was occasionally clever enough to attract a wide audience. Many listeners were curiosity seekers wanting to hear how far Stern would push the FCC envelope. By 1985, he'd pushed it too far, at least in his station's estimation; his show was canceled after a segment called "Bestiality Dial-a-Date." Moving to New York, Stern built up a national following with the same format of jokes, parodies, sexual innuendo, and a rock 'n' roll play list. Despite chronic violations of FCC rules, with resultant fines, Stern continued to push the boundaries of good taste. In 1995, his syndication network (Infinity) was forced to pay a $1.7 million FCC fine. The nearly constant scrutiny by the FCC provoked Stern to leave traditional radio broadcasting and sign a contract with Sirius Satellite Radio in 2004. He has since flourished in the pay-to-listen format.

Stern's Disciples

Just as Rush Limbaugh generated imitators, Stern found imitators in nearly every regional audience. Each large city seemed to spawn their own home-grown "bad boy" (or girl), one who pushed buttons of tastelessness and profanity. Among the most controversial was Doug Tracht, whose on-air personality was "Greaseman." Constantly in trouble for racist slurs, Greaseman was hired and fired more often than Stern, but his career came to an abrupt end when he cracked jokes about James Byrd, the black man in Texas who was dragged to death in 1998. Another "shock jock" who retained the proudly offensive persona was Mancow Muller, based in Chicago, a self-described "conservative libertarian" who was also a frequent guest on Fox News. Mancow had his share of battles with the FCC, resulting in fines, for "indecency," and one out-of-court settlement of $1.6 million for "defamatory statements" about Keith Van Horne, a Chicago Bulls basketball player, as well as another defamatory suit for calling another Chicago deejay's wife a "slut" and then, redundantly, a "whore."

Savage Radio

One of the most vitriolic of the shock jocks was Michael Savage, whose real name, Michael Weiner, was not as effective at projecting the persona he craved. After earning a doctorate in "nutritional ethnomedicine" at the University of California-Berkeley, Savage wrote books about homeopathy and nutrition. However, his political conservatism supplanted his career as New Age avatar. He began his radio act relatively late in his career, in 1994, on San Francisco stations. His show's motto was "To the right of Rush and to the left of God." Soon, "The Savage Nation" was syndicated nationally, reaching 10 million listeners on 410 stations, third behind only Limbaugh and Sean Hannity. Savage, like Dr. Laura Schlesinger, failed to translate well to television. His MSNBC television show lasted less than a year and was canceled after he called one caller "a sodomite" who "should only get AIDS and die, you pig ... Go eat a sausage and choke on it. Get trichinosis."[6] Nonetheless, Savage continued to host a nationally syndicated radio show in 2008.

Savage Woman

The distaff Savage was Laura Ingraham, one of the few women to carve a niche in political talk radio. Her biggest beef was with "the Elites," which included all liberals who she deemed to be, by definition, "anti-American." Scandal followed her from her earliest foray into political commentary, as editor of the *Dartmouth Review*, which she filled with such observations as calling the Gay Students Association "cheerleaders for latent campus sodomites." Based on her writing talent, she was hired as a speechwriter for President Ronald Reagan and then as a clerk for conservative Supreme Court Justice Clarence Thomas, for whom she led the attacks on Anita Hill. (*See also* "Clarence Thomas Confirmation Hearings.") She became the host of a radio talk show, on which she regularly claimed that "true Americans" were "white, southern, Christian, and Republican." Simultaneously, she decried liberals, the United Nations, and Europeans. She was a staunch supporter of the Iraq war and George W. Bush's policies.

PSEUDO SCIENCE IN BROADCASTING

Medicine Women

Ten years before the rise of Dr. Laura Schlesinger, the widely syndicated psychological advice giver, another self-proclaimed "relationship expert" named Dr. Toni Grant ruled the airwaves. *The Dr. Toni Grant Show* was aimed at "feminist-infected" women. Grant, who had a degree in clinical psychology from Syracuse University, often chided listeners for their problems, advising them to act "more feminine" rather than battle with the men in their lives. Among the controversial insights Dr. Grant shared with her listeners—conveniently found in her bestselling self-help books, which she promoted on the air—was that "the new assertive woman was abnormal precisely because she asserts herself." She also called feminism "a set of big lies" and said that feminists "conjure up images of a devouring, consuming monster, a Lady Macbeth completely divorced from her feminine feeling." For her millions of listeners, Grant's solution was simple, and controversial: "Surrender into being a woman." The ultimate goal of all this was to find a husband. It was Old School philosophy couched as New Age radio wisdom.

Dr. Laura Schlesinger picked up Dr. Toni Grant's baton when the latter "retired" in 1989 to become a "corporate wife" of a millionaire industrialist. Dr. Laura's show was a clone of Dr. Toni's show. In fact, because Grant's noontime slot was filled by another relationship expert, Barbara De Angelis,

Schlesinger was given De Angelis's former night slot on Los Angeles station KFI, and, when De Angelis left, Schlesinger took over the noon slot. Her three-hour show aired from noon to 3 P.M. each weekday. After guest-hosting Sally Jessy Raphael's ABC Radio show, Dr. Laura was syndicated nationally in 1994, making her the best-known radio call-in advice show host in the country. Politically conservative, she constantly bemoaned the nation's lack of morality and slammed adultery, divorce, and unmarried couples sharing a home (which she called "shacking up"). A scandal ensued when it was learned that Schlesinger had herself violated nearly every edict with which she berated her listeners. She'd had an affair with a married man, who then divorced his wife to "shack up" with Schlesinger for eight years before they married. She had also posed for nude photographs, many of which ended up on the Internet. Like Grant, Schlesinger put much of her on-air advice between the covers and plugged her best-selling books. She briefly had a syndicated TV show called, simply, *Dr. Laura*, but it did not reach anywhere near the size of her radio audience. Her TV career was hurt, in part, by her characterization of homosexuality as a "biological error" and her insistence that gay people should simply avoid sexual relations. Her TV show was canceled in 2001, barely one year after its debut.

Scandals of Television Broadcasting

Television existed in a crude form as early as 1930, after Vladimir Zworkyn, director of electronic research at RCA, demonstrated his kinescope, the first cathode ray television picture tube. A number of television systems were unveiled, to great fanfare, at the New York World's Fair in 1939, but World War II curtailed plans for development of commercial programming. After the war, the medium became a fixture of American life. In 1946, there were only 6,000 television sets in the United States, but by 1952, nearly 22 million sets were in American homes. A genuine cultural phenomenon was born, the fallout from which is still being felt. Since that time, television has been blamed for everything from juvenile delinquency (comic books, James Dean, and rock 'n' roll also stood accused of this), illiteracy, aliteracy, and, in recent years, violence, racism, promiscuity, misogyny, incivility, and pandering to the lowest common denominator. However, it's worth noting what Edward R. Murrow, one of the guiding lights at the inception of the Television Age, said, "This instrument can teach, it can illuminate; yes, and it can even inspire. But it can do so only to the extent that humans are determined to use it to those ends. Otherwise it is merely wire and lights in a box."

See It Now with Edward R. Murrow

Edward R. Murrow was the most respected television newsman of his day, a fearless pursuer of journalistic truth who cut his teeth reporting live on CBS Radio from Europe during World War II. After the war, he led the CBS news organization, just as television was coming into its own. Through the reporters he hired (Eric Sevareid, William Shirer, Howard K. Smith, and Don Hollenbeck), he made CBS the most respected name in TV news—and the most controversial. Hollenbeck's opinionated critiques of the right wing drew the wrath of William Randolph Hearst as well as FBI Director J. Edgar Hoover, who dubbed CBS "Communist Broadcasting System." As the Communist witch hunts heated up in the 1950s, CBS news staffers were forced to take loyalty oaths to the United States, and many were blacklisted, including Hollenbeck, who was driven to suicide by the insinuations of the right-wing press. Undeterred, Murrow used his televised current-events series, *See It Now* (1951–58), to attack those forces in American society that were undermining press freedoms. Murrow and producer Fred W. Friendly often sparked controversy with their broadcasts. For example, one prescient program, aired on June 25, 1952, simulated a terror bombing of New York City. More frequently, Murrow and Friendly sought to defuse the pervasive paranoia and fear generated by the likes of Senator McCarthy. Murrow's *See It Now* program on March 9, 1954, in fact, tossed the gauntlet at the senator's feet. After devoting most of his half-hour broadcast to a point-by-point assessment of McCarthy's career, allowing the footage of the senator in action to speak for itself, Murrow closed by warning viewers, "This is no time for men who oppose Senator McCarthy's methods to remain silent ... We can deny our heritage and our history, but we cannot escape responsibility for the result ...The actions of the junior senator from Wisconsin have caused alarm and dismay amongst our allies abroad and given considerable comfort to our enemies." This riveting broadcast is credited with beginning the process that led to McCarthy's downfall. On November 25, 1960, Murrow broadcast a controversial documentary, "Harvest of Shame," that offered Thanksgiving-stuffed Americans an unwelcome but riveting look at the miserable plight of America's migratory workers. Eight years later, CBS aired a sequel to Murrow's broadcast, called "Hunger in America," that would shame the federal government into taking action to address the issue of malnutrition on Indian reservations and among migrant workers.

In Murrow's Shadow

The spirit of Edward R. Murrow continued to inhabit CBS News, largely in the groundbreaking *60 Minutes*, which premiered in 1968 and became the most watched (and imitated) investigative new "magazine" program on television. It was produced by former Murrow associate Don Hewitt and hosted by the original "gotcha" interviewer, Mike Wallace, as well as a veritable Who's Who of broadcast journalism (and scandal): Dan Rather, Morley Safer, Ed Bradley, Harry Reasoner, Christiane Amanpour, and the ageless personality, Andy Rooney. A show of this stature, longevity, and mission naturally provoked its share of scandals. Among the most noteworthy included the following:

In 1982, the *60 Minutes* staff produced a documentary for "CBS Reports," narrated by Wallace, called "The Uncounted Enemy, a Vietnam Deception." The report accused General William Westmoreland, former military commander in Vietnam, of lying to Congress about the progress of the war, in order to give political cover to the White House and the Pentagon. Westmoreland sued CBS for libel, calling the show a "hoax." He eventually dropped the suit before it went to a jury.

In 1995, *60 Minutes* was able to get Jeffrey Wigand, a former tobacco executive, to admit that his firm, Brown and Williamson, suppressed information about the harmful and addictive effects of their cigarettes, as well as added unlabeled ingredients like fiberglass and ammonia to exacerbate the nicotine's addictive powers. However, the threat of a potentially bankrupting lawsuit caused CBS News to be uncharacteristically timid in airing the show. Because *60 Minutes* hesitated, the *Wall Street Journal* scooped them and won a Pulitzer Prize for their reporting. The series of events was depicted in the 1999 film *The Insider*, co-scripted by *60 Minutes* producer Lowell Bergman, who had worked on the quashed piece. Long after the tobacco cat was out of the bag, *60 Minutes* broadcast a severely trimmed and gutted segment about Wigand and his charges, prompting the *New York Times* to note that CBS News "had betrayed the legacy of Edward R. Murrow."

TABLOID TELEVISION

The Forerunners

Before Mike Wallace became the anchorman for *60 Minutes*, the "magazine show" that did the best investigative reporting CBS News ever produced, he was the originator of "gotcha" TV on his *Night Beat* show. Breaking the mold of the say-nothing interview format that prevailed before 1955, when his show began, Wallace was relentless in his interrogations, whether it was a second-tier actress like Zsa Zsa Gabor or a world leader. Of his show, *Newsweek* said, "For his guests' pains, he has been called a muckraker and a scandal monger ... as well as the bravest man on TV." Prior to this gig, the then-39-year-old Wallace hosted game shows and was an announcer on *The Lone Ranger* and *The Green Hornet*. In a pot-calling-the-kettle-black observation, the scandal magazine *Hush-Hush* described Wallace's *Night Beat* this way: "His wasn't the cliché interview program.... Mike's gimmick was to club his guests with queries on video's four taboo subjects—religion, politics, sex, and personal habits."

By 1957, Wallace was garnering 1.5 million viewers a night on ABC's New York City affiliate alone. When his show went national the following year as *The Mike Wallace Interview*, tabloid TV was born. As Jeannette Walls wrote,

Night Beat was "the young medium's first real foray into the world of tabloid journalism and the true precursor to the 'tabloid television' of the eighties." *The Mike Wallace Interview* was broadcast by ABC on Sunday nights at 9:30. His first guest was slated to be Senator Joe McCarthy, no stranger to national scandals himself. By this time, however, McCarthy's "scandal" value was waning, his health was shot (he would die a month later), and he canceled. A bad omen. Gloria Swanson filled in at the last moment, to little fanfare.

The next week, Wallace scored a coup with his guest Mickey Cohen, the "reformed" mobster who shocked a national audience with his vindictive attacks on Los Angeles police chief Bill Parker, calling him a "sadistic degenerate" and a "reformed thief." Parker sued ABC for $33 million. The network retracted the comments, apologized, and settled with Parker out of court. *Newsweek* intoned, "What are his rebuttals to the charge that he is an untrained reporter and a sensation hound, and that his show ... is no better than the TV equivalent of *Confidential* magazine?" Soon after this, Wallace's guest was investigative reporter Drew Pearson. Pearson had made enemies of the Kennedy family by insisting in his interview that Senator John F. Kennedy had not written *Profiles in Courage*, the book that had won him the Pulitzer Prize, but that it had been ghostwritten by Theodore Sorenson. The senator's father, Joe Kennedy, threatened a massive lawsuit unless ABC made a full retraction. Wallace refused. Pearson refused. Nonetheless, ABC president Oliver Treyz made a full retraction on the air. Wallace's trailblazing show was canceled the next year. Pearson was right. Kennedy's book, it is now known, was ghostwritten by Sorenson.

The promise of investigative journalism on television was realized by Wallace's second incarnation as host of *60 Minutes*. The same strict adherence to journalistic ethics and reputable reportage was evident on a number of other shows that sprung up in the wake of *60 Minutes*, including ABC's *Nightline*, hosted by Ted Koppel, and *20/20*, hosted by veteran Hugh Downs, who was later joined by Barbara Walters.

Donahue Phils a Void

Phil Donahue created the daytime TV talk show, a format that eventually turned into "freak shows" hosted by the likes of Jerry Springer and Ricki Lake. Donahue began his career in 1963 in Dayton, Ohio. In his four years as a radio host on WHIO-AM in Dayton, Donahue's *Conversation Piece* program offered a rare platform for liberal views. He interviewed Martin Luther King Jr., Malcolm X, war resisters, and other activists. His all-talk format was adapted for Dayton television in 1967 as *The Phil Donahue Show*, which proved popular enough to go into national syndication in 1970. By the time the program had run its course in 1996, *The Phil Donahue Show* was the longest continuous broadcast of any syndicated talk show on television. Donahue's popularity was due to his gift of gab, but also for the unpredictability of the conversations and his courting of audience participation. Donahue made this a part of every broadcast, running up and down the aisles with microphone in hand and an earnest look on his face. Donahue's show was credited with generating sensitive and thought-provoking discussions on topics that had previously been taboo on television. However, the show began to lose viewers to the more shocking imitators of Donahue's format, like Springer and Lake. Donahue, to win back viewers, featured a show called, "Woman Wins 8-Year Battle to Care for Disabled Lesbian Lover," sported a dress during a discussion of cross-dressing, and hit his highest rating in 1991 with a segment called "Transvestite Shopping Spree."

No News Is Good News

The vast majority of the "news" shows that arose in the wake of *60 Minutes'* runaway success were hybrids of "news" and "entertainment," with emphasis on the sensational or trendy. Indeed, hoping to emulate the success of tabloid newspapers, TV executives began a series of syndicated celebrity-watching shows like *Access Hollywood*, *Hard Copy*, and *A Current Affair*. *A Current Affair*, the most popular of the three shows, was pioneering in one unique sense: it was the horse upon which the controversial Australian media mogul Rupert Murdoch rode to prominence. Murdoch had continued to raise hackles and cause scandal with his purchases of print media venues like the *Chicago Sun-Times*, *Boston Herald-American*, *New York* magazine, *Village Voice*, and half interest in Twentieth Century Fox and Metromedia, a collection of seven television stations in big-city markets (New York, Chicago, D.C., and Los Angeles). Out of all this multimedia "synergy" rose Murdoch's Fox Network, founded in 1985 as a division of his larger News Corporation, to produce TV and movies. Having made his fortune on tabloid newspapers, Murdoch simply transferred that formula to television. His first show along these lines was *A Current Affair*, created in 1986 and hosted by Maury Povich (Murdoch's third choice, after Tom Snyder and Geraldo Rivera turned him down over pay). Povich had worked previously at Murdoch's Washington, D.C., affiliate. *A Current Affair's* bottom line was sensationalism. Povich devoted broadcasts to such topics as UFOs, nude beaches, and surrogate mothers who decided to keep their babies. He showed videos of Rob Lowe having sex with an underage woman. *A Current Affair* proved so popular that by 1988 it was syndicated to more than a hundred stations. After Povich aired a story about Steven Spielberg's divorce from Amy Irving, and his alleged affair with actress Kate Capshaw, Spielberg threatened never to work with Barry Diller, head of Fox, Inc., again.

Other syndicated news-hybrid shows popped up in imitation of *A Current Affair*, including *Inside Edition*, started in 1988 and hosted by Bill O'Reilly, and *Hard Copy*, started in 1989, which earned such notoriety for scandal by

1996 that actor George Clooney led a successful boycott of the show. These new tabloid television shows began competing with each other for titillating and scandalous material. In the shuffle of competition for a finite number of stories, journalistic ethics and even basic rules of journalism often went by the wayside. In 1991, tabloid TV shows were handed a gift when William Kennedy Smith was accused of rape by Patricia Bowman. The rape trial was covered by every tabloid TV outlet. *A Current Affair* led the pack, with its producers paying for news tips and scouring the Palm Beach area—where the rape allegedly occurred—for sources. Every news outlet was tainted by the need for fresh information, even printing the alleged rape victim's name (previously a journalistic taboo) because one of the newspaper tabloids had already done so. The *New York Times*, of all papers, was among the biggest offenders. Under the guise of writing a background story on Bowman, *Times* reporter Fox Butterfield, a friend of the Kennedy family, wrote what amounted to a scathing attack on her character, much of the information provided by the Kennedy family's private investigator. Even the *Times* staff was outraged at Butterfield's story. Indeed, the *National Enquirer* ended up looking like a more ethical bastion of news, for not including Bowman's name in its own coverage of the trial.

As Jeannette Walls wrote, "*A Current Affair* not only provided the definitive coverage of the trial, they influenced its outcome in a way that may have been unprecedented in legal history, and in doing so permanently redrew—and in the view of some, obliterated—the lines between the tabloid and the establishment press ... In the end, the trial damaged almost everyone it touched. Patricia Bowman was forever scarred. The Kennedy family's reputation had received another serious blow. The editorial judgment of the *New York Times* had been denounced throughout the country. Cable television, however, had profited handsomely." CNN's audience rose 71 percent on opening day and 142 percent on the day Bowman testified.[7]

Oprah Winfrey Rules

In 1984, Oprah Winfrey began her career as a TV talk show host in Chicago. Within a year, her show was the highest rated in the city; by September 8, 1986, *The Oprah Winfrey Show* was syndicated nationally by King World. Winfrey's mix of personal testimony and seeming sincerity proved popular, and her show was soon the number one daytime talk show in the country. Within five years, Winfrey was arguably the most popular person on television and certainly, between her show's syndication and her spin-off magazine and book club empire, one of the richest. She was also seen as an important voice of moderation and decency in the middle of the cesspool of daytime TV. Any scandals that her show initiated were unintended, or grew out of good intentions. On one show in April 1996, for example, Winfrey discussed outbreaks of Mad Cow disease with a guest expert. After the expert explained how the

Oprah Winfrey waves to supporters outside an Amarillo, Texas, courtroom on February 26, 1998. She had been sued by a group of Texas cattlemen after she made some anti-beef remarks on her television show, which they said hurt their sales. The jury ruled in her favor, agreeing that her remarks fell within First Amendment protection. AP Photo/LM Lotero.

disease might have resulted from the manner with which beef cattle were fed, Winfrey remarked, "That just stopped me cold from eating another burger." A group of Texas cattlemen and the National Cattlemen's Beef Association (NCBA), citing a 1995 state law making it a felony to "make false and disparaging statements about perishable food products," sued the show, claiming that it provoked a precipitous drop in beef sales. A jury didn't agree; Oprah was acquitted three years later. After the verdict, Winfrey told the gathered press, "Free speech not only lives, it rocks!" The irony of the media storm that followed Winfrey's remarks about beef were how other media figures who themselves had been hounded by lawyers came to the defense of the beef industry. Geraldo Rivera, in particular, was fit to be tied. "There's still an awful lot of whining, exaggerated reporting about the dangers of this or that additive," said Rivera on *Rivera Live*. "The story's always about the one person who gets sick, not the 20 billion people who are fine and well and thriving on—you know, on Double Whoppers with cheese."

A potentially more damaging scandal for Winfrey was created by her championing the book *A Million Little Pieces* by James Frey, because it endangered something that Rivera did not have—her spotless reputation. Equally damaging, potentially, was the October 2007 scandal involving a South African "leadership academy" for girls underwritten by Winfrey's charitable fund. Fifteen girls at the academy came forward to accuse a member of the staff (a "dorm matron") of sexually abusing and physically assaulting dorm residents. The case shook Winfrey, who herself had been a victim of sex abuse as a child. Rather than greet the scandal with silence, Winfrey aggressively sided with the abused girls, congratulated them for speaking out, and resolved to change the way students were overseen in the dorms. What could have been a terrible scandal turned into another victory for Winfrey.

In 2007, Winfrey was criticized for entering the political arena when she endorsed Barack Obama for president and then campaigned for him. She had never risked her considerable media power by specifically endorsing any candidate in the past, and some of her viewers were dismayed at the direction she pursued. The media went into a frenzy, trying to determine the impact of what became known as the "Oprah factor."

Paging Dr. Phil

Oprah Winfrey's biggest scandal may prove to be her elevation of "celebrity therapist" Phil McGraw to national prominence. After meeting him in 1998 during the course of her beef lawsuit, Winfrey was impressed enough with the self-proclaimed "relationship expert" to offer him a regular slot on her popular show. By 2002, McGraw had his own syndicated daily advice show, *Dr. Phil*. One problem: Because of sanctions imposed on him for "unethical behavior" in 1989, McGraw was not licensed to practice psychology. Nonetheless, he dispensed psychological advice to millions of Americans who seemed to respond to his brash style. Despite his popularity as a TV host, author, and weight-loss champion, scandal followed *Dr. Phil* like a virus. In 2003, the Federal Trade Commission probed his weight-loss products and, under pressure, he pulled them off the market, not before a successful class action suit was filed. In 2006, he was sued by two brothers whom he'd interviewed in connection with Natalee Holloway, the American student who disappeared in Aruba. According to the suit, McGraw had manipulated the footage of the interview to suggest that the brothers were criminals. Among the charges in their defamation suit was that McGraw invaded their privacy, deceived and defrauded them, causing emotional distress. McGraw got into further hot water in January 2008 when, unsolicited, he inserted himself into pop star Britney Spears's marital and mental health crises, hoping to film an "intervention" for his show. He later apologized to the Spears family and to his powerful sponsor, Oprah Winfrey, perhaps fearing the loss of his syndicated show.

Geraldo Rivera

Rivera's career might be described as one long scandal. He began as a legitimate and energetic investigative reporter for WABC-TV in New York City, and exposed some terrible abuses with his reports on migrant labor, drug addiction, senior citizens' care, and, most noteworthy, a report from Willowbrook State School for the Mentally Retarded in 1972. He managed to get inside the school with his camera crew, which filmed retarded children, unclothed, wallowing in their own excrement. He told the camera, "This is what it looked like, this is what it sounded like. But how can I tell you how it smelled? It smelled of filth, it smelled of disease, and it smelled of death."

The ensuing scandal over health-care abuses, some of which were redressed by state legislation, won Rivera top press awards and parlayed his new fame into

Every part of Geraldo Rivera was a magnet for scandal, including his nose, which was broken by a guest on his syndicated television show on November 3, 1988. AP Photo/ Richard Drew.

high-paying gigs with ABC's national news desk. He, along with co-anchors Hugh Downs and Barbara Walters, transformed *20/20* into an investigative news program that almost achieved the status of *60 Minutes*. His biggest scoop may have gotten him fired—a piece about Marilyn Monroe, the Kennedy family, and the Mob that was set to run on September 26, 1985. The story was killed by ABC president Roone Arledge, a friend of the Kennedys, and the livid Rivera started his own production company soon thereafter. He created and syndicated his own show, *Geraldo*, which was noteworthy for breaking new ground in taboo-busting. He took on serial killers, male strippers, sat inside prison to interview a manacled Charles Manson, who made physical threats against him, and televised a man's sex change operation. In one famous episode devoted to "teen hate mongers," a guest threw a chair, breaking Rivera's nose.

Tabloid Television: Geraldo Springers a Leak

The ratings for shows like Rivera's soared, especially when the conversation turned nasty and incited the studio participants. Rivera kicked open the door for tabloid television, making possible the careers of Jerry Springer, Maury Povich, Montel Williams, Sally Jesse Raphael, Ricki Lake, and so forth starting in the 1980s and 1990s. Each were hosts of their own daytime TV talk show. Like newspaper tabloids, they competed by one-upping each other in sensationalism. One of the techniques used to create scandal was the ambushing of guests. That is, guests who thought they were booked to talk voluntarily about one topic would find themselves unexpectedly confronted—on live television with a national audience—by an antagonistic family member or acquaintance, who would accuse the guest of some embarrassing act or reveal unsavory secrets. The Jerry Springer and Jenny Jones programs developed ambushing into a high art. In some cases, the guest would react violently, spinning the show out of control with hair-pulling, fistfights, and other audience-titillating mayhem. Men who dressed in their mothers' clothes competed against women who slept with their fathers or mothers who slept with their daughters' boyfriends. Jerry Springer was, arguably, the most talented of the lot simply because he did not take himself, or what he was doing, seriously. Springer, in fact, referred to himself as "the godfather of the decline of Western civilization."

Beyond the individual dramas provoked by specific episodes, the larger issue for critics was whether the shows were harmful to viewers. Some academics argued that the shows were the first forum people on society's fringe ever had (this was before the advent of the Internet), while others claimed that the shows harmed society by making aberrant behavior appear normal. The discussion came to a halt, briefly, in March 1995, when a guest on the *Jenny Jones Show* devoted to "Secret Admirers" later murdered another gay guest on the show who had confessed to having a crush on him. While the killer was convicted of second degree murder, the victim's family successfully sued

Warner Bros. for $25 million in damages. In response to this scandal, *The Jerry Springer Show* cut back on the hysteria that characterized its broadcasts. However, by the end of the first week, the show's ratings had plummeted 8 percent. In order to rescue his tumbling ratings, Springer returned to the tried and true "freak show" formula. His ratings went up, reaffirming a truth by which the media is now seemingly ruled: Scandal sells.

In the wake of the Oklahoma City terrorist bombing masterminded by Timothy McVeigh, President Clinton took aim at these television talk show and radio shock jocks, calling them "the purveyors of hatred and division." In an April 1995 speech, Clinton further decried the broadcasting trend by saying, "They leave the impression, by their very words, that violence is acceptable." Piling on these shows was Senator Joe Lieberman, who sided with the religious right in denouncing these types of shows as "pornographic" and "degrading," and decried that "the preponderance of perversion on daytime talk shows is affecting our entire society … pushing the envelope of civility and morality in a way that drags the rest of the culture down with it."[8]

Geraldo's Biggest Breach

Rivera's free fall from what had been a promising career reached bottom in 2003, when Fox News hired him as a war correspondent. Though not officially "embedded" with the 101st Airborne Division of the U.S. Army, Rivera was nonetheless traveling with them. He broadcast live from Iraq as the American military pushed toward Baghdad, telling Fox News anchorman John Gibson where he and the troops were by drawing a map in the sand and saying, "First, I want to make some emphasis here that these hash marks here, this is us. We own that territory. It's 40 percent, maybe even a little more than that." He went on at length with more specifics about the timing of attacks and planned strategies. Pentagon officials were horrified. "He actually revealed the time of an attack prior to its occurrence," a Central Command spokesman told the press. After notifying Fox's parent company, the News Corp., of Rivera's breach, a Pentagon official said, "We are giving the news organization an opportunity to do the right thing and pull him out. If they don't, we will." Rivera was pulled off the beat. No charges were filed against him, or Fox, for this breach of national security. More than ever, Rivera became the butt of jokes. Conan O'Brien, host of NBC's *Late Night*, quipped, "This means Saddam Hussein will once again be the most hated man in Iraq."

Backlash against Bill O'Reilly

Like his counterparts on the left, Bill O'Reilly had a knack for provoking political foes. His broadcasts have often fueled backlashes on rival networks, most recently from Keith Olbermann on MSNBC, whose left-leaning show aired opposite O'Reilly's after 2003.[9] Even more than what he says, though,

O'Reilly is controversial for what he claims as his credentials. Before he was given his own show by Fox News in 1995 (*The O'Reilly Factor*), he was an anchor on *Inside Edition*. For a time after leaving *Inside Edition*, O'Reilly insisted that the show had won two Peabody Awards, the most prestigious honor in broadcast journalism. However, neither he nor *Inside Edition* had won a Peabody Award. In fact, the show won a Polk Award, a year *after* he had left it and for something with which he was not connected (he did win two Emmy Awards for local news coverage early in his career). In his book *Lies and the Lying Liars Who Tell Them*, Al Franken used this example of O'Reilly's distortion of the truth as emblematic of his larger issues of news distortion. Individual scandals spawned by O'Reilly are legion. One in particular, spoke to his brand of bellicose partisanship. This occurred on February 4, 2003. His guest on *The O'Reilly Factor* was Jeremy Glick, whose father was killed in the 9/11 attacks on the World Trade Center. Glick said O'Reilly evoked "9/11 to rationalize everything from domestic plunder to imperialistic aggression world-wide," and O'Reilly exploded in anger, saying (on the air), "That's a bunch of crap. I've done more for the 9/11 families by their own admission—I've done more for them than you will ever hope to do." He also told Glick to "shut up," and then instructed his staff to cut Glick's microphone. This move only widened the gap between O'Reilly's fans and foes, with the former applauding it as the latter loudly denounced the host's insensitivity and bullying. Glick told *Rolling Stone* magazine that, off the air, O'Reilly said, "Get out of my studio before I tear you to f__ pieces."[10] Undercutting his carefully crafted image as an arbiter of morality, O'Reilly faced a sex scandal in October 2004, when one of his show's producers, Andrea Mackris, accused him of sexual harassment. After O'Reilly accused her of a attempting a "shakedown," Mackris filed a lawsuit that alleged a chronic pattern of sexual harassment, including explicit talk about telephone sex, masturbation, and his sexual fantasies. Rather than face the possibility of a protracted, humiliating trial, O'Reilly settled out of court with Mackris for a reported $2 million.[11]

Keith Olbermann's Worst Person Alert

Among the least likely people to don Edward R. Murrow's mantle may have been Keith Olbermann, a former ESPN sportscaster who left that network in a dispute with management. In 2003, Olbermann began hosting MSNBC's *Countdown*, and in homage to his hero, he closed the show with Murrow's famous sign off: "Good night and good luck." Olbermann's format resembled a sportscast, with the five biggest news stories of the day ranked and then dissected. One of his regular features, which generated angry denunciations from many of his targets, was "Worst Persons in the World," and Bill O'Reilly often finished in one of those top three places. Another of his popular features was his "Special Comment," in which he often, like Murrow, passionately defended the First Amendment and decried the fear-mongering of the right wing. Olbermann was one of the few unbending critics of the Bush administration and the Iraq war. In his first three years, ratings for *Countdown* steadily grew, and Olbermann was given a contract extension through 2011.

Colbert Channels O'Reilly

A more subtle critique of Bill O'Reilly was made by Stephen Colbert. Colbert first developed his alter-ego—an unapologetically biased, right-wing news correspondent named Stephen Colbert—on *The Daily Show*, where he started as a writer and performer in 1997. In 2005, his spin-off show, *The Colbert Report*—created in part with *Daily Show*-host Jon Stewart—debuted on Comedy Central and immediately achieved high ratings. Using this right-wing persona as a disguise behind which he hid his own personal views, Colbert skewered the pomposity of egomaniacal political pundits. He pretended to hero-worship O'Reilly in particular, whom he called "The Bear." Because his show was coy, viewers were never certain what Colbert believed. O'Reilly even agreed to appear on Colbert's show, and he himself seemed confused as to whether Colbert was praising or mocking him. However, the "real" Colbert unleashed a political scandal on April 29, 2006, as guest speaker at the White House Correspondents' Association annual dinner. Hiding behind his persona, Colbert skewered both the assembled journalists for their timidity and lack of skepticism and President Bush, seated only a few feet away on the stage. Among Colbert's comments were: "I stand by this man. I stand by this man because he stands for things. Not only for things, he stands on things. Things like aircraft carriers and rubble and recently flooded city squares. And that sends a strong message, that no matter what happens to America, she will always rebound—with the most powerfully staged photo ops in the world."[12]

REALITY TELEVISION

Since the days of *Candid Camera*, a television show that debuted in 1948 and has survived to the present day, Americans have been fascinated with watching themselves, or people like them, caught on hidden cameras doing inappropriate or embarrassing things. *Candid Camera*, cohosted for many years by the genial pair of Allen Funt and (after 1961) Durwood Kirby, planted a stationary camera at a staged scene and filmed the reactions of passersby. For example, Harpo Marx was placed inside the shell of a soda machine, and when people tried to purchase a drink, the silent comedian personally handed them the bottle, making for some impromptu high jinks. This early version of *Candid Camera* was innocent and gentle compared to its later incarnation under Peter Funt, who eschewed his father's witty musings on human behavior (Woody Allen wrote some of the earlier shows' material) for ruder pranks, mirroring the pathology of then-popular daytime programs like *The Jerry Springer Show*. After one particularly harsh stunt in which a person was injured, *Candid Camera* was successfully sued in 2003.

From Rude to Crude

This later incarnation of *Candid Camera* inspired shows like *Punk'd*, *Girls Behaving Badly* and *Jackass*. *Jackass*, which aired on MTV from 2000 to 2002, was hosted by Johnny Knoxville. Knoxville's cast of daredevils performed dangerous, destructive, and ill-advised stunts that often ended in injuries. The show was popular with impressionable adolescents, some of whom—against posted disclaimers and warnings—attempted to re-create the stunts at home. *Jackass* came to the attention the U.S. Congress in January 2001, when a Connecticut teenager allowed friends to douse him with lighter fluid and then set him on fire—a stunt based on one he'd seen on *Jackass*. The teen suffered severe burns, requiring numerous skin grafts, and Senator Joseph Lieberman denounced MTV and its parent company Viacom for its failure to protect its young viewers. Under pressure from the senator, *Jackass* was rescheduled later in the evening and reruns of episodes were curtailed.

Dysfunctional Families

Television's original dysfunctional family was the Bunkers, the fictional characters from the comedy-drama-saga *All in the Family*. As soon as this Norman Lear-created show began airing on CBS on January 12, 1971, it sent shockwaves through America. The show's lead character, Archie Bunker (portrayed by Carroll O'Connor), was one of the most memorable ever created on television. He was unapologetically racist, sexist, xenophobic, and homophobic, but his profound ignorance and cultural insensitivity drew laughter, not derision. Lear, an unrepentant liberal, discovered a formula that worked: to defuse the beliefs of bigots like Archie Bunker, one must hold them up to ridicule. For four straight years (1972–76), *All in the Family* was the number one-rated show in America. After Archie, virtually any "edgy" character was possible on network television.

Television's original "real-life" dysfunctional family was the Louds, the subject of a series called *An American Family*, aired on PBS in 1973. The Louds, of upscale Santa Barbara, California, allowed cameras to document their lives over a period of months in 1971; the resultant 300 hours of footage was culled into twelve episodes that captivated a national audience. During that time, the parents' marriage fell apart, and divorce proceedings were initiated, while one of the sons, the camera-hungry Lance, announced to America that he was a homosexual (it was no secret to his family). For its time, *An American Family* was controversial, sparking editorials (pro and con) and condemnation from conservatives who complained about its depiction of a crumbling nuclear family. Years later, when the revelations on the show were no longer controversial, PBS filmed a follow-up broadcast, *Lance Loud: A Death in an American Family*, chronicling the last days of the charismatic son, who was HIV positive and died soon after the taping ended. This "final" episode of the show aired in 2003.

In the Louds' wake, family dysfunction was a staple of reality television. Perhaps because the explosion of cable channels and the advent of Internet-based YouTube had dissipated the concept, these outrageous "unrehearsed" shows caused little scandal. (*See also* Chapter 7, "Internet Scandals.") The most controversial shows were *The Osbournes*, as it "starred" the foul-mouthed heavy-metal-rock icon Ozzy Osbourne, and *The Anna Nicole Show*, because the troubled silicon-inflated "star" eventually died of a drug overdose. Such shows went from the ridiculous to the surreal, with *Hogan Knows Best*, chronicling the life of pro wrestler and paterfamilias Hulk Hogan, and *Tommy Lee Goes to College*, chronicling the intellectual odyssey of Motley Crue's former singer.

More controversial were the shows that evoked novels like George Orwell's *1984* and William Golding's *Lord of the Flies*. These "reality competitions" were set in exotic, isolated, and/or insulated locations; they tested the psychological and physical endurance of the contestants. One of the shows took its name from Orwell. That was *Big Brother*, launched in the United States in 2000 (versions of the show were also produced worldwide). In *Big Brother*, contestants resided in the same house where every activity was filmed. Similarly themed, *Survivor* was launched in 2000 and also proved a success. Rather than being trapped inside the same house, contestants were confined to an isolated location, where they lived off their wits. These types of shows reached a nadir, of sorts, on *Celebrity Rehab with Dr. Drew*, launched in 2007. On this show, fading stars like Brigitte Nielsen, porn actors, and pro wrestlers grappled with their addictions on camera. This grew out of the popularity of *Breaking Bonaduce*, a reality show that chronicled the chemical abuse and suicidal tendencies of a former child star.

Everybody Famous for Fifteen Minutes

Less bleak but no less controversial was the TV genre devoted to showcasing star-struck amateurs and undiscovered stars as they display previously hidden, or nonexistent, talents. This concept originated with the radio show *Major Bowes' Amateur Hour*, first broadcast in 1934 and adapted for television by Ted Mack in 1948. From 1958 to 1970, *Ted Mack and the Original Amateur Hour* was a staple on CBS. The concept was updated on *Star Search*, hosted by Ed McMahon (1983–95). However, the most popular show in this genre is *American Idol*, launched on the Fox Network in 2002. Each week, contestants perform for a trio of "celebrity judges," including the razor-tongued Simon Cowell, as well as the viewers at home, who vote for the winners by phone. Because each season's winner has gone on to a lucrative career in the music business, the stakes are high. Partly because of this, *American Idol* has been accused of manipulating viewers to vote according to a preordained script. Elton John, a guest judge, accused the show of racism for voting off the talented African American singer Jennifer Hudson in the semifinals. The shows most talked about have involved the judge Paula Abdul, whom one contestant claimed had initiated a sexual relationship with him. After a scandalously protracted probe, Fox determined that Abdul was innocent, at least of this affair. Spin-off shows, like *America's Next Top Model* and *Dancing with the Stars*, have emulated the formula of *American Idol*.

TELEVISION CREATES ITS OWN SCANDAL

Quiz Show Scandals

The quiz show was a staple of American television in the 1950s. This format was popular with network executives because it was cheap to produce and offered reliable profits, with ad revenues generating a profit margin of up to 800 percent. By the 1970s, quiz and game shows accounted for 60 percent

Charles Van Doren, a contestant on the quiz show *Twenty-One*, was celebrated for his string of victories. He was a fraud, coached by the show's producers and provided with the answers, creating the biggest scandal in television broadcasting. Courtesy of Library of Congress, Prints and Photographs Division.

of the networks' gross income.[13] The format was also popular with audiences because it offered live drama with changing casts—everyday people, like themselves—and made viewers feel that they could win the prizes if they were the contestants.

However, the quiz show also generated scandal. The most popular quiz show in television history—measured by audience share—was *The $64,000 Question*, which debuted on June 5, 1955. The show was so popular that CBS created a spin-off, *The $64,000 Challenge*, in April 1956. The shows were the number one- and two-rated shows on television. To compete, NBC launched its own prime-time quiz show, *Twenty-One*, in 1957. The show didn't fare well until Charles Van Doren became a contestant. The scion of a distinguished literary family, he was handsome and humble. When he defeated *Twenty-One*'s champion, Herbert Stempel, whom viewers saw as prickly and crude, Van Doren was an overnight sensation. By the time he lost to contestant Vivienne Nearing, Van Doren had won $129,000, and was famous. He landed a job cohosting NBC's *The Today Show*. However, the miffed Stempel contacted the press to tell them that *Twenty-One*'s producers had rigged the contest to assure that Van Doren would beat him. He claimed that producers Dan Enright and Albert Freedman had told him to "purposely lose" to the more popular contestant. At first, the press sat on the story, but by 1958, similar claims were made by other miffed quiz show contestants, on *The $64,000 Question*, *The $64,000 Challenge*, and *Dotto*, as well as *Twenty-One*. Stempel's story was printed in the *New York Journal-American*, sparking a New York grand jury probe lasting nine months and involving 200 witnesses. A similar probe was undertaken by the U.S. House Legislative Oversight Committee in October 1959. Van Doren testified on November 2, 1959, and admitted, "I was deeply involved in a deception." He said the show's producers provided him with answers, coached him on how to behave, ad-lib, and even how to "pat his brow to build suspense." President Eisenhower proclaimed the quiz shows' deception as "a terrible thing to do to the American public."[14]

Payola to Play-ola, on Television and Radio

Soon after the quiz show scandal ended in firings, fines, and cancellations, television was hit by a bigger scandal. This one also involved radio broadcasting. In early 1960, a disc jockey at Detroit's WJBK admitted to a Congressional committee that he accepted payola, in cash and gifts, from record companies to play their new singles. This was the culmination of a long investigation of the record industry by the Federal Trade Commission. The most scandalous revelation was that Dick Clark, host of the television music variety show *American Bandstand*, was among those facing charges. Clark, whose squeaky-clean image was bolstered by his youthful looks, owned large interests in three record companies whose product he played on his show, without revealing the conflict of interest to viewers. Evidence against Clark included his playing "Sixteen Candles" by the Crests twenty-seven times in thirteen weeks after he'd become part owner of the record company (though he'd only played it four times in ten weeks prior to this deal), as well as the fact that he had a financial stake in 27 percent of the records he played over the two years the FTC probed *American Bandstand*. When Clark testified before Congress, he displayed the proper deference to the committee and was, in the words of one Congressman, "a fine young man." Though he escaped prosecution, he had to sever all ties with businesses that presented a conflict of interest with his show. The majority of the payola occurred at AM radio stations, the main conduit for rock 'n' roll, country music, and "race records." Another big name caught by the feds in the payola probe was Alan Freed, the radio deejay generally credited with coining the term "rock 'n' roll." Freed admitted to taking more than $30,000 from record companies, was fined, and given a suspended sentence. He was indicted the following year for income tax evasion, but, his health ruined, he died in the hospital before he could face the judge. Freed was among 207 radio deejays in forty-two cities found to be part of the payola scam. As a result of this media scandal, Congress passed an anti-payola amendment to the Federal Communications Act on September 13, 1960.

Fade to Black (List)

In 1950, three former FBI agents published an influential pamphlet called *Red Channels*, subtitled "The Report of Communist Influence in Radio and Television." In it, they listed 151 people working in these media "reported" to have Communist leanings. Among the names cited were radio icons like Orson Welles and William Shirer, as well as folksingers, blues and jazz musicians, composers, writers, producers, directors, and renowned actors like Zero Mostel and Burgess Meredith. This blacklist sent a wave of paranoia through broadcasting circles; the major networks walked on eggshells, especially with sponsors wary about having their products affiliated with "Commies." Even CBS, the home of Edward R. Murrow and Shirer, instituted a staff loyalty oath. One particularly tragic blacklisting involved Philip Loeb, an actor who'd starred in the comedy radio show *The Goldbergs*, which was adapted for television in 1949. Because Loeb's name had appeared in *Red Channels*, CBS felt pressured by the show's sponsor, General Foods, to remove him from the cast. Three years later, Loeb committed suicide; the blacklist, resulting in his inability to find work, was blamed. Though few others took the drastic step of suicide, all 151 people in *Red Channels* found their careers curtailed, if not ended. Orson Welles simply left the country, thus effectively ending the radio and TV career of one of America's native geniuses.

The Television Hoax That Canned Soupy

Comedian and television host Soupy Sales (born Milton Hines) was renowned for his manic on-air behavior and endless pranks (including throwing a pie in Frank Sinatra's face). This behavior found him constantly in hot water with the network and censors, but endeared him to his youthful fans. Sales's most notorious prank cost him his job in 1962, when he told all of his young viewers to find their parents' wallets and purses, extract from them the "green paper," and mail it to him. Parents deluged WNET-TV with enraged phone calls, and Soupy was canned.[15]

Longtime game show producer and host Chuck Barris was the next incarnation of Soupy Sales, utilizing the same manic energy to underscore his creation, *The Gong Show* (1976–89). Part parody/part amateur talent show, Barris's creation was carefully monitored by network censors who barred the risqué moments from being broadcast. Some, however, made it past the censors. When these were broadcast, they caused uproars, but also accounted for the show's enduring popularity. One of the most controversial shows involved a pair of teenage girls known as "The Popsicle Twins," who were filmed suggestively slurping on frozen phallic-shaped popsicles. Another time, one of the *Gong Show*'s judges, Jaye P. Morgan, bared her breasts during a contestant's dance routine. Pee Wee Herman (Paul Reubens) was not unlike a combination of Soupy Sales and Chuck Barris. His manic, frantic, surrealistic, and childlike persona was on display every Saturday morning on *Pee Wee's Playhouse* (1986–91) on CBS. In 1991, at the height of his success, Reubens was arrested during a police raid of a pornographic movie theater. Given Pee Wee's popularity with children, CBS was terrified of being affiliated with this scandal and would not allow reruns of the show to be seen. Reubens's career essentially came to an end.

Smothering Two Brothers

During the 1960s, only a few television programs reflected the growing unrest in the nation, as well as the flowering counterculture of the young. Ironically, the most relevant shows on television were comedy venues like the *Smothers Brothers Comedy Hour* (1967–75) and *Rowan and Martin's Laugh-In* (1968–73). Tom and Dick Smothers rose from the ranks of the same politically aware folk-music crowd that spawned rebels like Bob Dylan, Phil Ochs, and Joan Baez. In fact, Baez's appearance on a March 1969 show resulted in the Smothers Brothers being removed from the air by CBS, the network objecting to Baez's dedicating the song "Green Green Grass of Home" to "my husband David [Harris], who is going to prison soon." Harris was a draft resistor whose imprisonment was a cause célèbre within the antiwar movement. Earlier, CBS had censored a song by Pete Seeger, "Waist Deep in the Big Muddy," for its antiwar theme, and objected to a jocular monologue about the meaning of

Easter by comedian David Steinberg. Though soon reinstated, the *Smothers Brothers Comedy Hour* had a wobbly ride for the duration, eventually airing on—and being canceled by—all three networks. Regular guests like Pat Paulsen and George Carlin kept the scandal fires burning. Well in advance of Watergate, Paulsen's mock-presidential campaigns reflected the degraded status of the highest office in the land in the eyes of an increasingly skeptical electorate. The network, in fact, asked him to tone down the act for fear of having to offer equal time to other candidates.

The Rocking Beat of Scandal

Arguably, the first rock 'n' roll TV scandal involved Elvis Presley. The young star had taken America by storm in 1956, with the unprecedented feat of seven hit singles and $6 million in royalties. Earlier appearances on the Dorsey Brothers and Steve Allen television variety shows drew high ratings, but nothing like the ratings for his first appearance on the *Ed Sullivan Show* on September 9, 1956, when nearly 83 percent of America's television sets tuned in, the biggest single audience in TV history. Many parents did not like what they saw, and *New York Times* critic Jack Gould claimed that Elvis "injected movements of his tongue and indulged in wordless singing that were singularly distasteful" and performed a "gross national disservice" by arousing teenagers. The biggest scandal occurred on January 6, 1957, on Presley's third Sullivan show appearance. Buckling to pressure from critics and parents, CBS agreed to allow the cameras to film Presley only from above the waist, so as not to allow his hip-shaking and thigh-rubbing to corrupt the morals of the young.

Ed Sullivan played host to another (nonmusical) scandal on October 18, 1964, when comic Jackie Mason was alleged to have made an obscene gesture on live television. Apparently, Mason mistook Sullivan's offstage directions as a taunt and began making gestures back at Sullivan. The camera caught an angry Sullivan, who tore up Mason's contract, alleging the comic had made an obscene gesture at him. Mason filed a libel suit against Sullivan, who invited him back two years later, after which the suit was dropped.

On September 17, 1967, the Doors were Sullivan's musical guest. The group was scheduled to perform their popular single "Light My Fire," and CBS officials demanded that the word *higher* be deleted from the song, for its drug connotations. Though the group allegedly agreed ahead of time to do so, singer Jim Morrison defied them when the group performed live. Earlier that same year, the Rolling Stones had, at CBS's request, changed the lyrics of their song "Let's Spend the Night Together" to "let's spend some time together."

Two days earlier, on September 15, 1967, the Smothers Brothers played host to the British pop band the Who. Though CBS's fire marshals forbade pyrotechnics, the Who's drummer Keith Moon packed his kit with extra explosives, to blow out the front of his bass drum at the end of the set (a Moon trademark). The explosion, occurring after Who leader Pete Town-shend destroyed his guitar and speaker, was nearly catastrophic. It set Town-shend's hair on fire and temporarily deafened him, sliced open Moon's arm, and knocked singer Roger Daltry off his feet. The show was nearly canceled for thwarting CBS policy, and when it aired two days later it is safe to say that American viewers had never seen anything like it.

MTV, which became a cable television staple, debuted on August 1, 1981, as a venue for rock music videos. Up until 1987, MTV's programming was devoted almost entirely to musical performances. Some of these videos generated scandals for their language, sexual connotations, and attacks on organized religion or advocacy of "Satanism." Madonna's career was launched partly by her early videos and appearances on MTV, which generated controversy for their profound influence on the fashions and attitudes of adolescent girls, particularly the vacuity of sentiments in hits like "Material Girl" and "Like a Virgin." Her live performance of "Like a Virgin" at the first MTV Music Awards ceremony in 1984 shocked as many parents as the teenagers it entertained, complete with her writhing on top of a wedding cake wearing sex-shop fashions and a "Boy Toy" belt. By 1989, needing a career boost, Madonna debuted a video of "Like a Prayer" on MTV that featured Catholic icons and salacious scenes of murder and racial prejudice. Adding to the controversy, Madonna simultaneously aired the video as a Pepsi commercial for which she was paid $5 million. She was attacked for her material crassness and for her expropriation of sacred symbols.

Many other videos have generated scandals since that time, but the following music videos were banned from MTV in the wake of criticism from viewers: "A Tout Le Monde" (Megadeth); "American Life" (Madonna); "Arise" (Sepultura); "Be Chrool to Your Scuel" (Twisted Sister); "Body Language" (Queen); "Erotica" (Madonna); "Ghost Ride It" (Mistah F.A.B.); "In My Darkest Hour" (Megadeth); "Jesus Christ Pose" (Soundgarden); "Justify My Love" (Madonna); "Lacquer Head" (Primus); "Reckoning Day" (Megadeth); and "Vans" (The Pack).

As the network's programming expanded to include game shows, reality shows, and dramatic series, conservative critics like the Parents Television Council accused MTV of broadcasting "sleaze" and "smut" that is "family-unfriendly." The American Family Association has called MTV "pro-sex, anti-family, pro-choice drug culture."[16] The fundamentalist lobby Focus on the Family has long warned against the "dangerous messages" broadcast by "MTV Culture." Perhaps the embodiment of that culture was found in MTV's cartoon series, *Beavis and Butt-head*, which aired from 1993 to 1997. The show "starred" a pair of downwardly mobile Texas teens enamored of heavy metal music, tasteless pranks, and crude, but unconsummated, sexual come-ons to teenage girls. They created havoc at school and the fast food restaurant where they worked. Their language offended many parents, and their antics were blamed for two separate fatalities alleged to have been sparked by imitators. Subsequent lawsuits were dropped when it was learned that in each instance the perpetrator had no cable access to the show. Senator Fritz Hollings (D-SC) decried the show's excesses on the floor of the Congress, but botched its name, calling it Buffcoat and Beaver, which then became a recurring motif in the show. The show had as many famous fans as foes, including David Letterman, who often touted it on his talk show. Because the show was deemed too provocative for its intended audience, MTV moved its original 7 P.M. slot to 11 P.M., and the show's creator, Mike Judge, added a disclaimer: "Beavis and Butt-head are not role models. They're not even human, they're cartoons. Some of the things they do could cause a person to get hurt, expelled, arrested ... possibly deported. To put it another way, don't try this at home." (*See also* "Reality Television.")

Maher's 9/11 Comments Get Him 86'ed

The American press was on tenterhooks in the wake of the 9/11 terrorist attacks. Mirroring the collective feeling of the nation, the media was united behind the efforts to take the battle to the terrorists. Dan Rather, the anchorman on *CBS Evening News*, expressed the posture of the media when he told David Letterman, "[Bush] is my commander in chief. All he has to do is tell me where to line up and I'll do it." That this came from a veteran newsman trained to be skeptical sent chills through newsrooms across America. Bill Maher, the comedian host of ABC's *Politically Incorrect*, was not willing to "go along to get along." Less than one week after the attacks, in response to remarks by guest Dinesh D'Souza about the terrorists not being "cowards," Maher said, "We have been the cowards lobbing cruise missiles from 2,000 miles away. That's cowardly. Staying in the airplane when it hits the building, say what you want about it, it's not cowardly. Stupid maybe, but not cowardly." For this offense—and backlash from angry viewers—ABC canceled Maher's contract. Further fanning the scandal, White House press secretary Ari Fleischer, responding to a question about the remarks, said, "All Americans need to watch what they say, watch what they do." Ironically, the scandal made Maher a "free speech" hero, and he has since achieved wider success with *Real Time with Bill Maher*, on HBO cable network, and in bestselling books filled with his irreverent observations.[17]

Dan Would Rather Not

Dan Rather was forced to resign his position as the anchor of *CBS Evening News* in March 2005 when sources for his story on George W. Bush's military record were called into question by the White House and political supporters of the president, who claimed the documents on which the story was based were forgeries. The Rather-narrated story, originally aired in September 2004, claimed Bush had shirked his Air National Guard duties and that his commanding officers were pressured to remove negative material from his service record. Rather maintained the accuracy of his broadcast, and, because he was forced to apologize publicly, he was made to be the scapegoat. After the story aired, CBS fired the producer (Mary Mapes) and asked for the resignations of three other executives, while Rather was forced out of the anchor seat after twenty-four years. On September 19, 2007, Rather filed a $70 million lawsuit in New York's state Supreme Court against CBS, former parent company Viacom, Inc., CBS president and CEO Leslie Moonves, Viacom chairman Sumner Redstone, and former CBS News president Andrew Heyward. The scandal was exacerbated when Katie Couric, a morning show host with no news anchor experience, replaced Rather as the anchor of *CBS Evening News*.

TELEVISION SPORTS SCANDALS

Death in the Ring

Live boxing matches were a weekly staple of television in the 1950s and 1960s. One bout in particular generated a scandal for the simple fact that a boxer died. On March 24, 1962, Emile Griffith and Benny Paret fought their third welterweight championship bout. Griffith had won the first, lost the second (and thus his championship belt), and this "rubber match" was anticipated by millions of fans. Tension was heightened by prefight enmity between the boxers, especially after Paret called Griffith a *maricon*, the Spanish slang word for homosexual. The fight was brutal on both sides. In the twelfth round, Griffith pounded Paret senseless. When the referee tried to separate the boxers, Griffith continued to punch Paret—thirteen times in all. The comatose Paret died ten days later, having never regained consciousness. As a result of the scandal, NBC canceled live boxing broadcasts, and the sport went into decline. Boxing recovered with the emergence of Cassius Clay/Muhammad Ali, who sparked his own share of scandal with his mouth, his religious affiliation, and his antics in the ring.

Heidi Game

On November 17, 1968, the New York Jets and Oakland Raiders played a nationally broadcast football game that, with just over one minute to play, was preempted for a previously scheduled made-for-TV movie, *Heidi*. In the final seconds of the game—denied to viewers—the Raiders scored twice and beat the Jets, 43–32, one of the most improbable comebacks in pro football history. The Raiders were the defending American Football League champs, while the Jets were led by popular and flamboyant quarterback Joe Namath (who would cement his legend at the end of the season, when his upstart Jets beat the Baltimore Colts in Super Bowl III). However, the game ran past its three-hour allotted scheduling slot, and, at a commercial break, NBC cut to the start of *Heidi*. The ensuing backlash from fans was unprecedented. Millions of Americans called NBC switchboards, affiliates, newspapers, and even police departments to register their complaints. NBC was forced to make a public apology. Many fans angry with the network sent NBC numerous items of Heidi paraphernalia in various states of defilement.

Howard Cosell Told It like It Was

Howard Cosell was a self-made gadfly among professional sports journalists. This set him apart from his colleagues, most of whom were part of what he called a "jockocracy." Cosell made his name as the foil of Muhammad Ali, and the verbal sparring between the two made for the most compelling TV sports broadcasts of their day. Cosell took heat for his unwavering support of Ali when the boxer had his championship belt rescinded for refusing military service during the Vietnam War. Cosell also was at the center of the coverage at the 1972 Munich Olympic Games, when Palestinian terrorists killed eleven Israeli athletes. He unleashed another scandal when he made the offhand comment, "There it is, ladies and gentlemen, The Bronx is burning" while broadcasting Game 2 of the 1977 World Series from Yankee Stadium. An abandoned building near the park had caught on fire; Cosell used it as a backdrop for his acerbic social commentary. Cosell never flinched from criticizing the games he covered. He was especially harsh about professional boxing, which was filled with corruption and excess. After Ray Mancini killed Duk Koo Kim in the ring in 1982, Cosell expressed disgust with boxing during a heavyweight bout between Larry Holmes and Randall Cobb, a one-sided fight that should have been stopped when it was clear Holmes could maim the nearly defenseless Cobb. The one stain on Cosell's career was his exclamation, "Look at that little monkey go!" after Washington Redskins receiver Alvin Garrett ran with a pass reception. Because Garrett was black, the phrase was seen as a racial slur, though Cosell had often used it in the past to refer to swift, small white players. Nonetheless, the controversy soured Cosell on sports, and he quit *Monday Night Football* at the end of the season.

Death on the Ring

Though some critics insist that professional wrestling is more of a choreographed dance than sport, the television world was shocked at the death of Owen Hart on May 24, 1999. Just prior to a live pay-per-view television broadcast at Kansas City's Kemper Arena, Hart fell to his death in the ring when a harness to which he was strapped broke loose. As the audience gasped, Hart—known professionally as the "Blue Blazer"—plummeted fifty feet and hit one of the ring's turn buckles. He was declared dead at the scene. It was a body blow to the World Wrestling Federation, which had expanded its weekly audience to 35 million viewers. This unprecedented popularity (and wealth) prompted David Usborne to note in the *Independent*: "It is a revival that has not escaped controversy. Much more than just a sport, wrestling is now a swill of pyrotechnics, soap opera, rock music and, above all, maximum bodily violence. Groins are punched, chairs are smashed and lewdness is celebrated with prostitutes, swearing, homophobia and even simulated sex." This inexplicable tragedy—Hart was being lowered into the ring from the rafters as part of the prefight fanfare—focused attention on the sport's excesses.

ESPN Gives Limbaugh the Bum's Rush

Rush Limbaugh made an inauspicious debut as a television commentator when he was hired in September 2003 by ESPN for its pregame show, *NFL Sunday Countdown*. In only his fourth week on the job, Limbaugh made what were construed as racist remarks about Philadelphia Eagles quarterback Donovan McNabb. Limbaugh attributed McNabb's past success to his preferential treatment by the media because of his black skin. "The media has been very desirous that a black quarterback do well. There is a little hope invested in McNabb and he got a lot of credit for the performance of this team that he didn't deserve." Boycotts of ESPN were organized by Reverend Al Sharpton, and even presidential candidates Howard Dean and General Wesley Clark weighed in on the scandal, insisting that ESPN fire Limbaugh. Limbaugh resigned October 2, 2003, and returned to his radio berth where such remarks were tolerated by his fan base, his so-called "Ditto-heads."

TELEVISION NEWS SCANDALS

Peter Arnett—CNN's Loose Cannon?

The massive air attack on Baghdad that signaled the start of the Persian Gulf War in February 1991 seemed ready-made for television. Indeed, TV was the predominating medium of the conflict, with its video-game-like air attacks and "smart bombs" and the arrival of Ted Turner's Cable News Network (CNN), which could supply twenty-four-hour live coverage of unfolding events. Among Turner's correspondents in Iraq was Peter Arnett, Pulitzer winner for his Vietnam War coverage as a print journalist for the Associated Press. Arnett was not content to cover aspects of the war approved by the Pentagon and White House. Secretary of Defense Dick Cheney placed unprecedented restrictions on the press and the free flow of information at this time. Thus, when Arnett reported on civilian casualties, he provoked the Bush White House into calling him a "traitor." Arnett further inflamed Cheney and the White House by reporting on a U.S. air strike at a civilian shelter in which 400 women and children were killed. Despite these scandals, CNN won the ratings wars with the other networks, as American viewers were transfixed by the live dispatches and the unvarnished inside look at the war.

Another journalist who felt Cheney's wrath was *Time* photojournalist Warren Bocxe who, for allegedly violating Department of Defense press restrictions, was blindfolded and detained for thirty hours by American troops. Though Cheney had always had a contentious relationship with a free press, his dander kicked into high gear during the Gulf War. Working in tandem with General Colin Powell, Cheney restricted access to information, released reports that exaggerated the accuracy of U.S. missile strikes, covered up mistakes, and, in the words of one ABC News producer, "duped" the media. Army Colonel David Hackworth, a decorated war hero who covered the war for *Newsweek*, said, "The American people did not get the truth."[18]

A Mighty Tailwind

Arnett created a more serious scandal for the CNN/*Time* magazine report that aired June 7, 1998, on *NewsStand*. The broadcast made the ominous charge that U.S. Army commandos used sarin nerve gas in a secret mission called "Tailwind," which targeted Americans who'd defected to Laos in 1970, as part of President Nixon's war policy. These soldiers were allegedly hiding out in a Laotian village, all residents of which were wiped out in a matter of minutes. This was alleged to be a "black operation," a covert mission made to look like the enemy had done it and designed to offer the covert perpetrators "plausible deniability." April Oliver and Jack Smith spent eight months researching the story and conducting interviews with firsthand witnesses. However, once the broadcast aired, CNN was bombarded with complaints from former Nixon administration officials and military commanders. Rather than stand by their reporters—Oliver, Smith, and Arnett were all highly regarded veterans—CNN and *Time* issued apologies and retractions, fired Oliver and Smith, and reprimanded Arnett, whose contract was not renewed at CNN. (Arnett had minimal connection to the story, though his name was on the byline of the *Time* article). Oliver and Smith continued to maintain that the Tailwind story was true and their sources rock solid. They even proposed that all of the Tailwind material they gathered for CNN be released to the public (tapes, transcripts, notes, and memos). "Let's make Tailwind a case study for our journalism schools," they told *Brill's Content*. This has yet to happen.

However, the scandal that has effectively ended Arnett's career was his granting of an interview to Saddam-controlled Iraqi TV after U.S. troops invaded the country in March 2003. At the time, Arnett was in Iraq filming a special for *National Geographic*, and Cheney was no longer secretary of defense but vice president under George Bush. Arnett's broadcasts from war zones raised uncomfortable questions for other journalists. Foremost among them were: To whom do journalists owe their allegiances first, their country or the truth?

Should a journalist suppress an atrocity that he has witnessed in order to protect "his" side? Even if he or she does suppress an atrocity during a war, once hostilities have ceased, should he then report what he has seen, and of which he has documentary evidence? In a world of YouTube and instant round-the-clock news outlets and analysis, these are increasingly relevant questions.

Guerilla Marketing Bites

On January 31, 2007, the "guerilla marketing campaign" for a cable TV show backfired horribly. To generate media buzz for the Cartoon Network show *Aqua Teen Hunger Force*, magnetic light boxes depicting the show's cartoon characters making obscene gestures were placed in ten different cities, including Boston, New York, Los Angeles, and Chicago. Only in Boston did people mistake the light boxes—which blinked and had electric wires dangling from them—for bombs. City officials declared an emergency, closing subway lines, bridges, and highways. Bomb squads were dispatched to "defuse" the boxes. The hoax cost the city of Boston millions of dollars, as well as an unquantifiable amount of mental anguish. Turner Broadcasting, sponsors of the show, paid $2 million to settle all legal claims out of court. The real media scandal underlying this unfortunate incident was "guerilla marketing" itself. Though a modern advertising concept, guerilla marketing has roots in wartime propaganda campaigns of deception, psychological gamesmanship, and brainwashing. It also went to the very nature of terrorism, and its intended goal—to foment terror. While critics used the Boston incident to call for an end to such practices, they also admitted that such deception was unlikely to stop. After all, because of the media scandal and panic, the nation suddenly knew about *Aqua Teen Hunger Force*. As they say in advertising, you can't buy that kind of publicity. Edward Bernays would have been proud.

Warning: Infomercial Ahead

Infomercials are a hybrid television genre that grew out of a similar hybrid used in print media, *advertorials* (advertisement copy disguised as an article). Infomercials and advertorials appealed to editors and programmers because they filled space that would otherwise require editorial content costing the network (or newspaper) money. Because media outlets were part of publicly traded telecommunications corporations, owners were more deferential toward shareholders' demands for higher profits than they were committed to the higher calling of journalism. Infomercials were offered free of charge to the networks; they made money for the infomercial producers from sales generated by their broadcast. Though infomercials are required to be labeled "advertising," they can be so cleverly made that viewers don't make that distinction. The self-proclaimed "King of the Infomercial" is Kevin Trudeau, a former car salesman who spent time in prison for credit card fraud. He has also been prosecuted for perpetrating pyramid schemes and agreed to a $1 million out-of-court settlement with the Federal Trade Commission for false advertising. After leaving prison in the early 1990s, Trudeau founded the American Memory Institute, a front for his infomercials. His reputation for salesmanship was made by parlaying products like Mega Memory and Mega Speed Reading—his claims for which defy belief and are impossible to verify—into millions of dollars in sales. His talent was to make infomercials look like actual news broadcasts or network talk shows. One of his techniques was to pretend to talk to guest experts "live via satellite" when, in fact, the "expert" was seated only a few feet away in the studio and filmed on a separate camera. Though he was required to include disclaimers that his "talk show" was actually an advertisement—lasting anywhere from twenty-five to twenty-seven minutes, in order that networks can use the segments for standard thirty-minute programming slots—Trudeau only did so at the end of the broadcast. His slippery practices were perfected on cable venues like Home Shopping Network and Shop America. After years of scrutiny by the FTC, which he described as "extortion of an honest businessman," Trudeau moved to the more forgiving Internet. (*See also* Chapter 7, "Internet Scandals.") He had little choice. In 2004, the FTC banned Trudeau "from appearing in, producing, or disseminating future infomercials that advertise any type of product, service, or program to the public, except for truthful infomercials for informational publications."[19] He also had to pay another $2 million fine the same year.

Chapter 7

INTERNET SCANDALS

The Internet enjoys the same First Amendment protection as print media, which has helped make it an invaluable part of our everyday existence. However, the Internet is also a double-edged sword. On the one hand, it can be a bastion of unfiltered news and opinion, a vehicle for community activism, and a great leveler of the field in an age when corporations own most media outlets and control the messages therein. On the other hand, there are people like Matt Drudge, the fedora-wearing—in homage to Walter Winchell (*see also* Chapter 5, "Newspapers and Magazines")—proprietor of *The Drudge Report*, a popular news Web site he began in 1994 that traffics in undocumented rumor, innuendo, and partisan attacks against anyone with whom he disagrees politically. Drudge is, said Jeannette Walls, television columnist, "the personification of how scandal had hijacked the news."[1]

Prior to creating his site, Drudge had no previous journalism experience, never went to college, and was a clerk at CBS Studios' gift shop near Hollywood. Nonetheless, he came into prominence on January 16, 1998, when his Web site carried this headline: "*Newsweek* KILLS STORY ON WHITE HOUSE INTERN BLOCKBUSTER REPORT: 23 YEAR OLD FORMER WHITE HOUSE INTERN, SEX RELATIONSHIP WITH PRESIDENT." Drudge didn't report the story; he reported the story of *Newsweek*'s *not* reporting the story. He was tipped off by an unnamed source inside the magazine, which had decided not to run the story about Monica Lewinsky. Once he reported on it, the mainstream media now felt compelled to do so too. Drudge appeared on the TV news show *Meet the Press* on January 25, 1998, where he portrayed himself as "the little guy," an "outsider," and a "citizen reporter." He hailed the Internet as the field leveler for citizens shut out of mainstream media's conversation.

Drudge continued to traffic in scandal, predominantly of a political nature, and has been regularly attacked by the targets of his stories and media experts. Soon after the Lewinsky revelation, Drudge faced a $30 million libel lawsuit filed by White House assistant Sidney Blumenthal over the story that he beat his wife, then retracted the story the next day, blaming "bad information."

The sources cited in his "story" were "top GOP operatives" who, of course, went unnamed. But the story was out there, accepted by some as fact, which Drudge's critics said was his real motive to begin with. Blumenthal sued Drudge for libel, but later settled out of court. Other fabrications that Drudge reported as fact didn't end up in a courtroom: that Bill Clinton had a bald eagle tattooed on his penis, that Ken Starr had seventy-five photographs of Monica Lewinsky and Bill Clinton "together," and that Hillary Clinton was going to be indicted. Again, during the 2004 presidential campaign, Drudge ran a story insinuating that John Kerry's campaign would collapse because of the senator's alleged affair with an intern. The story proved false, but, again, the suggestion of impropriety had already made its way around the Internet. That it had echoes of the damaging revelations about Bill Clinton was no coincidence, according to Drudge's critics, who've charged the gossip hound with being in league with the Republican Party. When confronted with his egregious errors, Drudge claimed 80 percent accuracy. His only allegiance, said Walls, "was to scandal."

NO LONGER LEFT BEHIND

On the other side of the political fence, Salon.com, one of the first Internet-only magazines, broke a story about Representative Henry Hyde, a high-ranking Republican leading the effort to impeach Clinton for the Lewinsky affair. According to the story, Hyde was himself guilty of sexual misconduct, having carried on a seven-year affair with a married woman. Only the persistence of Norman Sommer, a retired businessman upset over the hounding of Clinton, brought the story about Hyde's behavior to light. Sommer contacted fifty-seven media outlets before David Talbot, at Salon.com, agreed to talk to him about the Hyde affair. When the story broke, Hyde chalked it up to a "youthful indiscretion" (he was in his 40s when the affair ended, and it destroyed the woman's marriage, but not his own). Salon.com's story kicked off a series of events that drove the impeachment effort into the gutter. Blumenthal, blamed for leaking the Hyde story, was dragged before special prosecutor Ken Starr. "In a way, it was the law of unintended consequences," said Sommer. "It slowed the push for impeachment long enough to get Newt [Gingrich] sniffed out, then [Representative Robert] Livingstone had to resign after being outed by *Hustler*, who got the idea from *Salon*. Hyde was a sure bet for Speaker of the House, but not after the *Salon* story."[2]

Fake Journalist/Fake News

The credentials of journalists who claim to represent Internet news outlets have also been a source of skepticism, if not scandal. The most egregious example was the case of James Dale Guckert, who wrote under the byline "Jeff Gannon" and claimed to represent an Internet venue called Talon News in

2003. In reality, Guckert had no journalism experience; his training consisted of a two-day seminar at the "Leadership Institute Broadcast School of Journalism," said to be for "conservatives who want a career in journalism"; his only "published" work was found on Web sites of homosexual escort services under the name "Bulldog." Regardless of his thin resume, Guckert was given full White House press credentials from 2003 to 2005 and never subjected to the intense security scrutiny others in the press corps regularly faced. Further, Gannon was the one reporter on whom President George W. Bush was said to rely for a friendly question. Gannon's questions were, in fact, so friendly that he was soon suspected of being a "plant." For example, at a January 26, 2005, press conference, Gannon did not so much ask a question as deliver an editorial, one with which the president agreed. Gannon's verbatim "question" was: "Senate Democratic leaders have painted a very bleak picture of the U.S. economy. Harry Reid was talking about soup lines. And Hillary Clinton was talking about the economy being on the verge of collapse. Yet in the same breath they say that Social Security is rock solid and there's no crisis there. How are you going to work—you've said you are going to reach out to these people—how are you going to work with people who seem to have divorced themselves from reality?"[3]

After Guckert's dubious press credentials came to light, it was discovered that regardless of the fact that he was using a fake name, he had still been given clearance by the Secret Service to attend White House press events. His organization, Talon News, did not have an office and was underwritten by GOPUSA, a Republican-run Web site. Talon News was essentially a front for the fictional Gannon to get White House press credentials. Neither the White House press office nor Guckert faced any legal consequences for this elaborate ruse. And Gannon continued to pose as a journalist.

PARTISAN POLITICS

The Internet—and its "cousins" e-mail and blogs—gave journalists new weapons with which to deceive, or enlighten and empower, their readers. The shadow of Edward R. Murrow looms over some of the best of these sites, including Talking Points Memo, or TPM, an Internet-only news organization founded and edited by Joshua Micah Marshall, a historian and literary scholar turned political pundit.

Founded as a political blog in late 2000, mostly in opposition to the tainted presidential election, TPM soon established itself in the cacophony of competing voices for its professionalism, knowledge of complicated issues, and intelligent political commentary. Typical of news organizations in the past, TPM was relentless in its pursuit of a story. Indeed, TPM was credited with keeping alive a number of political scandals ignored by the mainstream media, including the 2006–2007 U.S. Attorney firing scandal, the corruption case of

Representative Duke Cunningham, and the pro-segregation speech of Senator Trent Lott. Cunningham went to prison for his corruption and Lott lost his post as Senate Majority Leader, largely because of TPM. By 2007, TPM had a fulltime staff of ten, with interconnected Web sites (TPM Café, TPM Muckraker, TPM Election Central, and the main Talking Points Memo) and an average daily readership of 400,000. Many TPM readers and contributors have connections to Washington, D.C., power circles and, like Drew Pearson and Jack Anderson's "Washington Merry Go Round" column in the heyday of print journalism, TPM is read and feared by the power brokers in Washington, D.C. Collectively, Marshall and his staff and users pore over thousands of pages of government documents. TPM also does serious political reporting, with two fulltime Washington-based investigators on its staff.

Blogs on the Political Beat

The influence of daily print journalism and traditional television news has waned as politically partisan Internet sites have become part of Americans' daily reading habits. Often personality-driven and always opinionated, Weblogs (or blogs) have also empowered individuals to engage themselves, and their readers, in the political process. Among the most prominent of the blogs and political news sites, the following have been sources of scandals, big and small.

Daily Kos

Started by Markos Moulitsas Zuniga in 2002, Daily Kos had attracted one million visitors per day by 2005—more than the top fifty conservative blogs combined. It is now the most trafficked left-wing blog in the world, with an average of 519,000 visits each weekday and 14 to 24 million per month. Opinionated and partisan, Daily Kos is driven by a wide array of provocative voices known by screen names (e.g., Meteor Blades, DarkSyde, Georgia10, Hunter, mcjoan, MissLaura), as well as establishment figures like Representative John Conyers, Senator Jon Tester, former Governor Eliot Spitzer, General Wesley Clark, and former president Jimmy Carter. Daily Kos has been credited with energizing the political grassroots via the Internet, what Zuniga calls "the Netroots." The site was successful enough by 2007 to initiate a fellowship program to groom young progressive activists. Some guest bloggers on Daily Kos have gone on to start their own sites, including Steve Gilliard (NewsBlog), who died in June 2007. Daily Kos has come under fire for alleged conflicts of interest. Bill O'Reilly has called it a "hate site." During the 2008 presidential campaign, Hillary Clinton's supporters complained about the amount of negative commentary their candidate was receiving, in deference to Senator Obama's campaign. Many staged a "strike" of the site, to which Zuniga responded that Senator Clinton "doesn't deserve fairness on this site" and suggested her supporters seek other sites more in tune with her campaign.[4]

MyDD

Jerome Armstrong started the site, one of the most informed on the inside workings of political campaigns, in 2001. Rather than face conflict-of-interest charges—that he would promote the campaign of someone by whom he was being paid—Armstrong shut the site down in 2003 after he was hired as a consultant by Howard Dean's presidential campaign. MyDD resumed posting in 2004. Armstrong and Zuniga collaborated on an influential book, *Crashing the Gate: Netroots, Grassroots, and the Rise of People Powered Politics* (2006).

Firedoglake

A collaborative blog founded by Jane Hamsher and Christy Hardin Smith, Firedoglake rose to prominence for its live blogging from the Supreme Court during the confirmation hearing for Samuel Alito and John Roberts, as well as the trial of Lewis Libby. They created a scandal for their heated attacks on the campaign of Senator Joe Lieberman, and impassioned (some said, too impassioned) support for Lieberman's challenger, Ned Lamont, in the 2006 Connecticut Senate race.

InstaPundit

Started in 2001 by University of Tennessee law professor Glenn Reynolds, Instapundit is a conservative political blog. Though Reynolds more often than not sides with Republican policies, InstaPundit has castigated both political parties for falling prey to lobbyists' money.

Free Republic

Free Republic was founded by Jim Robinson in 1997. In 2004, after being accused of mistreating visitors to his site with whom he disagreed, Robinson posted a letter that has since served as Free Republic's mission statement. The letter said, in part, "Free Republic is pro-God, pro-life, pro-family, pro-Constitution, pro-Bill of Rights, pro-gun, pro-limited government, pro-private property rights, pro-limited taxes, pro-capitalism, pro-national defense, pro-freedom, and-pro-America. We oppose all forms of liberalism, socialism, fascism, pacifism, totalitarianism, anarchism, government enforced atheism, abortionism [*sic*], feminism, homosexualism [*sic*], racism, wacko environmentalism, judicial activism, etc. We also oppose the United Nations."[5] The extremism of some of Free Republic's members has been criticized. Though some remarks that are racist or incite violence have been removed, many are allowed to remain posted. The site has also drawn fire for "Freeping" online opinion polls—enlisting its members to, en masse, vote on polls, thus skewing them toward the right wing.

MoveOn.org

Arguably the most controversial of the political sites, Moveon.org is a progressive political advocacy network started in 1998 by Joan Blades and Wes Boyd, cofounders of Berkeley Systems. Upset by the attempt to impeach Bill Clinton, they began an e-mail petition campaign to "censure President Clinton and move on." The success of that drive led to the formation of MoveOn.org as a permanent site to promote progressive causes and candidates. The zealousness of Moveon.org's efforts sparked scandals that hurt their causes. Most recently, Moveon.org was attacked for its full-page ad in the *New York Times* on September 10, 2007. In the ad, Moveon.org suggested that General David Petraeus, commander of U.S. forces in Iraq scheduled to testify in Congress, should be called General "Betray Us" for what the group felt was his propagandizing on behalf of the Bush White House's failed war policy. Republicans seized the issue, exploiting Moveon's ad to fortify their shaky political fortunes. Representative John Cornyn proposed a resolution, which passed 341–79 in the U.S. House, to "condemn personal attacks on the honor and integrity of General Petraeus." A similar bill passed the U.S. Senate, putting Democrats on the defensive. The *Times* was criticized for giving the group a discount ad rate and violating its own policy, which forbids "attacks of a personal nature." President Bush weighed in on the scandal, saying the ad was "disgusting" and insisting "most Democrats ... are more afraid of irritating [MoveOn] than they are of irritating the United States military."[6]

Right Makes Might

The most extreme right-wing Internet site that attracts a wide audience is Overthrow.com, which was founded in 2002 by William White, "commander" of the American National Socialist Workers' Party in Roanoke, Virginia. The Southern Poverty Law Center has called Overthrow.com "the second most popular racist site on the Internet."[7] White unleashed a national scandal, and drew widespread notoriety, when he praised Dylan Klebold and Eric Harris, the pair who murdered twelve students and a teacher at Columbine High School in Colorado. In 2005, the *New York Times* reported that White "laughed" when U.S. district court judge Joan Lefkow's husband and mother were murdered, after Lefkow ruled against white supremacist Matthew Hale in a trademark dispute.[8] He told the *Roanoke Times* that he hoped for "further killings of Jews and their sympathizers." White is also virulently anti-Semitic, as well as a professed Holocaust denier. In September 2007, Overthrow.com was investigated by the FBI for posting the addresses and phone numbers of the families of the "Jena Six," black teenagers charged with a racially motivated attack on a white student in hurricane-ravaged New Orleans. An FBI spokeswoman said that the site "essentially called for their lynching." Some of the families received repeated threatening phone calls as a result.

INTERNET DANGERS

Shark-infested MySpace Waters

The social-networking Web site MySpace, founded in 2003, has become a source of concern to parents and law enforcement officials. MySpace users are mostly in their teens. As of September 2007, MySpace had 200 million accounts worldwide. Because the site is interactive, it contains content that the registered users post themselves. The intimate nature of MySpace encounters with unseen strangers created nearly perfect conditions for sexual predation. Indeed, numerous criminal cases have resulted when young MySpace users arranged rendezvous with older predators they "met" on the Internet and have been sexually assaulted. In July 2007, MySpace found and deleted 29,000 profiles belonging to registered sex offenders. The company also implemented account restrictions for users under age sixteen.

Kevin Trudeau, the Sequel

After being banned from making infomercials on cable television, Kevin Trudeau moved on to the Internet to peddle his controversial wares. He became a regular guest on iTV in 2006, which streams television programming over the Internet. He also turned his hand to writing books, which are essentially his infomercials that he self-published. As Salon.com's Christopher Dreher wrote, "By shifting his business model from selling supposed cure-all products to peddling books, which are protected by the First Amendment, Trudeau has been able to slip past federal regulators and continue to sell snake oil to the masses—first through his infomercial and now via mainstream book retailers like Amazon.com and Barnes & Noble."[9] His books include *Natural Cures "They" Don't Want You to Know About* (2005) and *The Weight-Loss Cure "They" Don't Want You to Know About* (2007). While both books have become bestsellers, through Trudeau's constant iTV exposure, the contents are under FTC investigation. Trudeau has been accused of inaccurate sourcing, bogus statistics (that conveniently buttress all of his diet and health tips), citing "experts" who have no medical credentials, and perhaps even causing health problems for unsuspecting readers who take his advice seriously.[10]

A Tube Just for You

Founded in February 2005, the Internet online video service YouTube has already spawned a revolution in entertainment and politics. Almost instantly, footage of a scandalous nature can be uploaded onto the YouTube site and shared with millions of people. Because of its timeliness and wide reach, YouTube was instrumental during the 2006 election campaign. It essentially ended the political career of one U.S. Senate incumbent, thus reshaping the makeup of the U.S. Congress. On August 13, 2006, YouTube picked up some footage from a campaign stop in rural Virginia by Senator George Allen. A heavy favorite to win reelection, as well as the front runner for the 2008 Republican presidential nomination, Allen found his career in free fall when he addressed some racist comments at an Indian-American college student named S. R. Sidarth, who was filming the event as a volunteer for Allen's opponent, James Webb. Sidarth, stationed near the front of the hall, filmed Allen saying he was "going to run this campaign on positive, constructive ideas."[11] Then, pointing at Sidarth, Allen said, "This fellow here, over here with the yellow shirt, macaca, or whatever his name is. He's with my opponent. He's following us around everywhere. And it's just great ... Let's give a welcome to macaca, here. Welcome to America and the real world of Virginia." Not only is the word *macaca* a racist epithet (meaning "monkey"), but Sidarth needed no "welcome" to America. He was American-born and graduated as an honors student from his Virginia high school. Once Allen's insensitive remarks were made available on YouTube, they were the death knell of his career. Allen's past association with Confederate memorabilia and previous racist comments were resurrected and made the YouTube rounds. A nearly prohibitive underdog in the race, Democrat James Webb won the Senate seat. Allen's "Macaca moment" was a watershed event for the Internet. Since then, candidates have become more vigilant, lest one of their gaffes become the "Macaca moment" at their own career's end.

Because of the sheer volume of video streamed on YouTube and the number of registered users, Google, Inc. purchased the site for $1.65 billion in Google stock in November 2006. YouTube (and Google) have since been sued for posting videos without permission from the creators, a copyright infringement. As a result of this litigation, YouTube has implemented a self-policing "flagging" feature, whereby users can report videos of questionable or obscene content, or that they believe violate copyrights. The site that had, prior to YouTube, been instrumental in disseminating such footage on the Internet was Crooks and Liars, founded in 2004 by John Amato. It contained an extensive and frequently updated archive of audio and video clips of political events, television, and radio shows. In 2005, the site began offering original audio interviews with news makers on the edges of political scandal.

Wikimedia

Wikipedia is a vast online encyclopedia that was created in 2001 and is sustained by thousands of unpaid volunteers who contribute their money, research, and writing. The mission of its American founder, Jimmy Wales, was to "distribute a free encyclopedia to every single person on the planet in their own language." By 2007, the mission was all but accomplished, as Wikipedia contained more than one million articles in 200 languages and received as many as 14,000 hits per second.[12] Among the many appeals of Wikipedia are that it costs nothing to use or for membership, and it has "open editing." Open editing allows anyone with Internet access to become a Wikipedia member and work on encyclopedia articles, either by producing new entries or editing already existing ones. Because Wikipedia is a nonprofit corporation and takes no advertising, the vast majority of the contributions are made by these thousands of members around the world, most of whom remain anonymous to encyclopedia users. This egalitarian approach to knowledge has also proved to be an Achilles heel. That is, if anyone can contribute, anyone will contribute, including those with vested interests in how an article is worded or a subject presented. For example, a Holocaust denier might doctor the entries for Nazi Germany, World War II, or anti-Semitism, "softening" the language to minimize the horror. Wikipedia users, literally, do not know where the information is coming from. They are, as Blanche DuBois in Tennessee Williams's *A Streetcar Named Desire* put it, "dependent upon the kindness of strangers"— or the honesty and integrity of strangers.

This has caused a series of scandals for Wikipedia that, to be fair, are symptomatic of the hidden dangers of the Internet in general. When one "surfs" this vast network, one is bound to gather some bad or unreliable information, unless it is taken from a site that is openly vetted or attached to a reputable institution (e.g., the Library of Congress, Harvard University, etc.) whose imprimatur signifies legitimacy. The biggest scandal involved one of the most prolific volunteers on Wikipedia, an "administrator" who went by the screen name Essjay. A Wikipedia administrator not only writes entries, but he/she has the power to overrule those who also do this. Essjay claimed, "I hold the following academic degrees: Bachelor of Arts in Religious Studies (B.A.); Master of Arts in Religion (M.A.R.); Doctorate of Philosophy in Theology (Ph.D.); Doctorate in Canon Law (JCD)." Largely due to Stacy Schiff's *New Yorker* reportage in 2006, Essjay lost his cloak of online anonymity. He turned out to be a twenty-four-year-old from Kentucky named Ryan Jordan, who had earned no degrees. Given the stature Jordan/Essjay had achieved in the Wikipedia community and the amount of work he'd done, questions were raised about the accuracy of any, or all, material on the site.

Wikipedia's reputation was further damaged by revelations in the wake of the Essjay scandal. The anonymity of "open editing" was tantamount to inviting the world's wolves into the chicken coop. Indeed, many corporate publicists tampered with Wikipedia articles to reflect the "spin" they want. For example, Exxon-Mobil publicists altered the material about the Exxon Valdez oil spill—the worst manmade environmental disaster in world history—to minimize the damage it did. Other companies caught doing similarly brazen acts of spin-doctoring were Dell, McDonald's, Starbucks, Apple, and Microsoft. Corporations weren't the only entities who breached the wall. Politicians, or members of their staff with official approval, did this. Among the biggest culprits was Representative Marty Meehan (D-MA), whose staff changed his

Wikipedia entry to delete negative (but factual) material. (Meehan went on to become the chancellor of the University of Massachusetts-Lowell). Staff for Senator Conrad Burns (R-MT) and Senator Norm Coleman (R-MN) did the same. Conversely, politicians have also had their biographical entries vandalized by political opponents, with negative, unsubstantiated material added, or positive information deleted. As a result of all these mini-scandals, Wikipedia was forced to change the way it vetted the credentials of administrators. Also, new software was developed (WikiScanner) that tracks all articles or edits back to their source computers, providing both a safety net for abuse and a deterrent against those who would contemplate abusing their membership.

Hookering Up on the Internet

A huge Internet-generated political scandal took place in March 2008, when an FBI investigation of an international prostitution ring called The Emperor's Club V.I.P. uncovered the identity of Eliot Spitzer, New York's governor, as one of the club's regular clients. Within days of his bust—as the club's "Client 9"—Spitzer resigned, bringing to an end a promising political career. The club, based in New York but with prostitutes in Washington, D.C., Miami, London, and Paris as well, secured its "appointments" online, with the fees ranging from $1,000 to $5,500 an hour, paid with credit card or wire transfers of funds; these Internet transactions drew the attention of the FBI. The club rated its prostitutes by diamonds (the more diamonds the higher her fee), but like most online "escort services," circumvented the law by touting itself as a "social introduction service" for "an evening date, a weekend travel companion, or a friend to accompany you during your next business/social function."[13] The club was the tip of an Internet iceberg, with both male and female prostitution having found a lucrative, largely unregulated home in cyberspace. Prostitutes have their own Web sites, contact clients by e-mails and text messages on cell phones, and can be paid discreetly, eliminating the need for pimps. Mayor James West of Spokane, Washington, was forced to resign in December 2005 after he was caught in a gay Internet sex scandal, and U.S. Representative Mark Foley was forced to resign in October 2006 after sending sexually explicit e-mails and instant messages to underage Congressional pages. However, most people who utilize the Internet for the purposes of sex are never caught.[14]

Perfect Match: Paris and Perez Hilton

The closest thing to a grocery store gossip magazine on the Internet may be www.perezhilton.com, a popular blog created in late 2004 by gay activist Mario Armando Lavandeira Jr. Originally called www.PageSixSixSix.com, the blog's name was changed in 2006, playing off the notoriety of heiress-celebrity Paris Hilton, whom Lavandeira claimed as a friend. Generally known for his irreverence, Lavandeira touched off several scandals by "outing" celebrities and public figures, claiming that they were homosexual. Members of the gay community criticized these tactics as irresponsible and, if the information was inaccurate and unsourced, destructive to one's career. Indeed, Lavandeira has reported false news on his blog, including the death of Fidel Castro in August 2007. PerezHilton.com has also been the target of several lawsuits for posting video, audio, and photographic content without permission from the creators. Lavandeira claimed that his was acceptable behavior under the "fair use" clause in the Copyright Act. The outcomes of the lawsuits have yet to be decided.[15]

Googling Along

As one of the Internet's major players, Google Inc., founded in 1998, has an impact far beyond cyberspace. One of their most controversial initiatives has been Google Book Search, an effort to "scan every book ever published and to make the full texts searchable."[16] While this monumental undertaking was touted as a democratization of information, Google is one of the most profitable companies in the world. Thus, many critics have called into question the real motives of this effort. Book publishers and authors are particularly wary of Google Book Search, as it would virtually eliminate any need for future hardbound editions of most books. Two lawsuits have been filed in federal court against Google, one by the Authors Guild and another by a consortium of publishers, claiming Google Book Search is a violation of U.S. copyright law. Not only are the authors of the scanned books not notified or asked for permission for their work being scanned and made available for free on the Internet, but authors worry that this effort sets a precedent for the future.[17]

Google has been similarly criticized for hosting pirated copies of feature films without permission or knowledge of the copyright owners. This is in addition to the $1 billion suit filed by Viacom against Google for allegedly posting approximately 150,000 copyrighted works on its popular YouTube Web site. (*See also* "A Tube Just for You.")

NOTES

INTRODUCTION

1. Posner, *Law and Literature*, 308; Kalven, *A Worthy Tradition*, 40.
2. McLuhan and Fiore, *The Medium Is the Message*, 26.
3. Ibid., 63.

CHAPTER 1

1. A facsimile of *Publick Occurrences Both Forreign and Domestick* is available online at: http://www.masshist.org/database/query3.cfm?queryID=219.
2. Ghiglione, *The American Journalist*, 14.
3. Rossiter, *The First American Revolution*, 125–26.
4. Ibid., 127–28.
5. Ibid., 129.
6. Mott, *American Journalism*, 384.
7. Wikipedia, "Muckraker."
8. Ghiglione, 50.
9. Steffens, *Autobiography*, 373.
10. These events, and Reed's character, were depicted in Warren Beatty's 1981 film, *Reds*.
11. Kaplan, *Lincoln Steffens*, 250.
12. Anderson, *Confessions of a Muckraker*, 19.
13. Ibid., 106–7.
14. Bisbort, *What Happened Here?*, 17.
15. Anderson, 213.
16. Oudes, ed., *From: The President*, xxxvi.
17. Kershaw, *Hitler*, 194.
18. Hersh, *My Lai 4: A Report on the Massacre and Its Aftermath*.
19. Hersh, *The Target Is Destroyed: What Really Happened to Flight 007*.
20. *CNN Late Edition with Wolf Blitzer*, aired March 9, 2003.
21. Ungar, *The Papers*, 11–19.
22. Ibid., 14–15.
23. Ibid., 136–46.
24. Ibid., dust jacket.

25. Mount Holyoke College has the full "Gravel" edition of the Pentagon Papers available for free, online at: http://www.mtholyoke.edu/acad/intrel/pentagon/pent1.html.

26. Shabecoff, *A Fierce Green Fire*, 107–10.

27. Nader, *Unsafe at Any Speed*.

28. *LIFE*, March 19, 1951.

29. Fireman, ed., *TV BOOK*, 264.

30. Ibid.

31. To hear and read the transcript of Welch and Senator McCarthy, go to: http://www.americanrhetoric.com/speeches/welch-mccarthy.html.

32. Ghiglione, 92.

33. Transcript of Thomas hearings, October 11, 1991.

34. Boorstin, *The Image*, 66–70.

35. Blumenthal, *The Clinton Wars*.

36. FOX News, November 8, 2005.

37. Academy Awards ceremony, March 23, 2003.

38. Kornbluh, "Storm over Dark Alliance," *CJR*, January/February 1997.

39. Rich, *New York Times*, November 7, 2007.

40. Haskew, ed., *The World War II Desk Reference*, 476–81.

41. Tye, *Father of Spin*, 24.

42. McGinnis, *Selling of the President*, 178.

CHAPTER 2

1. Ghiglione, *The American Journalist*, 34–42.

2. Ibid., 51.

3. Watkins, *On the Real Side*, 93.

4. Bisbort, *Books That Shook the World*.

5. Watkins, 87.

6. Larson, *Civilization*, February/March 1997, 46–55.

7. Watkins, 307.

8. Ibid., 308.

9. Palmer, *Dancing in the Street*, 82–83.

10. Baise, *Twentieth-Century Literary Criticism*, Vol. 82, 201.

11. Campbell, *Talking at the Gates*, 167–75.

12. Griffin, *Black Like Me*.

13. *Time* magazine, "Will the Real Nat Turner Please Stand Up?," July 12, 1968, 43.

14. Cleaver, *Soul on Ice*, 82.

15. Cleaver, *Post-Prison Writings*, 203–4.

16. Fraser, *Bell Curve Wars*, 112.

17. Churchill, *On the Justice of Roosting Chickens*, 19.

18. Baise, *Twentieth-Century Literary Criticism*, Vol. 58, 26.

19. Ibid.

20. "God's Law," an interview with Kahane, 1985.

21. Gates, "The Charmer," *Thirteen Ways of Looking at a Black Man*, 123–54.

22. Ibid.

23. Ibid.

24. Baise, *Twentieth-Century Literary Criticism*, Vol. 58, 31.

25. Goldberg, *Salon*, July 29, 2002.

26. CNN, October 9, 2003.

CHAPTER 3

1. Haffercamp, "Un-Banning Books."
2. Teachout, *The Skeptic*, 225–28.
3. Hutchison, *Tropic of Cancer on Trial*, 46–47.
4. Ibid.
5. Miles, ed. *Allen Ginsberg Howl*, Appendix III, "Legal History of HOWL," 169–74.
6. Ginzburg, press release, 1962.
7. Hutchison, 244–45.
8. Ibid.
9. The American Library Association sponsors an annual Banned Books Week and compiles updated lists of banned books in the United States, www.ala.org.
10. Kunitz and Haycraft, *Twentieth Century Authors*, 423.
11. Wright, *The Looming Tower*, 12.
12. Makower, *Boom!*, 117–18.
13. Ibid. 150–52.
14. Faludi, *Backlash*, 281–90.
15. Ibid., 319–20.
16. Ibid.
17. Yalom, "The Last Taboo," *Stanford Magazine*.
18. Hutchison, 87–88.

CHAPTER 4

1. Levin, *The Holocaust*.
2. Sward, *The Legend of Henry Ford*, 132.
3. Ballantine Books, *I, Libertine* back flap copy.
4. Park, "Mehta Fiction," *Village Voice*, May 16, 2006.
5. *New York Times* coverage.
6. Lee, *New York Times*, January 12, 2008, C1.
7. Rich, "Gang Memoir … Is Pure Fiction," *New York Times*, March 4, 2008.
8. Plotz, *Slate*, January 11, 2002.
9. Greenstein, February 2000, *Brill's Content*, 32.
10. Cleaver, *Soul on Ice*, 31–39
11. Dardis, *The Thirsty Muse*, 3–4.
12. Fenster, *Ether Day*, 85–110.
13. Bouton, *Glad You Didn't Take It Personally*, 16.
14. Hubbard, *Dianetics*, 6.
15. Carroll, *The Skeptic's Dictionary*, entry for "Dianetics."
16. www.bookscan.com.
17. *Punch*, February 19, 1988, 46.
18. Makower, *Boom!*, 85–86.
19. Brill, *Brill's Content*, February 2000, 68.

CHAPTER 5

1. Mencher, *News Reporting and Writing*, 68–69.
2. Ghiglione, *The American Journalist*, 58.
3. Ibid., 129–30.

4. Jones, "She Had to Die!" *American Heritage*, 1979, 20–31.
5. Ibid.
6. Knightly, *The First Casualty*, 55.
7. Ibid., 56.
8. Ghiglione, 62.
9. Burnam, *The Dictionary of Misinformation*.
10. Gabler, *Winchell*, 252–53.
11. Ibid., 186–91.
12. Ghiglione, 70–71.
13. Krassner, *Confessions*.
14. Author interview, 2007.
15. Reidelbach, *Completely Mad*, 26–28.
16. Ibid.
17. Blair, *Burning Down My Masters' House*.
18. Morrison, *USA Today*, March 19, 2004.
19. Toppo, "Educ. Dept. paid commentator to promote law," *USA Today*, January 7, 2005.
20. Walls, *Dish*, 13–14.
21. Ellroy, *Destination Morgue!*
22. Walls, 36–50.
23. Ibid.
24. Ibid., 299–300.
25. Ibid., 298.
26. Ibid., 293.
27. Ibid., 292–98.
28. *60 Minutes*, September 1, 1997.
29. Walls, 325.
30. Carlson, "Focusing on the New Paparazzi," *Washington Post*, C5, April 1, 2008.
31. Pearson, "The Britney Beat; Riding with the Paparazzi," Associated Press, April 5, 2008.
32. Brill, *Brill's Content*, September 1999, 99.
33. *Atlanta Journal Constitution*, October 28, 1996.

CHAPTER 6

1. Brinkley, *Voices of Protest*, 97.
2. Ghiglione, *The American Journalist*, 87.
3. To hear the "War of the Worlds" broadcast, go to www.mercurytheatre.info.
4. Eliot, *Death of a Rebel*, 133–34.
5. The events inspired a one-man play by Eric Bogosian, which was adapted for the film *Talk Radio*, directed by Oliver Stone (1988).
6. MSNBC, "The Savage Nation," July 6, 2003.
7. Walls, *Dish,* 238–43.
8. Senator Lieberman's Web site is: http://lieberman.senate.gov.
9. Colapinto, "Mad Dog," *Rolling Stone*, August 11, 2004.
10. Ibid.
11. Kurtz, "O'Reilly, Producer Settle Harassment Suit," *Washington Post*, October 29, 2004.
12. National Press Club, transcripts.

13. Fireman, ed., *TV BOOK*, 89.

14. Ibid.

15. Makower, *Boom!*, 117.

16. American Family Association.

17. www.billmaher.com.

18. Sharkey, "Collective Amnesia," *American Journalism Review*, October 2000.

19. Dreher, *Salon*, July 29, 2005.

CHAPTER 7

1. Walls, *Dish*, 2.

2. Bisbort interview, August, 20, 2003.

3. Savage, "White House-friendly Reporter under Scrutiny." *Boston Globe*, February 2, 2005.

4. www.dailykos.com, March 17, 2008.

5. www.freerepublic.com.

6. Luo, and Zeleny, "Behind an Antiwar Ad, a Large and Powerful Liberal Group," *New York Times*, September 15, 2007.

7. www.Overthrow.com.

8. Wilgoren, "Shadowed by Threats, Judge Finds New Horror," *New York Times*, March 2, 2005; Cramer, "White Supremacist Comments on Case," *Roanoke Times*, March 3, 2005.

9. Dreher, *Salon*, July 29, 2005.

10. Oliver and Smith. *Brill's*, February 1999, 58–61.

11. http://www.youtube.com/watch?v=9G7gq7GQ71c.

12. Schiff, "Know It All," *The New Yorker*, July 31, 2006.

13. www.thesmokinggun.com.

14. Rhodes, "Internet Cathouse," Associated Press, March 12, 2008.

15. Abcarian, "Perez Hilton Takes Their Best Shots," *Los Angeles Times*, December 17, 2006.

16. Toobin, "Google's Moon Shot," *The New Yorker*, February 5, 2007.

17. Ibid.

BIBLIOGRAPHY

Aaron, Daniel. *Writers on the Left.* New York: Harcourt, Brace and World, 1961.

Ackroyd, Peter. *Ezra Pound.* London: Thames and Hudson, 1987.

Anderson, Elliott, and Mary Kinzie, eds. *The Little Magazine in America: A Modern Documentary History.* Yonkers, NY: Pushcart, 1978.

Anderson, Jack. *Confessions of a Muckraker.* New York: Random House, 1979.

Baise, Jennifer, ed. *Twentieth-Century Literary Criticism.* Topics Volume. Vol. 82. Detroit: Gale, 1999.

Beinecke Rare Book and Manuscript Library. *Red Letters/Black Lists: Communism and Literary America,* exhibit, 2005.

Bisbort, Alan. "Nobody Is a Nobody, Norman." *Hartford Advocate,* July 24, 2003.

Bisbort, Alan. *What Happened Here? Washington, D.C.* San Francisco: Pomegranate Publications, 2003.

Bisbort, Alan. *When You Read This, They Will Have Killed Me: The Life and Redemption of Caryl Chessman, Whose Execution Shook America.* New York: Carroll and Graf, 2006.

Bisbort, Alan, and Parke Puterbaugh. *Rhino's Psychedelic Trip.* San Francisco: Backbeat, 2000.

Blair, Jayson. *Burning Down My Masters' House: My Life at the New York Times.* Beverly Hills, CA: New Millennium, 2004.

Blumenthal, Sidney. *The Clinton Wars.* New York: Farrar, Straus and Giroux, 2003.

Boorstin, Daniel J. *The Image.* New York: Penguin, 1962.

Borjesson, Kristina, ed. *Into the Buzzsaw: Leading Journalists Expose the Myth of a Free Press.* New York: Prometheus Books, 2002.

Brill, Steven. "How Woodward Goes Wayward." *Brill's Content,* September 1999.

Brill, Steven. "Selling Snake Oil." *Brill's Content,* February 2000.

Brinkley, Alan. *Voices of Protest: Huey Long, Father Coughlin and the Great Depression.* New York: Vintage, 1983.

Brock, David. *Blinded by the Right: The Conscience of an Ex-Conservative.* New York: Crown, 2002.

Burnham, Tom. *The Dictionary of Misinformation.* New York: Thomas Crowell Co., 1975.

Burnham, Tom. *More Misinformation.* New York: Lippincott and Crowell, 1980.

Callow, Simon. *Orson Welles: The Road to Xanadu.* New York: Viking, 1995.

Campbell, James. *Talking at the Gates: A Life of James Baldwin.* New York: Viking, 1991.

Cantril, Hadley. *The Invasion from Mars: A Study in the Psychology of Panic.* Princeton, NJ: Princeton University Press, 1940.

Carlson, Peter. "Focusing on the New Paparazzi." *Washington Post,* April 1, 2008.

Carroll, Robert Todd. *The Skeptic's Dictionary.* Hoboken, NJ: John Wiley, 2003.

Churchill, Ward. *On the Justice of Roosting Chickens.* Oakland, CA: AK Press, 2004.

Clarke, John Henrik, ed. *William Styron's Nat Turner: Ten Black Writers Respond.* Boston: Beacon Press, 1968.

Cleaver, Eldridge. *Soul on Ice.* New York: Dell, 1968.

Cleaver, Eldridge. *Post-Prison Writings and Speeches.* Robert Scheer, ed. New York: Random House/Ramparts, 1969.

Cockburn, Alexander, and Jeffrey St. Clair. *Whiteout: The CIA, Drugs and the Press.* New York: Verso, 1999.

Cooper, Matthew. "Too Good to Check." *Time,* March 29, 2004.

Curcio, Vincent. *Chrysler: The Life and Times of an Automotive Genius.* New York: Oxford University Press, 2000.

Dardis, Tom. *The Thirsty Muse: Alcohol and the American Writer.* New York: Ticknor and Fields, 1989.

Dearborn, Mary. *Mailer: A Biography.* Boston: Houghton Mifflin, 1999.

Draper, Theodore. *A Very Thin Line: The Iran-Contra Affairs.* New York: Hill and Wang, 1991.

Dreher, Christopher. "What Kevin Trudeau Doesn't Want You to Know." *Salon,* July 29, 2005.

Drosnin, Michael. *Citizen Hughes.* New York: Henry Holt, 1987.

Edwards, Bob. *Edward R. Murrow: And the Birth of Broadcast Journalism.* Hoboken, NJ: John Wiley and Sons, 2004.

Eliot, Marc. *Death of a Rebel: Starring Phil Ochs and a Small Circle of Friends.* Garden City, NY: Anchor, 1979.

Ellroy, James. *Destination: Morgue! L.A. Tales.* New York: Vintage, 2004.

Faludi, Susan. *Backlash: The Undeclared War against American Women.* New York: Crown, 1991.

Faulk, John Henry. *Fear on Trial.* New York: Simon and Schuster, 1964.

Fenster, Julie. *Ether Day. The Strange Tale of America's Greatest Medical Discovery,* New York: HarperCollins, 2001.

Fireman, Judy, ed. *TV BOOK: A Celebration of Television.* New York: Workman, 1977.

Foner, Eric, and John A. Garraty, eds. *The Reader's Companion to American History.* Boston: Houghton Mifflin Co., 1991.

Ford, Mark. "The Dream of Allen Ginsberg." *The New York Review of Books,* September 27, 2007.

Frank, Thomas. *What's the Matter with Kansas? How Conservatives Won the Heart of America.* New York: Henry Holt, 2004.

Franken, Al. *Rush Limbaugh Is a Big Fat Idiot, and Other Observations.* New York: Delacorte, 1996.

Fraser, Steven, ed. *The Bell Curve Wars.* New York: HarperCollins, 1995.

Friedrich, Otto. *Decline and Fall.* New York: Harper and Row, 1970.

Gabler, Neal. *Winchell: Gossip, Power and the Culture of Celebrity.* New York: Alfred A. Knopf, 1994.

Gallagher, Robert S. "The Radio Priest." *American Heritage,* 1972.

Gariepy, Jennifer, ed. *Twentieth-Century Literary Criticism,* Vol. 58. Detroit: Gale, 1995.

Gates, Henry Louis. *Thirteen Ways of Looking at a Black Man.* New York: Vintage, 1998.

Ghiglione, Loren. *The American Journalist: Paradox of the Press.* Washington, DC: Library of Congress, 1990.

Glenn, David. "The Marshall Plan." *Columbia Journalism Review,* September/October 2007.

Goldberg, Michelle. "Fundamentally Unsound." *Salon,* July 29, 2002.

Goodman, Amy. *Democracy Now!* radio broadcast, February 2005.

Greenstein, Jennifer. "Snow Job." *Brill's Content*, February 2000.

Greif, Mark, "The Hard Sell." *New York Times Book Review*, December 30, 2007

Griffin, John Howard. *Black Like Me*. Boston: Houghton Mifflin, 1961.

Guardian Unlimited, June 8, 2005.

Haffercamp, Jack. "Un-Banning Books: Part Two." *Libido: The Journal of Sex and Sensibility*, Fall/Winter 1996.

Halberstam, David. *The Powers That Be*. New York: Knopf, 1979.

Halliday, E. M. "The Man Who Cleaned up Shakespeare." *Holiday*, 1961.

Hallinan, Joseph T. *Going up the River: Travels in a Prison Nation*. New York: Random House, 2001.

Haskew, Michael E., ed. *The World War II Desk Reference*. New York: HarperCollins, 2004.

Hatfield, J. H. *Fortunate Son*. Brooklyn: Soft Skull Press, 2001.

Herndon, Booton. *Praised and Damned: The Story of Fulton Lewis, Jr.* New York: Duell, Sloan and Pearce, 1954.

Hersh, Seymour M. *My Lai 4: A Report on the Massacre and Its Aftermath*. New York: Random House, 1970.

Hersh, Seymour M. *The Target Is Destroyed*. New York: Random House, 1986.

Hertzberg, Hendrik. *Politics: Observations and Arguments, 1966–2004*. New York: Penguin Press, 2004.

Hoffman, Abbie. *Steal This Book*. New York: Pirate Editions, 1971.

Hutchison, E. R. *Tropic of Cancer on Trial: A Case Study of Censorship*. New York: Grove Press, 1968.

Jones, Ann. *Women Who Kill*. New York: Holt, Rinehart and Winston, 1980.

Kalven, Harry. *A Worthy Tradition: Freedom of Speech in America*. New York: Harper and Row, 1988.

Kanfer, Stefan. "From the Yellow Kid to Yellow Journalism." *Civilization*, May/June 1995, 32–37.

Kaplan, Justin. *Lincoln Steffens: A Biography*. New York: Simon and Schuster, 1974.

Kershaw, Ian. *Hitler: 1889–1936 Hubris*. New York: Norton, 1998.

Knightly, Philip. *The First Casualty: The War Correspondent as Hero, Propagandist, and Myth Maker*. New York: Harcourt Brace Jovanovich, 1975.

Krassner, Paul. *Confessions of a Raving Unconfined Nut*. New York: Simon and Schuster, 1993.

Krementz, Jill. *The Jewish Writer*. New York: Henry Holt, 1998.

Kunitz, Stanley, and Howard Haycraft, eds. *Twentieth Century Authors: A Biographical Dictionary of Modern Literature*. New York: H. W. Wilson Co., 1942.

Larsen, Jonathan Z. "Tulsa Burning." *Civilization,* February/March 1997, 46–55.

Lavine, Harold, and James Wechsler. *War Propaganda and the United States*. New Haven, CT: Yale University Press, 1940.

Lee, Felicia R. "A Romance Novelist Is Accused of Copying." *New York Times*, January 12, 2008.

Lehmann-Haupt, Christopher. "Life with Father: Incestuous and Soul-Deadening." *New York Times*, February 27, 1997.

Levin, Nora. *The Holocaust: The Destruction of European Jewry 1933–1945*. New York: Schocken Books, 1973.

Lipstadt, Deborah E. *Denying the Holocaust: The Growing Assault on Truth and Memory*. New York: Free Press, 1993.

Lubow, Arthur. *The Reporter Who Would Be King: A Biography of Richard Harding Davis*. New York: Scribner's, 1992.

Luo, Michael, and Jeff Zeleny. "Behind an Antiwar Ad...." *New York Times*, September 15, 2007.

Lyons, Louis M. *Newspaper Story: One Hundred Years of the Boston Globe*. Cambridge, MA: Belknap Press, 1971.

Makower, Joel. *Boom! Talkin' About Our Generation*. Chicago: Contemporary, 1985.

Maraniss, David A. "Post Reporter's Pulitzer Prize Is Withdrawn." *Washington Post*, April 16, 1981.

Margolin, Leo. *Paper Bullets: A Brief Story of Psychological Warfare in World War II*. New York: Froben Press, 1946.

Mashberg, Tom. "Repeat Offender." *Salon*, August 20, 1998.

McCarthy, Colman. *Inner Companions*. Washington, DC: Acropolis, 1975.

McCarthy, Mary. *The Mask of State: Watergate Portraits*. New York: Harcourt, Brace, Jovanovich, 1974.

McGinnis, Joe. *The Selling of the President 1968*. New York: Simon and Schuster, 1969.

McLuhan, Marshall, and Quentin Fiore. *The Medium Is the Message*. New York: Bantam, 1967.

Mencher, Melvin. *News Reporting and Writing*, 8th ed. New York: McGraw-Hill, 2000.

Michaelis, David. *Schulz and Peanuts*. New York: Harper, 2007.

Miles, Barry, ed. *Allen Ginsberg Howl: Original Draft Facsimile...* New York: Harper and Row, 1986.

Miller, Jim. *Democracy Is in the Streets: From Port Huron to the Siege of Chicago*. New York: Simon and Schuster, 1987.

Miller, Russell. "See You in Court." *Punch*, February 19, 1988.

Morris, Errol, director. *The Fog of War: Eleven Lessons from the Life of Robert S. McNamara*. Documentary film, 2003.

Morris, James McGrath. *The Rose Man of Sing Sing: A True Tale of Life, Murder and Redemption in the Age of Yellow Journalism*. New York: Fordham University Press, 2003.

Morrison, Blake. "USA Today Reporter Resigns after Deception." *USA Today*, January 13, 2004; and "Ex-USA Today Reporter Faked Major Stories." *USA Today*, March 19, 2004.

Morrison, Joseph L. "A View of the Moon from the Sun: 1835." *American Heritage*, 1968.

Morthland, John. "The Payola Scandal." In *The Rolling Stone Illustrated History of Rock and Roll*, ed. Jim Miller, 101–3. New York: Random House, 1980.

Mott, Frank Luther. *American Journalism, A History: 1690–1960*. New York: Macmillan, 1962.

Nader, Ralph. *Unsafe at Any Speed*. New York: Pocket Books, 1966.

New York Times editors. "Correcting the Record: Times Reporter Who Resigned Leaves Long Trail of Deception." *New York Times*, May 11, 2003.

Ohmann, Richard. *Selling Culture: Magazines, Markets and Class at the Turn of the Century*. New York: Verso, 1996.

Oliver, April, and Jack Smith. "Implausible Deniability." *Brill's Content*, February 1999, 58–61.

Oudes, Bruce, ed. *From: The President, Richard Nixon's Secret Files*. New York: Harper and Row, 1989.

Palmer, Robert. *Dancing in the Street: A Rock and Roll History*. London: BBC, 1996.

Parry, Robert. *Lost History: Contras, Cocaine, the Press, and "Project Truth."* Media Consortium, 1999.

Peacock, Scot, and Jennifer Gariepy. *Twentieth-Century Literary Criticism*, Vols. 70, 78, Detroit: Gale, 1997.

Pearson, Ryan. "The Britney Beat; Riding with the Paparazzi." Associated Press, April 5, 2008.

Peck, Abe. *Uncovering the Sixties: The Life and Times of the Underground Press*. New York: Pantheon, 1985.

Plotz, David. "The Plagiarist: Why Stephen Ambrose Is a Vampire." *Slate*, January 11, 2002.

Pogrebin, Abigail, and Rifka Rosenswein. "Not the First Time." *Brill's Content*, September 1998.

Pooley, Jeff. "Tenured Chairs Fly." *Brill's Content*, September 1999.

Posner, Richard A. *Law and Literature: A Misunderstood Relation*, Cambridge, MA: Harvard University Press, 1988.

Randi, James. *Flim-Flam! Psychics, ESP, Unicorns, and Other Delusions*. Buffalo, NY: Prometheus Books, 1982.

Reidelbach, Maria. *MAD: A History of the Comic Book and Magazine*. Boston: Little, Brown, 1991.

Rendall, Steven. *The Way Things Aren't: Rush Limbaugh's Reign of Error*. New York: New Press, 1995.

Rideout, Walter B. *The Radical Novel in the United States 1900–1954*. New York: Hill and Wang, 1956.

Rosman, Katherine. "King of the Pitch." *Brill's Content*, June 1999.

Rossiter, Clinton. *Seedtime of the Republic*. New York: Harcourt, Brace and World, 1953.

Saulny, Susan. "To Fox, 'Fair and Balanced' Doesn't Describe Al Franken." *New York Times*, August 12, 2003.

Schiff, Stacy. "Know It All: Can Wikipedia Conquer Expertise." *The New Yorker*, July 31, 2006.

Shabecoff, Philip. *A Fierce Green Fire: The American Environmental Movement*. New York: Hill and Wang, 1993.

Sharp, Harold S. *Footnotes to American History*. Metuchen, NJ: Scarecrow Press, 1977.

Shenkman, Richard. *Legends, Lies and Cherished Myths of American History*. New York: William Morrow, 1988.

Sims, Patsy. *The Klan*. New York: Stein and Day, 1978.

Steffens, Lincoln. *Autobiography*. New York: Literary Guild, 1931.

Stein, Gordon. *Hoaxes!: Dupes, Dodges and Other Dastardly Deceptions*. Canton, MI: Visible Ink Press, 1995.

Stewart, James B. *Blood Sport: The President and His Adversaries*. New York: Simon and Schuster, 1996.

Stone, Robert. "Tabloid Days." *The New Yorker*, October 16, 2006.

Sward, Keith. *The Legend of Henry Ford*. New York: Rinehart, 1948.

Teachout, Terry. *The Skeptic: A Life of H. L. Mencken*. New York: HarperCollins, 2002.

Time. Unsigned review, "Will the Real Nat Turner Please Stand Up?" July 12, 1968.

Toobin, Jeffrey. "Google's Moon Shot." *The New Yorker*, February 5, 2007.

Tosches, Nick. *Country: The Biggest Music in America*. New York: Delta, 1979.

Tye, Larry. *The Father of Spin: Edward L. Bernays and the Birth of Public Relations*. New York: Crown, 1998.

Ungar, Sanford J. *The Papers and the Papers: An Account of the Legal and Political Battle over the Pentagon Papers*. New York: E. P. Dutton, 1972.

Wagner, Margaret E., et al., eds. *The Library of Congress Civil War Desk Reference*. New York: Simon and Schuster, 2002.

Walker, Brian. *The Comics before 1945*. New York: Harry N. Abrams, 2004.

Wallechinsky, David. *The People's Almanac*. New York: Doubleday and Co., 1978.

Walls, Jeannette. *Dish: The Inside Story on the World of Gossip*. New York: Avon, 2000.

Watkins, Mel. *On the Real Side*. New York: Simon and Schuster, 1994.

Wells, Tom. *The War Within: America's Battle over Vietnam*. Berkeley: University of California Press, 1994.

Wilgoren, Jodi. "Shadowed by Threats." *New York Times*, March 2, 2005.

Wolfe, Tom. *The Pump House Gang*. New York: Farrar, Straus, Giroux, 1968.

Worth, Robert F. "Jailhouse Author Helped by Mailer Is Found Dead." *New York Times*, February 11, 2002.

Wright Lawrence. *The Looming Tower*. New York: Alfred A. Knopf, 2006.

Yalom, Marilyn. "The Last Taboo." *Stanford Magazine*, 1998.

Young, Art. *His Life and Times*. New York: Sheridan House, 1939.

Zuniga, Markos Moulitsas, and Jerome Armstrong. *Crashing the Gate*. White River Junction, VT: Chelsea Green, 2006.

WEB SITES

The Center for Investigative Reporting. http://centerforinvestigativereporting.org. The center is "a nonprofit news organization dedicated to exposing injustice and abuse of power through the tools of journalism." Bill Moyers and Seymour Hersh are advisors.

The Center for Public Integrity. http://www.publicintegrity.org/default.aspx. The center is a nonprofit, nonpartisan organization that "produces original investigative journalism about significant public issues to make institutional power more accountable."

Crooks and Liars. http://www.crooksandliars.com. This site offers both video and print links to augment breaking news stories and media events.

Media Matters for America. http://mediamatters.org. A Web site started by former conservative David Brock to serve as a corrective to biased reporting.

The National Coalition against Censorship. http://www.ncac.org. The coalition is an alliance of fifty national nonprofit organizations committed to defending freedom of thought, inquiry, and expression, guaranteed by the First Amendment. It disseminates information to the public about attempts to suppress free speech.

Poynter Institute. http://www.poynter.org. One of the eminent journalism schools in the country and the host site for Jim Romenesko's blog, which offers a "daily fix of media industry news, commentary, and memos."

Project Gutenberg. http://www.gutenberg.org. The first and largest single collection of free electronic books. Founded by Michael Hart, who invented eBooks in 1971, the project offers classic muckraker texts and magazines including issues of *McClure's*.

The Smoking Gun. http://www.thesmokinggun.com. This site provides original documents, from incriminating photographs to arrest reports, which would otherwise require a prolonged effort, including Freedom of Information Act filings.

INDEX

Bly, Robert, 82
Bonds, Barry, 106
Book of Mormon, 57–58
The Boondocks, xxii
Boorstin, Daniel, 29
Boston Globe, 131–32
Bouton, Jim, 105–6
Bowman, Patricia, 176
Bradley, Ed, 172
Brennan, William J., 151
Brill, Steven, 97–98, 112
Brill's Content, 145, 196
Brinkley, Alan, 155
broadsides, 5
Brock, David, 29–30, 222
Brosnan, Jim, 105
Brown, Helen Gurley, 78–79
Bryant, Paul ("Bear"), 152
Burnett, Carol, xxi, 140
Burroughs, William S., 104–5
Burroughs, William S., Jr., 104–5
Bush, George H. W., 28–29, 40–41, 164
Bush, George W., xxiii, 28, 32, 34,
    41–43, 62–63, 98, 135, 170,
    183, 196, 204
Butler, Nicholas Murray, 149
Butts, Wally, 152
By Bread Alone (Friedman), 9

Calley, William, 16–17
Callow, Simon, 158–60
Cameron, William J., 90
Candid Camera, 183–84
Canseco, Jose, 106
Capa, Robert, xix
Capote, Truman, 130
Carlin, George, 132, 168, 190
Carroll, Robert Todd, 107, 110
Carson, Johnny, 140
Carson, Rachel, 20–21
Carto, Willis A., 61–62
Casey, William, 97
Castaneda, Carlos, 105, 109
Cayce, Edgar, 107–9
CBS News, 25–26, 171–74, 192
CBS Radio, 157–61

The Center for Investigative Reporting,
    222
The Center for Public Integrity, 222
Chapin, Charles, 117
Cheney, Dick, 42, 195–96
Chessman, Caryl, 100–101
Chicago Tribune, 118, 134
Churchill, Ward, 56
City Lights Books, 72–73
Clark, Dick, 187–88
Clay, Cassius, 43
Cleaver, Eldridge, 54–55, 100
Clinton, Bill, xxii, 29–32, 97, 165, 167,
    181, 199–200
Clinton, Hillary, xxii, 29–32, 97,
    200, 202
The Closing of the American Mind
    (Bloom), 81
CNN, xxi, 176, 195–96
Cohn, Roy, 139
Colbert, Stephen, xxiii, 183
Collier's, 9
Columbia Journalism Review, 140
Comfort, Alex, 79–80
comic books, 126–31
Common Sense, xvii, 5
Comstock, Anthony, xviii, 68–70, 77
The Confessions of Nat Turner
    (Styron), 53
Confidential, 136–40, 174
conspiracy theories, 16
Cooke, Janet, 131
Coolidge, Calvin, 38
Cooper, Matthew, 41–42
Cooper, Paulette, 111
Correll, Charles, 48–49
Cosby, William, 4–5
Cosell, Howard, 194
Cosmopolitan, 79
Costello, Frank, 139
Coughlin, Charles E., xviii, 155–57,
    161, 163
Coulter, Ann, 31–32, 34–35
Couric, Katie, 193
credibility gap, 16
Creel, George, 35–36

About the Author

ALAN BISBORT has authored or coauthored 16 books on history, biography, travel, as well as social and cultural issues. He has worked for the Library of Congress on *World War II: A Library of Congress Desk Reference* (2007). He is coauthor of *The Nation's Library: The Library of Congress* (2000), the official guide for the Library's bicentennial, and was a contributor to *The Civil War: A Library of Congress Desk Reference* (2002).